Strong State and Economic Interest Groups
The Post-1980 Turkish Experience

Editor: Metin Heper

Strong State and Economic Interest Groups
The Post-1980 Turkish Experience

Edited by Metin Heper

Walter de Gruyter · Berlin · New York 1991

Editor
Professor Dr. Metin Heper
Bilkent University
Faculty of Economics, Administrative and Social Sciences
Dept. of Political Science and Public Administration
06533 Bilkent, Ankara
Turkey

⊗ Printed on acid-free paper which falls within the guidelines of the ANSI to ensure permanence and durability.

Library of Congress Cataloging in Publication Data

Strong state and economic interest groups : the post-1980 Turkish experience / edited by Metin Heper.
p. cm.
Includes bibliographical references and index.
ISBN 3-11-012924-8 (alk. paper)
1. Turkey – Economic policy. 2. Turkey – Economic conditions – 1960. 3. Pressure groups – Turkey. 4. Industry and state – Turkey.
I. Heper, Metin.
HC492.S76 1991
338.9561 – dc20 91-29782
CIP

Die Deutsche Bibliothek – Cataloging in Publication Data

Strong state and economic interest groups: the post-1980 Turkish experience / ed. by Metin Heper. – Berlin; New York : de Gruyter, 1991
ISBN 3-11-012924-8
NE: Heper, Metin [Hrsg.]

Printing: WB-Druck, Rieden am Forggensee. – Binding: Dieter Mikolai, Berlin. – Cover Design: Johannes Rother. – Printed in Germany.

Preface and Acknowledgements

This volume looks at the relations between the State and economic interest groups in Turkey during the 1980s. Not unlike some western European countries such as France and Germany, Turkey, too, has had a State tradition. What makes the Turkish case interesting is that the State in Turkey has been stronger than its counterpart in the Fifth French Republic; the latter has been considered as the ideal-typical example of a strong State. A significant consequence of this difference has been that, while in France the monist State has shown signs of de-composition in its relations with interest groups, in Turkey the State-interest groups relations continued to evince monism. In fact, the State in Turkey of the 1980s has become even more isolated and autonomous from social groups. Post-1980 interest group politics in Turkey can be considered as a prime example of strong State-interest group relations.

The present volume also challenges earlier work on interest groups politics in Turkey, which viewed the Turkish case as another instance of a hybrid system. Interest group politics in Turkey was seen as manifesting either a predominantly state corporatist or a predominantly pluralist system. This volume shows that even in the Turkey of the 1980s, during which time there has been an effort to roll back the frontiers of the State in the economic sphere, a State-interest group relationship of the monist type continued unabated. This is explained in terms of the extraordinarily strong State tradition in Turkey, which earlier was structured in the civil bureaucracy and/or the military, and which during the 1980s was more and more structured in the political party in power.

The research leading to this volume was supported by the Friedrich-Ebert-Stiftung in Bonn. The Editor is grateful to the Foundation in question and in particular to its representatives in Istanbul - Mr Helmut Weber and Dr Matthes Buhbe - for their patience and enthusiastic co-operation. The Editor acknowledges with pleasure the extremely useful suggestions made by Dr Victor Funnell, who kindly took time off, and read the whole manuscript. The Editor would also like to thank Mrs Sibel Kurgan Bozkurt and Mrs Sibel Ramazanoğlu who carefully helped to prepare the manuscript for publication. Finaly, the Editor would like to express his debt to his collaborators in this volume who never lost their hope that the book would eventually see the light.

Ankara, March 1991.

Contents

Terms and Abbreviations

BMHPPF		[Board of] Mass Housing and Public Participation Fund
DISK		Turkish acronym for the Confederation of Revolutionary Trade Unions
DLP	:	Democratic Left Party
EBF	:	Extra-budgetary fund
EXIMBANK	:	Export Credit Bank
FERB	:	Foreign Economic Relations Board
FTCC	:	Foreign trade capital company
GDP	:	Gross domestic product
Hak-İş	:	Turkish acronym for the Confederation of 'Justice Seekers' Trade Unions
HC		Holding company
IMF		International Monetary Fund
ILO		International Labour Organization
ISI		Import-substitution industrialization
JP		Justice Party
JSC		Joint stock company
LDC		Less developed country
MISK		Turkish acronym for the Confederation of Nationalist Trade Unions
MP	:	Motherland Party
NSC	:	National Security Council
OECD	:	Organization for Economic and Cultural Development
PEA	:	Public Employers' Association
PPO	:	Public professional organization
RPP	:	Republican People's Party
SAL	:	Sectoral adjustment loan
SDPP	:	Social Democratic Populist Party
SEE	:	State economic enterprise
TAA	:	Turkish Association of Agriculturalists
TFF	:	Turkish Federation of Farmers
TİSK	:	Turkish acronym for Turkish Confederation of Employers' Associations
TOBB		Turkish acronym for Turkish Union of Chambers and Stock Exchanges
TUCA		Turkish Union of Chambers of Agriculture
TUCAE		Turkish Union of Chambers of Agricultural Experts
Türk-İş		Turkish acronym for the Confederation of Turkish Trade Unions
Türk-Trade		Turkish acronym for Turkish Foreign Trade Association
TÜSİAD		Turkish acronym for the Turkish Industrialists' and Businessmen's Association

Part One
INTRODUCTION

1

The State and Interest Groups with Special Reference to Turkey

Metin Heper

Introduction

Interest group politics constitutes a critical link between the State and civil society.[1] The primary function of interest groups is no longer perceived solely as that of articulating and transmitting demands of society into the political process;[2] in its stead, the interest groups are accorded a variety of roles, including socializing citizens, organizing consensus, contributing to the making of policy, implementing laws, and the like.[3]

Yet, in both the pluralist and corporatist studies of interest group politics, the dominant approach for the most part is a society-centred one. Pluralists hardly pay attention to the theory of the State; instead, they work with the theory of representative government.[4] Despite the fact that corporatist arrangements basically derive from a State-related notion - the general interest - State theory on the whole remains a crucial missing link in empirical analyses guided by corporatism.[5] In sum, for many, the purpose of looking at interest groups is generally that of broaching 'societal functioning and change'.[6]

Such an approach is less than adequate, because, as has been cogently argued by Pierre Birnbaum, the State, democracy and capitalism are independent variables with multiple relationships; all contribute, each in its own fashion, to the structuration of interest group politics.[7] The theory of corporatism, however, takes into account only

---

1 In this chapter, the State is taken in the sense cogently formulated by J.P. Nettl ['The State as a Conceptual Variable', *World Politics*, 21 (1968), pp. 559-92]. From this particular perspective, we talk about the phenomenon of the State to the extent to which we come across goals that do not essentially reflect the views and demands of civil societal elements because in formulating them hardly any attention is paid to those views and interests. For an elaboration, see Metin Heper 'Introduction', in *The State and Public Bureaucracies. A Comparative Perspective*, Metin Heper, ed. (New York, etc.:Greenwood Press, 1987). We return to some other characteristics of the State in question below.

2 A leading examplar of this approach is Gabriel A. Almond and G.Bingham Powell, Jr., *Comparative Politics. A Developmental Approach* (Boston and Toronto: Little, Brown, 1966), chap.4.

3 Suzanne Berger, 'Introduction', in *Organizing Interests in Western Europe. Pluralism, Corporatism and the Transformation of Politics*, Suzanne Berger, ed. (Cambridge: Cambridge University Press, 1981), p. 10.

4 For a further discussion of this matter, see Alan Cawson, *Corporatism and Political Theory* (Oxford: Basil Blackwell, 1986), p. 26.

5 For an elaboration, see Peter J. Williamson, *Corporatism in Perspective. An Introductory Guide to Corporatist Theory* (London, etc.: Sage, 1989), p. 136.

6 Berger, 'Introduction', p. 4.

7 Pierre Birnbaum, *States and Collective Action. The European Experience* (Cambridge, etc.: Cambridge University Press, 1988), p. 107.

'political regime'.[8] For instance, it is noted that in centralized systems of government, power is concentrated in the executive, and the ability of the policy makers to limit access to relatively few, favoured groups is high. Laws, also, can make it more or less difficult for interest groups to form.[9] However, the same theory of corporatism does not take into consideration the phenomenon of the State itself, whose existence precedes the particular regime associated with it at different historical periods.[10]

Indeed, it is the phenomenon of the State itself which has a significant impact upon politics and, for that matter, upon society in general,[11] and the structuration of interest group politics in particular.[12] Any study of interest group politics must be carried out with a systematic reference to the type of the State, or the degree and kind of 'stateness' encountered in the polity.[13] As Guillermo A. O'Donnell has shown, 'each type of corporatism is a function of the type of [S]tate'.[14] It follows that 'a generalized notion of the [S]tate' which makes no distinction between 'different types of State at the heart of capitalistic societies, let alone in diverse capitalistic societies', would not be useful.[15]

In fact, in his early and influential (institutional) model of corporatism, Philippe C. Schmitter attributed the variations in the nature and role of interest associations in Western European polities (with similar economic and social structures) to the degree to which their States had autonomy vis-à-vis civil society.[16] Similarly, the presence or absence of neo-corporatism has been seen to be closely tied to the degree of stateness; neither a too strong nor a too weak State furnishes an appropriate environment for the emergence of neo-corporatism.[17] The State should be strong enough to maintain its autonomy from interest groups, yet it should not be so strong that the state elites can impose their own notion of public interest to be imposed upon society.[18] A State relatively autonomous and able to act on its own initiative would hinder pluralism.[19] In fact, the pluralists like to see the State as the 'helpless victim of interest groups', unless interest groups hold each other in check.[20]

Thus, keeping in mind the significance of the State for interest groups, Peter J. Williamson has proposed that we use the words 'State' and 'government' when study-

---

8 Ibid.

9 See Graham K. Wilson, *Interest Groups* (Oxford: Basil Blackwell, 1990), pp. 138-9.

10 Birnbaum, *States and Collective Action*, p. 107.

11 Bertrand Badie and Pierre Birnbaum, *The Sociology of the State*, trans. by Arthur Goldhammer (Chicago: The University of Chicago Press, 1983).

12 Birnbaum, *States and Collective Action*, p. 116.

13 Guillermo A. O'Donnell, 'Corporatism and the Question of the State', in *Authoritarianism and Corporatism in Latin America*, James M. Malloy, ed. (Pittsburgh: The University of Pittsburgh Press, 1977), p. 47.

14 Ibid., p. 8.

15 Birnbaum, *States and Collective Action*, pp. 110, 112.

16 Philippe C. Schmitter, 'Models of Interest Intermediation and Models of Societal Change in Western Europe', in *Trends Toward Corporatist Intermediation*, Philippe C. Schmitter and Gerhard Lehmbruch, eds. (London: Sage, 1979).

17 Pierre Birnbaum, 'The State versus Corporatism', *Politics and Society*, 11 (1981), pp. 490-501.

18 Cawson, *Corporatism and Political Theory*, p. 225.

19 Frank L. Wilson, *Interest-Group Politics in France* (Cambridge, etc.: Cambridge University Press, 1987), p. 24.

20 Cawson, *Corporatism and Political Theory*, p. 224.

ing corporatism and pluralism, respectively, and otherwise utilize the phrase 'public authority'.[21] In the same fashion, Alan Cawson has suggested that the State and government should be conceptually distinguished.[22]

While making this distinction, however, one should not fall into the trap of reverting back to a generalized notion of the State, that is, seeing the State only as a capitalist State. Thus one should not argue, as Cawson has done, that the State 'has developed symbiotically - cause and effect - with the spread of capitalist rationality'.[23] In the same fashion, it is not possible to agree with R. Alford and R. Friedland who noted that the State in the area of production has an institutional logic made up of legal rules, explicit norms and implicit premises, supportive of the process of capital accumulation.[24]

States have their own distinctive logic based on explicit norms and implicit premises, but the sources of the State's rationale may be more variegated than implied in the works cited here and elsewhere.[25] As Theda Skocpol has persuasively argued,

> Politics in all of its dimensions is grounded not only in 'society' or in the 'economy' or in a 'culture' - if any or all of these are considered separately from the organizational arrangements and activities of [S]tates. The meaning of public life and the collective forms through which groups become aware of political goals and work to attain them arise not from societies alone but at the meeting points of [S]tates and societies. Consequently, the formation, let alone the political capacities, of such apparently purely socioeconomic phenomena as interest groups and classes depends in significant measure on the structures and the activities of the very [S]tates the social actors, in turn, seek to influence.[26]

Skocpol has also shown the likely sources of State norms. State norms are derived, firstly, from the exigencies of interstate relations; for instance, international economic policy and foreign policy often tend to be made behind closed doors. Secondly, critical problems of development and modernization, particularly when foreign models are emulated, are tackled by the State rather than by the political elites. Thirdly, the need for control and order - when these functions cannot be fulfilled by the political elites - pushes the State elites into the centre stage. Finally, increased specialization in public organizations leads to the emergence of State norms, especially when public officials are differentiated and insulated from weighty social groups because of their different socioeconomic backgrounds and/or organizational and educational socialization.[27]

It is patent that to the degree to which the above factors help to shape a polity, to

---

[21] Williamson, *Corporatism in Perspective*, p. 20, note 1.

[22] Cawson, *Corporatism and Political Theory*, pp. 57 ff.

[23] Ibid., p. 58.

[24] R. Alford and R. Friedland, *Powers of Theory* (Cambridge: Cambridge University Press, 1985), p. 428.

[25] See, *inter alia*, Ralph Miliband, *The State in Capitalist Society* (London: Weidenfeld and Nicolson, 1969); Nicos Poulantzas, *Political Power and Social Classes* (London: New Left Books, 1973); Bob Jessop, *The Capitalist State* (Oxford: Martin Robertson, 1982).

[26] Theda Skocpol, 'Bringing the State Back In: Strategies of Analysis in Current Research', in *Bringing the State Back In*, Peter B. Evans, Dietrich Rueschemeyer and Theda Skocpol, eds. (Cambridge, etc.: Cambridge University Press, 1985), p. 27.

[27] Ibid., pp. 9 ff.

that extent the State in that polity would have a structuring impact on the nature of society, including interest group politics. Thus, Schmitter asked for the development of a more convincing account of the State for better understanding the phenomenon of corporatism.[28] David Easton, too, has focused his attention on 'political institutions' for their function of integration in pluralistic contexts.[29] Furthermore, as has been rightly pointed out, if States can at certain places and periods to a great extent shape polities and societies there is a need for a theoretical account of the State from a historical and comparative perspective in order to have a better grasp of interest group politics.[30] Frank Wilson has shown the consequences of failing to adopt such a framework:

> ... discussions of the fit between a country's interest group politics and one of...[the interest group] models... are ultimately unsatisfying because they often lead to descriptive studies featuring the mechanical fitting of models with reality. They are disappointing because nearly all empirical studies end up with the conclusion that the overall pattern of interest-group politics in any country is a hybrid of two or more of the ideal-type models...but most are unable to explain how the mix develops. They are incomplete because they miss the more theoretically significant questions: why do certain patterns of interest-group politics occur in some settings and not in others?... Why are some groups prone to engage in this or that style of pressure wielding?[31]

It is, in fact, proper to go one step further and argue that depending upon the State or governmental tradition a polity has had in the past, interest group politics would tend to evince, during the later historical periods, not a *mix* of different patterns of interest group politics but one *dominant* pattern. That dominant pattern of interest group politics, I would like to suggest, would depend upon the particular configuration of the State-civil society relationship that has been established in the past, and which still lingers on. This is because each pattern of interest group politics has a particular logic behind it which closely fits one type of State, or government, and not others. Pluralism requires a government basically responsive to civil society; neo-corporatism necessitates a harmonious relationship between the State and civil society. Neither pattern of interest group politics would be encountered in a polity dominated by a strong State. It is not therefore possible to agree with Alan Cawson that '[t]he need for state theory [is] to comprehend the *coexistence* of corporatist practices and competitive pressures'.[32]

For example, it would not be tenable to argue that pluralism and/or neo-corporatism would exist, or constitute one dimension of its interest group politics, in France which,

---

28 Philippe C. Schmitter, 'Neo-Corporatism and the State', in *The Political Economy of Corporatism*, Wyn Grant, ed. (London: Macmillan, 1986), pp. 31 ff.

29 David Easton, *A Framework for Political Analysis* (Englewood Cliffs, New Jersey: Prentice-Hall, 1965).

30 Birnbaum, *States and Collective Action*, p. 108; F. Wilson, *Interest-Group Politics in France*, p. 45.

31 F. Wilson, *Interest-Group Politics in France*, p. 45.

32 Alan Cawson, 'Conclusion: Some Implications for State Theory', in *Organized Interests and the State. Studies in Meso-Corporatism*, Alan Cawson, ed. (London, etc.: Sage, 1985), p. 226. My emphasis.

as Birnbaum has shown, has had a strong State tradition. As Wilson himself has indicated, in France the 'government has worked to break interest-group monopolies, especially those representing interests more or less opposed to the position defended by the government'.[33] According to Wilson, France is a fertile ground neither for pluralism nor for neo-corporatism: '...the notion of "social partnership" is still poorly established in France. The government refers to interest groups as social partners but fails to accord genuine involvement to groups in the policy-making process'.[34] Then in Britain, although for a while functional representation was tried, the system never gained full legitimacy. Belief in the sovereignty of parliament clashed with the neo-corporatist practice of making concessions to economic interest groups.[35] Thus, as compared to its counterparts on the continent the National Economic Development Council in Britain came to have a rather modest impact on policy-making in that country.[36] As Peter J. Williamson deminds us, the institutional structures of different interest-group politics can exist in markedly different regime types but there were major differences in the processes which produced those structures. So it would be misleading if 'corporatism' or 'pluralism' are seized upon as terms to apply to particular phenomena without proper consideration being given to the connection between these and what mainstream students of that particular interest group politics consider as the core of that particular pattern.[37] For instance, corporatism is often used carelessly to characterize virtually any intimate interest group-public authority relations.[38]

Notwithstanding the view advanced by the sole significant work in its field that inter-

---

[33] F. Wilson, *Interest-Group Politics in France*, p. 129. In contrast to the situation in France, neo-corporatism is a product of a government's need to avoid acting in an authoritative manner; it is a diffusion of state power and purposes rather than a unity of control. See Reginald J. Harrison, *Pluralism and Corporatism. The Political Evolution of Modern Democracies* (London, etc.: George Allen and Unwin, 1980), p. 188.

[34] Ibid., p. 131. Also see Andrew Cox and Jack Hayward, 'The Inapplicability of the Corporatist Model in Britain and France: The Case of Labour', *International Political Science Review*, 4(1983): 217-40.

[35] G. Wilson, *Interest Groups*, p. 100. Also see A. G. Jordan and J.J. Richardson, *Government and Pressure Groups in Britain* (Oxford: Clarendon Press, 1987), p. 287.

[36] Jack Hayward, 'Interest Groups and the Demand for State Action', in *State and Society in Contemporary Europe*, Jack Hayward and R. N. Berki, eds. (Oxford: Martin Robertson, 1979), p. 34. On the basic contradiction between the corporatist state and liberal-democratic traditions, see Andrew Cox, 'Neo-Corporatism versus the Corporate State', in *The Corporate State. Corporatism and the State Tradition in Western Europe*, Andrew Cox and Noel O'Sullivan, eds. (Aldershot, England: Edward Elgar, 1988), pp. 36-7. Geoffrey Alderman argues that interest group politics in Britain may be referred to as functional corporatism characterized by 'cross fertilization of ideas' [*Pressure Groups and Government in Great Britain* (New York: Longman, 1984), p. 140].

[37] Williamson, *Corporatism in Perspective*, p. xii.

[38] Leo Panitch, 'The Development of Corporatism in Liberal Democracies', in *Trends Toward Corporatist Intermediation*, Schmitter and Lehmbruch, eds., p. 123.

est group politics in Turkey vacillated between state corporatism and pluralism,[39] the Turkish polity is a even better or pure example of the argument made here - that there is a virtually one-to-one relationship between the degrees of stateness and patterns of interest-group politics. The degree of stateness has been greater in Turkey than in continental European countries, including France, and, consequently, as compared to France, Turkey has been an even less fertile ground for the flourishing of pluralism or either variety of corporatism.[40] In order to elaborate the Turkish case, however, it is first necessary to place it in perspective by undertaking an historical and comparative survey of different State-civil society configurations and the related (dominant) patterns of interest group politics.

The State and Interest Groups in Western Europe

For a historical-comparative analysis along the lines noted above, a model suggested by Kenneth H. F. Dyson seems most appropriate.[41] Dyson suggests that we adopt a two- rather than one-dimensional model of historical evolution of different polities. That is, we should trace change not only in society (from the *Gemeinschaft* to the *Gesellschaft*)[42] but in the nature of public authority (to greater or smaller degrees of stateness). This is necessary because, as already noted, the nature of politics in general and interest group politics in particular are products of the recursive relationship between type of society and the conception of public authority. And, since once a political tradition is established it tends to linger on over different historical periods it is in order to look at the antecedent types of society and conceptions of authority if one wishes to make head or tail of interest group politics at a given time and place.

From this particular perspective, Joseph R. Strayer's distinction between centralized feudalism and decentralized feudalism is an appropriate starting point.[43] Medieval England provides a good example of centralized feudalism. During that era, English

39 Robert Bianchi, *Interest Groups and Political Development in Turkey* (Princeton: Princeton University Press, 1984). As Douglas A. Chalmers has shown, in some polities patterns of dependency would have not only informal, clientelistic but also formal dimensions, too - granting certain legal and financial privileges in return for political support, and the like. Sometimes the term 'corporatist' has come into use to describe some of these formal relationships, and, in particular, to emphasize the patterns of vertical dependency involved ('The Politicized State in Latin America', in *Authoritarianism and Corporatism in Latin America*, Malloy, ed., p. 34). In his work, Bianchi, too, refers to the latter phenomenon as 'state corporatism', and to those situations where the dependency in question is somewhat weakened, as 'pluralism'. In contrast the present chapter takes both corporatism and pluralism as different modes of policy-making

40 That the stateness in Turkey has been greater than that in France is elaborated below.

41 Kenneth H.F. Dyson, *The State Tradition in Western Europe. A Study of an Idea and Institution* (Oxford: Martin Robertson, 1980), pp. 48-78.

42 A transition from the *Gemeinschaft* to the *Gesellschaft* type of society implies a change from the corporate and communal to the individualistic and rational, from ascribed status to contract, and from the sacred-communal to secular-associational. This typology was developed by Ferdinand Tönnies in his *Gemeinschaft und Gesselschaft*, 1987. An English translation of this work is *Community and Society*, trans. and ed. by Charles Loomis (New York: Harper and Row, 1963).

43 Joseph R. Strayer, *On the Medieval Origins of the Modern State* (Princeton: Princeton University Press, 1970), passim.

kings and barons upheld each other's rights. By the beginning of the fourteenth century, a significant integration had taken place between the central and local authority structures. Travelling judges of the king's council were in close touch with the knights of the country courts, while local churches, the shires and boroughs contributed to the development of a polity with a strong sense of identity. One could thus begin talking about a 'national contract' rather than feudalism proper.[44]

The idea of a national contract was later structured in, and in turn further bolstered by, the *Ständestaat*, or polity of estates. In the English version of *Ständestaat*, Gianfranco Poggi has argued, the representatives of the estates rose above the petty political prerogatives of the individual estates.[45] In such *Ständestaaten*, powerful individuals and groups established the terms of their collaboration with the ruler and shouldered their share of the burdens of rule. So, from the beginning, it was possible for consensus to be reached through progressive resolution of conflicts about fundamental claims. Conflicts were resolved through multiple confrontations of the parties involved, that is, by means of 'politics'.[46]

Thus, in England, the dissolving feudal society was followed by a politically influential parliament; the formula of Crown-in-Parliament pre-empted a centralizing, bureaucratic polity. Political accommodation was reached in the fluid parliamentary arena through debate. In time, an adversary style of politics, that was hostile to the idea of power sharing, emerged. 'Political world views' were not informed by a deep institutional consciousness or constitutional awareness, but rather by the notion of politics as a game, in which the rules were often vague and subject to various interpretations between contestants who competed for the favour of the spectators.[47]

In such polities, the State emerged essentially in its Weberian garb, that is, as a transformatory structure.[48] Most issues were 'solved' primarily in terms of *procedural* rules and not with a view to *substantive* norms. For in these polities the sources of the State norms were essentially the exigencies of interstate relations and increased specialization in public organizations, and less the need for control and order and the critical problems of development and modernization. Thus, in these polities one came across only a handful of officials in some agencies who tended to operate independently of the political elites, and there was essentially an absence of the State elites who had a unified sense of ideology on the basis of which they wished to control, manipulate and/or transform polity and society.

With respect to decentralized feudalism, the best example is France. In the ninth to tenth-century France, feudal decentralization of authority was more complete than

---

44 Reinhard Bendix, *Kings or People. Power and the Mandate to Rule* (Berkeley: University of California Press, 1978), pp. 193-5.

45 Gianfranco Poggi, *The Development of the Modern State. A Sociological Introduction* (London: Hutchinson, 1978), p. 44.

46 Metin Heper, 'The State and Public Bureaucracies: A Comparative and Historical Perspective', *Comparative Studies in Society and History*, 27 (1985), p. 98.

47 Dyson, *The State Tradition in Western Europe*, pp. 62-7.

48 Richard Scase, 'Introduction', in *The State in Western Europe*, Richard Scase, ed. (London: Croom Helm, 1980), p. 11.

elsewhere.[49] There was a constant tug-of-war between the king and the local grandees, which culminated in the absolute rule of Louis XIV (1643-1715). But the conflict between the central and local authority structures in France was not resolved once and for all. The members of the *parlements* of late eighteenth-century France went on claiming the heads of political and economic reformers - the Turgots, Neckers, and others. In the process a State emerged that set the ideological parameters of politics.

Consequently, in France nationalism, for instance, has always been a more important norm than democracy.[50] While in England conflicts were resolved through multiple confrontations, that is, by means of 'politics', in France the parties in question organized themselves in (the continental European version of) estates, and 'law' became the rock on which they based their claims.

In countries with a heritage of decentralized feudalism the dissolving feudal society was replaced not by a politically influential parliament but by a strong executive. The pervasive conflict rendered 'politics' a less than adequate means of resolving contentious issues. The law became important both as a ratification of sectional interests and as a codification of the public interest. The inability of the parties to a conflict to resolve their differences dynamically, that is, through multiple confrontations and bargaining, led to the establishment of the hierarchical principle of the executive power and the *Sachlichleit* ideal - an executive frame of mind committed to the idea of objectivity. An 'inquisitorial' rather than an adversary style of politics - one that seeks the best solution rather than reconciling sectional interests - emerged. Politics was perceived in terms of a rational, objective framework of institutional values that focused upon duty, public service, proper procedure and efficiency.[51]

In such polities, the state was born as an admixture of Weberian-Hegelian entity.[52] The State was not primarily a transformatory structure. As compared to adversary politics, in the inquisitorial style of politics the scope of substantive norms was greater. In these polities the sources of State norms were not only the exigencies of interstate relations and increased specialization in public organizations but also the critical problems of modernization and development. The State elites came to have a virtually unified sense of ideology on the basis of which they tried to control, manipulate and/or transform politics and society.

These different paths of development have had significant implications for the structuration of interest group politics in the two categories of polities in question. The contrast between the two types of interest group politics is succintly clarified by the characterizations of 'socialization of the [S]tate' and the 'stratification of society'.[53] In Britain, the saliency of politics as a means of resolving conflicts and the dominant posi-

---

49 Samuel E. Finer, 'State- and Nation-Building in Europe: The Role of the Military', in *Formation of National States in Western Europe*, Charles Tilly, ed. (Princeton: Princeton University Press, 1975), p. 126.

50 David Thompson, *Democracy in France. The Third and Fourth Republics* (London: Oxford University Press, 1958), p. 146.

51 Dyson, *The State Tradition in Western Europe*, pp. 63, 65, 69.

52 Later, as in France, the Hegelian traits increased to the extent to which the executive frame of mind was represented by the bureaucratic elites, and as in Germany, the Weberian characteristics became stronger to the degree to which the political party became the carrier of the State norms.

53 Dyson, *The State Tradition in Western Europe*, p. 285.

tion of parliament led to the emergence, to use Philippe C. Schmitter's terminology,[54] of 'an un-specified number of multiple, voluntary, competitive, non-hierarchically ordered and self-determined interest group associations'. These associations were granted *de facto* power to influence public policy and implementation;[55] they did not need to be armed with *de jure* authority. In a comparative study of senior public officials, it was found that as compared to Italian, Dutch, Swedish and German officials the British were least fearful of interest groups. In Britain, lobbying was not looked upon with suspicion.[56]

In the latter context, the relations between interest groups and governments comprised a fluid, competitive and pluralistic politics of bargaining.[57] Formal and organized contacts with the interest group associations were not recognized as legitimate.[58] As already noted, the belief in the sovereignty of the elected bodies conflicted with the neo-corporatist logic of letting economic interest groups participate in policy-making. Thus, the establishment of stable tripartite arrangements between the government and both sides of industry proved an elusive quest. As compared to its counterparts on the continent, in Britain the National Economic Development Council has had a rather modest impact on policy-making.[59] It is true that during the Thatcherite years the State in Britain became 'stronger', yet the State was not structured on substantive norms and values.[60] What emerged was not macro- but meso- and micro-corporatism, which made it necessary for the bureaucrats to have inside knowledge of the industry or the firm concerned.[61] This requirement, however, did not lead to formal bargaining and joint decision-making but informal consultation, regular, sometimes daily, exchanges between interest group officials, civil servants and ministers by 'phone, over lunch or in London clubs'.[62]

In Britain, through the mechanism of consultations in question, society by itself reached the government and found an attentive ear. In continental western Europe, the State went to society and partially de-pluralised it - thus the notion of 'stratification of society'. Historically, an initial phase of estate representation in which interests

---

[54] Philippe C. Schmitter, 'Still the Century of Corporatism?', *Review of Politics*, 36 (1974): 85-131.

[55] Robert Salisbury, 'Interest Groups', in *Handbook of Political Science, Vol. IV, Nongovernmental Politics*, Fred I. Greenstein and Nelson W. Polsby, eds. (Reading, Massachusetts, etc.: Addison-Wesley, 1975), p. 181.

[56] Samuel Eldersveld, Sonja Hubee-Boonzaaijer and Jan Kooiman, 'Elite Perceptions of the Political Process in the Netherlands, Looked at in Comparative Perspective', in *The Mandarins of Western Europe. The Political Role of Top Civil Servants*, Mattei Dogan, ed. (New York, etc.: John Wiley, 1975), pp. 149-50.

[57] Dyson, *The State Tradition in Western Europe*, p. 66; Hayward, 'Interest Groups and the Demand for State Action', p. 34.

[58] Salisbury, 'Interest Groups', p. 216. Here, by formal and organized contacts the reference is to a corporatist interface between the government and interest groups and not to an organic affiliation of an interest group to a political party.

[59] Dyson, *The State Tradition in Western Europe*, p. 66; Hayward, 'Interest Groups and the Demand for State Action', p. 34.

[60] Cawson, *Corporatism and Political Theory*, p. 51.

[61] Ibid., pp. 62-4.

[62] G. Wilson, *Interest Groups*, p. 82.

coincided with the social system,[63] was followed by a 'liberal parenthesis' during the early part of the nineteenth century; representation was organized on an individual basis and association was entirely voluntary, hence fragmented and unstable.[64] The structuration of interest group politics along these lines could not last long. The traditionalists on the Right, whether statesmen such as Bismarck or Catholic corporatist writers, came to the conclusion that the liberal market worked to fragment communities and to incite revolutionary ideologies.[65] The solution was sought in corporatism now 'envisaged as being a means of resurrecting the positive attributes of medieval guild'.[66] Solidarity was to be provided for by loyalty to function or profession instead of class.[67] Corporatism helped to stratify society. Interest *intermediation* was substituted for interest *representation*. Again using Schmitter's terminology,[68] 'a limited number of singular, compulsory, non-competitive, hierarchically-ordered interest group associations' played a go-between role between the State and numerous interest groups.

Parallel to the formal recognition of the *legal* rights of the leaders of associations to participate in the economic decision-making process, the leaders in question were involved, vis-à-vis the rank-and-file members of associations, in interest intermediation. An inherent rather than an indirectly created notion of public interest was expected to inform the decisions jointly made. Decision-making tended to be seen as a rational rather than a political exercise. In some areas, that is, in matters of production rather than distribution, there was an effort to arrive at decisions that best reconciled the general and sectional interests rather than to make decisions that basically optimized sectional interests alone. Within the governmental and bureaucratic circles there was greater emphasis on specialists than on generalists. The specialists in governmental and bureaucratic agencies felt that they needed to meet regularly and make joint decisions with their counterparts in interest group associations.

The State and Interest Groups in the Ottoman-Turkish Polity

While medieval England was characterized by centralized feudalism and many countries on the continent by decentralized feudalism, the Ottoman-Turkish polity evinced unmistakable signs of bureaucratic centralism. The Ottoman-Turkish polity was bureaucratic-centralist in the sense that in contrast to the situation in feudal polities the centre in the Ottoman-Turkish polity did not face countervailing powers.

---

[63] As Alessandro Pizzorno has noted, 'in the system of representation by estates, all the interests represented were by definition "special" interests. The only bearer of general interest was the sovereign, himself a former bearer of a special interest in a given territorial area. The religions foundation of monarchical legitimacy excluded the conception of a state that was legitimized solely by its capacity to represent all interests' ('Interests and Parties in Pluralism', in *Organizing Interests in Western Europe*, Berger, ed., p. 256).

[64] Berger, 'Introduction', in *ibid.*, p. 14.

[65] Charles Maier, 'Preconditions for Corporatism', in *Order and Conflict in Contemporary Capitalism. Studies in the Political Economy of Western European Nations*, John H. Goldthorpe, ed. (Oxford: Clarendon Press, 1988), p. 41. First printed in 1984.

[66] Williamson, *Corporatism in Perspective*, p. 29.

[67] Ibid.

[68] See note 52 above.

In the establishment of the Ottoman Empire the military played a key role. Consequently, law and order as a norm of the State was always emphasized. The Ottoman statesmen were preoccupied with saving the empire from destruction by its external and internal enemies which led to a constant, and often exaggerated, fear of anarchy, rebellion and treason and, therefore, to an indiscriminate hostility towards representation of sectional interests.[69]

The State could remain aloof from civil societal elements because during the Ottoman golden age (from the middle of the fifteenth until the middle of the sixteenth centuries) the Ottomans for the most part dominated their enemies, and during their decline (from the middle of the sixteenth until the nineteenth centuries) they tried to arrest that process by modernizing (politically, administratively and culturally) rather than developing (economically) their realm; both phenomena had the consequence that the Ottoman statesmen were not obliged to mobilize social groups, and, therefore, to obtain their cooperation and consent.[70]

It follows that in the Ottoman Empire no need was felt for developing close ties between the State and civil society. For quite sometime, the primary function of the ruler was to achieve the 'military cooperation' of his subjects.[71] There could not be a constant tug-of-war between the State and civil society; power was tilted in a too lopsided fashion towards the former.

The Ottoman guild system, too, was the handiwork of the State rather than civil society. It functioned as an administrative link between the two. The chief officers of the guilds (the *kethüdas* or *kâhyas*) were generally agents of the State rather than spokesmen for the guilds; they were commonly recruited from among former civil servants.[72] If a member of a guild became too wealthy he could no longer stay as a craftsman; he had to become a merchant. His wealth being monetized, he could now be controlled more easily by the State.[73] In any case, economic life was controlled by the politically non-influential non-Muslims. The latter were organized under their *millet* systems, which again functioned as a one-way transmission belt from the State to civil society. The religious heads of these communities worked closely with the Ottoman government as partners in the administration of their respective ethno-communal system.[74] In the localities, notables did not form a nobility - a juridical class to which man belonged by birth. They also did not show characteristics of an aristocracy - a class able to

69 Şerif Mardin, 'Center-Periphery Relations: A Key to Turkish Politics?' *Daedalus*, 102(1973), p. 293.

70 For a contrasting pattern of evolution in continental western Europe, see Charles Tilly, 'Reflections on the History of European State-Making', in *The Formation of National States in Western Europe*, Tilly, ed., pp. 21 ff; idem, *Coercion, Capital and European States, AD 990-1990* (Oxford: Basil Blackwell, 1990), pp. 84 ff.

71 Kemal H. Karpat, 'Structural Change, Historical Stages of Modernization and the Role of Social Groups in Turkish Politics', in *Social Change and Politics in Turkey. A Structural-Historical Analysis*, Kemal H. Karpat, ed. (Leiden: Brill, 1973), p. 29.

72 Gabriel Baer, 'The Administrative, Economic, and Social Functions of Turkish Guilds', *International Journal of Middle East Studies*, 1(1970): 28-50.

73 Şerif Mardin, 'Turkey: The Transformation of an Economic Code', in *The Political Economy of Income Distribution in Turkey*, Ergun Özbudun and Aydın Ulusan, eds. (New York: Holmes and Meier, 1980), p. 25.

74 Kemal H. Karpat, 'The Ottoman Views and Policies toward the Orthodox Christian Church', *Greek Orthodox Theological Review*, 31 (1986): 131-55.

impinge upon the affairs of government.[75] These notables did not have any aspirations for forming horizontal links among themselves that could have led to the emergence of *Ständestaat*, or a polity of estates. Instead, they opted for vertical links with the State. They were interested in tax-farming privileges and not in productive enterprise.[76]

Consequently, the Ottoman polity showed neither the characteristics of a 'state as political organization of society' nor the dominant features of dual polities. Rather, it was a polarized polity. The setting was inappropriate not only for an adversary style of politics but also for an inquisitorial one. The mode of rule that was adopted was regulation from above. The subsidiarity principle adopted in continental western Europe (formulated by Pius XI in his Encyclical Quadragesimo Anno) that one should not withdraw from individuals and commit to the community what individuals can accomplish by their own enterprise and industry[77] had been alien both to the Ottoman and later to the Turkish polity. Starting from the middle of the nineteenth century the need for private entrepreneurial activities was recognized, yet the State considered it an utmost necessity to keep such activities under close supervision. An intermediate social class was considered necessary but it should not have had autonomy from the State.[78] At the turn of the century, Ziya Gökalp, the leading ideologue of modern Turkish nationalism, argued that there were three principal kinds of social groups - family, 'corporation', and the State. Of these, the State was the most important because it was an end in itself. When the situation demanded the family should subordinate itself to the corporation and the corporation to the State.[79] Atatürk, founder of the Republic (established in 1923), rejected the notion of social classes with different interests.[80] This view was shared even by the anti-Statist political parties founded following the installation of a multi-party regime in the mid-1940s. Fuad Köprülü, one of the founders of the *Demokrat* Party (1945-1960) stated: 'We cannot accept the fact that the social classes have irrenconcilable interests and have to struggle with each other.'[81] This view was also adopted by the Justice Party (1964-1980), another anti-Statist party.[82]

Consequently, when from the nineteenth century onwards the State began to pay attention to economic development it attempted to achieve it through administrative centralization. Even the adoption of development as one of the State norms did not persuade the State elites of the necessity of forming organic links with civil societal elements. The State continued to act without any allies in civil society. It did so by 'extending itself'.[83]

---

75 Metin Heper, 'Center and Periphery in the Ottoman Empire: With Special Reference to the Nineteenth Century', *International Political Science Review*, 1 (1980), pp. 87-8.

76 Şerif Mardin, 'Power, Civil Society and Culture in the Ottoman Empire', *Comparative Studies in Society and History*, 11 (1969), p. 266.

77 Alfred Stepan, *The State and Society. Peru in Comparative Perspective* (Princeton: Princeton University Press, 1978), p. 35.

78 Mardin,'Turkey: The Transformation of an Economic Code', p. 25.

79 Bianchi, *Interest Groups and Political Development in Turkey*, p. 97.

80 Ibid., p. 101.

81 Cited in ibid., pp. 104-5.

82 Ibid.

83 Faruk Birtek, 'The State and the Transition to Capitalism in England and Turkey: A Social-Structural Model', unpublished Ph.D. dissertation, University of California, Berkeley, 1978, p. 151.

Thus, from the mid-nineteenth century onwards the interest group associations (organized into various chambers) emerged as modified versions of traditional guilds, that is, as emanations of the State. During the *Tanzimat* (Reform) Period (1839-1876) and later, various chambers emerged as consultative bodies to and extensions of government, in addition to being professional associations. They were supposed to work in close cooperation with the Ministry of Trade to promote trade and later industry.[84]

During the Republican period, too, particularly during the single-party years (1923-1945), the chambers were expected to play a similar role. An Act enacted in 1924 defined the chambers as institutions serving the general interest. They were expected to carry out activities which would help to promote trade and industry. The secretary general of the Chamber of Trade and Industry was to be a civil servant from the Ministry of Trade.[85] The rationale behind another Act passed in 1943 was summed up as follows: 'The crises-ridden years we have been going through made it apparent that there is an absence in Turkey of professional morality and discipline on the part of businessmen and industrialists. It is well-known that such traits on the part of the members of private sector would induce them to function with a view to the general interest'.[86] This Act authorized the Ministry of Trade to set up chambers in places where there was a need for them. The Ministry could also expand or narrow down the jurisdictions of the chambers or dissolve and re-establish them, by having new members elected.[87]

That, during the Republican period chambers were perceived as a further arm of government was apparent in the way Act 5590 (1950) established Turkish Union of Chambers and Stock Exchanges. Article 62 enumerated the principal duties which were to be performed by the Union and, furthermore, stipulated that the Union had the responsibility 'to discharge any other duties to be assigned under the present Act and to function in an advisory capacity on economic affairs as may be requested by the Commissions of the Turkish Grand National Assembly or Ministries' and 'to fulfil such other functions as may be assigned by the Ministry of Economy and Commerce'.[88]

With the coming to power of the *Demokrat* Party in 1950 Turkish politics entered a period of relative liberalism. Consequently, the government's formal control over the chambers was somewhat relaxed. The tutelage over them of the Ministry of Economy and Commerce was abolished. The chambers could now themselves designate their secretary-general.[89] The 1961 Constitution, in turn, expanded the scope of basic rights and liberties, including the freedom to form associations. Government reaction to these developments was that of substituting informal controls for formal ones. During the 1950s, the *Demokrat* Party governments rewarded the members of the chambers which supported the party and harassed those chambers which opposed it. In the next two

---

84 Ayşe Öncü, 'Cumhuriyet Döneminde Odalar', *Cumhuriyet Dönemi Türkiye Ansiklopedisi*, 50 (1984), pp. 1567-8.

85 Ibid., p. 1569.

86 Ibid., p. 1570.

87 Ibid.

88 Kemali Saybaşılı, 'Chambers of Commerce and Industry, Political Parties and Government: A Comparative Analysis of the British and the Turkish Case', *Studies in Development* (Ankara), 11(1976), p. 122.

89 Öncü, 'Cumhuriyet Döneminde Odalar', p. 1571.

decades, the Justice Party did the same. [90] The Justice Party governments held summit meetings with chambers only when they figured they would not face opposition.[91] They consulted chambers 'only because they were semi-official bodies established for this purpose',[92] but paid no attention to their views when they clashed with their own. The Justice Party leaders were instrumental in the passing in 1972 of the rather restrictive Law of Associations. The spokesmen of the party had argued during the late 1960s that developments at the time represented not the emergence of a more truly pluralistic regime but a threat of anarchy and challenge to the authority of the State.[93] Armed with the powers the 1972 Act granted, the Justice Party governments continued to keep chambers at bay. Some of the powers of chambers such as to control and register prices of imports were withdrawn; at times, some chambers were dissolved.[94]

All in all, not unlike the situation in some continental western European countries, in Turkey, too, interest group associations were licensed, but in Turkey the purpose behind this arrangement was not to enable the leaders of these associations to intermediate economic interests but to control them politically.[95] This Turkish version of *parentala* relationship has been noted by Şerif Mardin:

> ...the central societal structuration in the Republic has always been a political structuration, and the leading industrialists and businessmen have been just as easily controllable as were moneylenders in the traditional Ottoman system. The top of the capitalistic entrepreneurial iceberg, the few leading industrialists and businesmen, were allowed to figure in the system because they could easily be manipulated.[96]

The situation was not different with regard to voluntary interest group associations, too. When asked in 1981 why employers did not articulate their demands unequivocally and in a straightforward fashion, the chairman of the Turkish Industrialists' and Businessmen's Association offered the following view:

> In this country, our philosophy has always been that of taking the paternal State ('*devlet baba*') as paramount, refraining from challenging it, and of pursuing an economic policy not in spite of, but along with the paternal State....Hesitancy on the part of members of the private sector to run for public office stems from the philosophy of not challenging the paternal State, from the belief that the State is still influential, and that alienating the State would not bode well for them.[97]

---

90 Bianchi, *Interest Groups and Political Development in Turkey*, p. 115.

91 Saybaşılı, 'Chambers of Commerce and Industry, Political Parties and Government', p. 129.

92 Ural Ayberk and Emre Boduroğlu, 'Turkish Interest Groups Facing the European Community', *Yapı Kredi [Bank] Economic Review* (Istanbul), 3 (1989), p. 142.

93 Bianchi, *Interest Groups and Political Development in Turkey*, p. 115.

94 Saybaşılı, 'Chambers of Commerce and Industry, Political Parties and Governments', p. 131.

95 From the Ottoman Empire to the present, all interest group associations, with the exception of the Organization for Cooperation of Industrial Chambers and the Turkish Businessmen's and Industrialists' Association, both founded during the 1970s, were established either by the State or with its support. See Kemali Saybaşılı, 'Türkiye'de Özel Teşebbüs ve Ekonomi Politikası', *Gelişme Dergisi* (Ankara), 13 (1976), p. 83.

96 Mardin,'Turkey: The Transformation of an Economic Code', p. 37.

97 Cited in Metin Heper, *The State Tradition in Turkey* (Walkington, England: The Eothen Press, 1985), p. 103.

In the event, unless governments were responsive to them, interest group associations in Turkey had little influence on economic decision-making. Their views were given shortshrift even in the preparation of five-year-plans.[98] Consequently, *individual* members of the private sector often by-passed their interest group associations and attempted establishing *clientala* relations with government officials. There has been an endless effort on their part to co-opt highly-placed bureaucrats to develop 'smooth' relations with the bureaucracy.[99]

Not unlike the situation in the Ottoman Empire, so during the Republican period, interest group politics in Turkey has been characterized by regulation from above. Interest group politics in Turkey has shown characteristics not of state corporatism, neo-corporatism, or pluralism but 'monism', to use Andrew Cox's terminology.[100] The State in Turkey has placed emphasis on rule from above; keeping civil societal elements at bay has not been a major issue; no need has been felt to let civil societal elements participate in government; the State has not felt itself obliged to be responsive to civil sociey.

This aloof attitude from civil society and the lingering impotence of civil society vis-à-vis the State, played a significant role in the evolution of the pattern of interest group politics in question. The passage to multi-party politics in the 1940s did not change this particular configuration of interest group politics. This was because of the particular conception of democracy held by the State elites and its impact on politics in Turkey. The strategy of defensive modernization, pursued from the end of the eighteenth century, made Westernization the most important item in the reform agenda of the Ottoman-Turkish State elites. Westernization among other things implied democracy.[101]

A democracy adopted by the conscious decision of the State elites rather than as a consequence of rising social groups, however, could not be conceived as a system of rule through which sectional interests would be reconciled. Instead, during the Ottoman period democracy was considered as the freedom of bureaucratic elites from the personal rule of the Sultan, and during the Republican era as the freedom of the intellectual- bureaucratic elites from the absolutism of the majority so that these elites could decide rationally, that is, through enlightened debate, what was best for the country. For long subordinated, if not virtually smothered, the representatives of the people for their part emerged as over-defiant or simply irresponsible which in turn fed on the prejudices towards them of the State elites.[102]

In the circumstances, it was difficult for a pluralistic interest group politics to flourish in Turkey. The State could not be seen as a 'helpless victim of interests'[103] for

---

98 Saybaşılı, 'Türkiye'de Özel Teşebbüs ve Ekonomi Politikası', p. 91.

99 Fehmi Yavuz, 'Özel Teşebbüs ve Planlı Kalkınmamız', in *Doç.Dr. Cem Sar'a Armağan*, no editor (Ankara: Ankara University Faculty of Political Science 1972), p. 641.

100 Cox, 'Neo-Corporatism versus the Corporate State', p. 46.

101 For an elaboration, see Metin Heper, 'Extremely "Strong State" and Democracy: The Turkish Case in Comparative and Historical Perspective', in *Modernity and Democracy*, Deborah Grenium, ed. for Israeli Academy of Sciences and Humanities (Leiden: Brill, forthcoming).

102 Heper, *The State Tradition in Turkey*, passim.

103 The phrase is borrowed from G. Wilson, *Interest Groups*, p. 151.

the Turkish State's autonomy and ability to act on its own initiative could not be denied. In their relations with the State, interest groups in Turkey, to use Wyn Grant's terminology, remained 'outsider' rather than 'insider groups'.[104] Insider strategies are adopted when access to ministers and civil servants is accorded to interest groups; outsider strategies involve campaigning, protest or partisan activities. In Turkey, faced with the strategy of *parentala* relations pursued by governments, interest groups could not engage even in partisan activities, and chose to stay out of politics.[105]

The Turkish Industrialists' and Businessmen's Association, considered by many as politically influential, often resorted in the late 1970s to public complaints and advertisement campaigns in the newspapers as a means of articulating their interests.[106] Roger King's delineation of non-efficacious interest groups aptly characterizes interest groups in Turkey: '...poorly organized groups formed voluntarily by individuals... which generally lacking close relations with government, rely on highly publicized campaigning activity to advance their cause'.[107]

That such activities would bear fruit was rather doubtful for in Turkey the State elites have had an incurably condescending attitude towards business groups. During the 1950s, the then Chamber of Commerce in Istanbul had to demand formally that bureaucrats be 'respectful' to businessmen and not to treat them as 'thieves with ties'![108] Similarly, in 1974, the Chairman of the Chamber of Commerce in Istanbul complained that the private sector should no longer be accused of playing the role of a 'middleman' (*aracı*), a derogatory term in Turkey.[109]

Turkish interest group politics has also been a far cry from neo-corporatism. Having a condescending and an aloof attitude towards civil society, the Turkish State was not 'woven with market', a *sine qua non* of neo-coorporatist interest group politics.[110] The sharp rift between the State and civil society was due to the absence historically in that polity of medieval corporatist forms, a point already made. Lack of a mercantilist tradition obviated the need for the development of Cameralism,[111] and therefore an orientation on the part of the State elites to make use of knowledge monopolized by business groups through seeking their cooperation in decision-making. Also, govern-

---

104 Wyn Grant, 'Insider Group, Outsider Group, and Interest Group Strategies in Britain', unpublished paper, 1977, cited in Ibid., p. 92.

105 Bianchi, *Interest Groups and Political Development in Turkey*, passim.

106 For elaborations, see Şebnem Gülfidan, 'Big Business and the State: The Case of TÜSİAD', unpublished Ph.D. dissertation, Boğaziçi University, Istanbul, 1989; Nazım İrem, 'Interest Groups-Government Interface: The Case of Turkish Businessmen's and Industrialists' Association', Unpublished M.A. Thesis, Bilkent University, Ankara, 1990. (TÜSİAD is the Turkish acronym for the Association in question.)

107 Roger King, *The State and Modern Society. New Directions in Political Sociology* (London: Macmillan, 1986), p. 121.

108 Doğan Avcıoğlu, *Türkiye'nin Düzeni. Dün, Bugün, Yarın* (Ankara: Bilgi Yayınevi, 1969), p. 250 and Metin Heper 'The Recalcitrance of the Turkish Public Bureaucracy to "Bourgeois Politics": A Multi-Factor Political Stratification Analysis', *The Middle East Journal*, 30(1976): 485-500.

109 At a panel discussion in Istanbul. See *Milliyet* (Istanbul daily), 5 May 1974.

110 The phrase is from Maier, 'Preconditions for Corporatism', p. 49.

111 For the lack of Cameralist tradition in Turkey see Metin Heper, 'A Methodological Note on Bureaucratic Modernization: Prevalent Attituds of the Turkish Civil Servants', *International Review of Modern Sociology*, 12 (1982): 75-103.

ments in Turkey did not feel it necessary to make resort to neo-corporatist arrangements for fostering their legitimacy. The notion of democracy prevalent in Turkey gave a particular twist to participation crisis. Political elites felt themselves vulnerable vis-à-vis the State elites and not the people; the state elites insisted that the political elites act within the framework of State norms they themselves formulated. In Turkey, democracy was viewed as an end in itself - that of finding the 'one best way'- and not as a means of satisfying group interests.[112] It must also be noted that before 1980, many other factors that elsewhere alone or in combination with other factors led to neo-corporatism were not present in Turkey - a strong presence of social democracy, need for creating and maintaining export viability, attempts at re-constructing the economy, perceiving long-term inflationary pressures as critical, growing international interdependency of the economy, a strong trade union movement, exacerbation of social cleavages, and the like.[113]

That social cleavages in Turkey remained moderate also obviated the need to resort to state corporatism. Çağlar Keyder has shown that until the 1980s many in Turkey viewed their relative standing in the economy in non-zero sum terms; depending upon the ups and downs in society either everybody gained or everybody lost.[114]

As already noted, the Left has not posed a threat as a social movement. The militancy on the part of some Leftist groups during the 1970s had no deep roots among the working class.[115] The Right could never brandish against the State the weapon of 'investment threat'. They were dependent on government in such areas as import allocation, credits, and investment.[116]

In the event, Turkey did not experience a personal dictatorship a la Portugal, a class-based authoritarianism as in Italy and Spain, or 'bureaucratic-authoritarianism' as in Latin America. Turkey did not have a Salazar, who tried to consolidate his own political base by removing autonomous sources of resistance.[117] Unlike what happened in Spain,[118] in Turkey working class organizations were not brutally destroyed. The Fascist practice of extending State control over the population through organized groups (for keeping at bay economic demands) had been alien, too. The Turkish case was also different from the Latin American one because in Turkey there was no sharing of

---

112 For an elaboration of this point, see Heper, 'Extremely "Strong State" and Democracy'.

113 That these factors contribute to the emergence of neo-corporatism is noted by, *inter alia*, Maier, 'Preconditions for Corporatism', passim, and Gerhard Lehmbruch, 'Concertation and the Structure of Corporatist Networks', in *Order and Conflict in Contemporary Capitalism*, Goldthorpe, ed. passim.

114 Çağlar Keyder, *State and Class in Turkey* (London: Verso, 1987), passim.

115 Kemal H. Karpat, 'Turkish Democracy at Impasse: Ideology, Party Politics and the Third Military Intervention', *International Journal of Turkish Studies*, 2 (1981): 1-43.

116 Nezih Neyzi, 'The Middle Classes in Turkey', in *Social Change and and Politics in Turkey. A Structural-Historical Analysis*, Karpat, ed., p. 129 and Ayşe Öncü, 'Inter-Organizational Networks and Social Structures: Turkish Chambers of Industry', *International Social Science Journal*, 21 (1979): 646-60.

117 On the Portuguese case, see Peter J. Williamson, *Varieties of Corporatism. A Conceptual Discussion* (Cambridge: Cambridge University Press, 1985), p.111.

118 Juan J. Linz, 'A Century of Politics and Interests in Spain', in *Organizing Interests in Western Europe*, Berger, ed., p. 387.

interests between the bureaucracy and the bourgeoisie.[119]

As Pierre Birnbaum has noted, State corporatism as defined by Schmitter has been a datum of authoritarian and totalitarian States which were not sufficiently differentiated from 'interests'.[120] For instance, in Franco's Spain the system was characterized by a complex network of influences and mutual favours between business, on one hand, and the ministries and bureaucracy, on the other;[121] in the (Spanish) Cortes there was a corporatist sector. In Fascist Italy, '[t]he State was not... the community's guardian but an amalgam of cliques of private interests'.[122] In Italy, Fascism never had its own governmental cadres, a new elite to run the corporate State. All the new corporatist agencies drew their staff notably from business.[123]

In Turkey, interest group politics could not take on a state corporatist form because there the State was distinctly differentiated from 'interests'. While elsewhere during the 1930s state corporatist practices were in full steam, during that decade Atatürk, was busy developing Atatürkism - a world view based in the last analysis on the value of reason - so as to separate rule from his person and endowing the State with a distinctive normative system of its own.[124] At the time, unlike the situation in state corporatist systems, the State in Turkey was not 'politicized' but to a large extent 'institutionalized' (around the Atatürkian principles of republicanism, nationalism, secularism, populism, étatism, and reformism). The State in Turkey came to have a notion of common good that one encounters in Catholic social philosophy - common good which can be known by 'right reason'.[125] It was not a liberal understanding of 'common good', but neither was it anti-democratic. This monist conception of public interest, developed by the State elites, was later adopted by the political elites. As already noted, the State-centred polity was replaced by a party-centred polity but not by a civil society-centred one. This led to the strategy on the part of the political elites to establish *parentala* relations with interest groups.

The State and Interest Groups: Turkey and France Compared

In terms of the interest group politics Turkey rather than France constitutes the

119 For the Latin American case, see the much debated thesis of Guillermo A O'Donnell in his, *Modernization and Bureaucratic-Authoritarianism. Studies in South American Politics* (Berkeley: Institute of International Studies, University of California, 1973). On the overlap between the public and private in Latin America, see Howard J. Wiarda, 'Corporatism and Development in the Iberic-Latin World: Persistent Strains and New Variations', in *The New Corporatism. Social-Political Structures in the Iberian World*, Fredrick B. Bike and Thomas Stritch, eds. (Notre Dame and London: University of Notre Dame Press, 1974), p. 14.

120 Birnbaum, *States and Collective Action*, p. 109.

121 Linz, 'A Century of Politics and Interests in Spain', in *Organizing Interests in Western Europe*, Berger, ed., p. 392.

122 Williamson, *Varieties of Corporatism*, p. 94.

123 Ibid., p. 95.

124 For an elaboration, see Metin Heper, 'Transformation of Charisma into a Political Paradigm: "Atatürkism" in Turkey', *Journal of the American Institute for the Study of Middle Eastern Civilization*, 1 (1980-81): 65-82.

125 For the notion of common good in Catholic social philosophy, see Stepan, *The State and Society*, p. 31.

polar type of a polity high in stateness. It is in Turkey and not in France that interest groups have been virtually ignored.

It is true, that in France, too, one comes across a concept of the State aloof from the squabbles of self-serving interests and the argument that the strength of the French State in the Fifth Republic makes it possible for the executive to act without consulting the affected interests.[126]

The State in France acts so, it is explained, because French culture is not so favourably disposed to interest groups as in America or even Britain and that French political discourse usually sets the interest groups with supposedly selfish concerns against the public interest which ought to be promoted by the State.[127] Consequently, in France one does not see even in limited areas pure forms of either neo-corporatism or pluralism. As already noted, in French neo-corporatism governments do not accord genuine involvement to groups in the policy-making process.[128] The French State co-operates with business for its own purposes.[129]

Yet, in France, interest groups play a more significant role in the polity than in Turkey. In the first place, as noted earlier, historically the French State has had less autonomy vis-à-vis civil society than the State in the Ottoman-Turkish context. Secondly, many top civil servants in France, during their training for such posts, spend some time in the private sector.[130] Thirdly, during recent decades, unlike the situation in Turkey, the State in France by its own volition began to narrow the gap between itself and civil society. In the early 1970s, Prime Minister Jacques Chaban Delmas undertook a bold effort to create a 'new society' in which interest groups could play a more important role.[131] Finally, in France democracy has been taken as a means rather than as an end: 'With the political fate of an incumbent government dependent in large part upon the economy's performance, government officials are likely to respond to argument that the businessmen's interests are theirs also.'[132]

Consequently, to use Allesandro Pizzorno's terminology,[133] in France the State seems to have been 'de-composed'; it no longer tends to speak with one 'voice' in the sense that not all agencies of the State have the same aloof attitude towards business: '...the senior civil servants may come, in terms of practical action, to identify the public interest (as it relates to a particular policy area) with the satisfaction of the claims of one or more private interests.'[134]

It is not therefore surprising that in France businessmen wield considerable political

---

126 F. Wilson, *Interest-Group Politics in France*, pp. 245-7.

127 G. Wilson, *Interest Groups*, p. 127. Also see George Lavau, 'Political Pressures by Interest Groups in France', in *Interest Groups in Four Continents*, Henry W. Ehrman, ed. (Westport, Connecticut: Greenwood Press, 1958), p. 60.

128 See note 32 above.

129 G. Wilson, *Interest Groups*, p. 133.

130 Ezra N. Suleiman, *Politics, Power and Bureaucracy in France. The Administrative Elite* (Princeton: Princeton University Press, 1974), chap. 3.

131 F. Wilson, *Interest-Group Politics in France*, p. 209.

132 Ibid., p. 92.

133 Alessandro Pizzorno, 'Interests and Parties in Pluralism', in *Organizing Interests in Western Europe*, Berger, ed., p. 262.

134 Cox and Hayward, 'The Inapplicability of the Corporatist Model in Britain and France', p. 231.

power. Unlike their brethren in Turkey, businessmen in France do not have to publicize their demands. They can 'present...[their] viewpoints in private, informal, bilateral contacts with elected government officials or civil servants'.[135] Sometimes businessmen are consulted prior to legislation affecting themselves.[136] In France, large enterprises usually have offices in Paris.[137] In 1979, businessmen, in response to an interview, expressed no anxiety about the government's infringement upon their 'autonomy'.[138]

This is not surprising. After the Second World War the idea of an *economie concertée* in which business would play a significant role pervaded French economic thinking. The State encouraged the strengthening and modernization of the *Conseil National du Patronat Français*, the major employers' association.[139] Over the years, different employers' chambers had been granted seats on the various government consultative bodies and committees. The French State gradually established quasi neo-corporatist relations with specific economic sectors.[140] Agriculture is one such sector.[141] Such relations flourished at the local level, too. In general, in France while trade unions evinced a weakness there has been a close partnership between government and 'powerful interests'.[142]

The Present Volume

Vis-à-vis interest groups, the State in the Ottoman-Turkish polity had always been more dominant than in France. In the Ottoman-Turkish polity the rift between the State and social groups had been greater than in France, and unlike France, that rift did not narrow down during the later historical periods under consideration here, that is, up to the 1980s The chapters that follow look at interest group politics in Turkey during the 1980s.

The 1980s are particularly important because one comes across developments that elsewhere contributed to the advent of pluralism or different versions of corporatism. Developments favourable for the emergence of corporatism included in the social sphere the crystallization of a zero-sum game notion of class relations,[143] in the economy a significant reconstruction (the strategy of import-substitution being replaced by that of export-orientation and the consequent increase in the internationalization of the

135 F. Wilson, *Interest-Group Politics in France*, p. 92.

136 Ibid., p. 164. Concerning certain policy measures various unions, too, had been invited to express views. See Janine Goetschy, 'The Neo-Corporatist Issue in France', in *Political Stability and Neo-Corporatism. Corporatist Integration and Societal Cleavages in Western Europe*, Ilja Scholten, ed. (London, etc: Sage, 1987), p. 179.

137 F. Wilson, *Interest-Group Politics in France*, p. 96.

138 Ibid., p. 185.

139 G. Wilson, *Interest Groups*, p. 151. Also see Graham K. Wilson, *Business and Politics. A Comparative Introduction* (London: Macmillan, 1985), pp. 80-6.

140 Ibid., pp. 36- 7.

141 Alan R. Ball and Frances Millard, *Pressure Politics in Industrial Societies. A Comparative Introduction* (London: Macmillan, 1986), pp. 130-64; John Keeler, *Politics of Neocorporatism in France* (Oxford and New York: Oxford University Press, 1987).

142 G. Wilson, *Interest Groups*, p. 36.

143 Keyder, *State and Class in Turkey*, passim.

economy),[144] and in politics a gradual weakening of the official ideology (Atatürkism)[145] that in the past was used by the State elites to achieve social and political integration. Developments favourable for the flourishing of pluralism included attempts at rolling back the frontiers of the State - privatization of state economic enterprises, decentralization of government and placing of emphasis on a market economy. Did these developments lead to at least glimmers of a transformation of interest group politics in Turkey into a pluralist or a corporatist pattern, or did the State in Turkey, perhaps in a different form, continue to dominate interest groups? The present volume addresses itself to this query.

---

144 Dankwart A. Rustow, 'Turkey's Liberal Revolution', *Middle East Review*, 12 (1985): 5-11.

145 Metin Heper, 'A *Weltanschauung*-turned-Partial Ideology and Normative Ethics', *Orient*, 1 (1984): 83-94.

Part Two

A NEW ERA: THE 1980s

2

Political Economy of Turkey in the 1980s Anatomy of Unorthodox Liberalism

Ziya Öniş

In 1980, a profound shift in philosophy occurred in Turkey concerning the role of the State in economic affairs. The new economic strategy aimed at decreasing both the scale of public sector activity as well as the degree of state intervention in the operation of the market. The structural adjustment initiated in 1980 embodied the following explicit objectives:(1) making prices flexible, (2) removing controls not only on prices but also on quantities, (3) reducing direct government participation in the economy, and (4) avoiding the de-stabilization of the economy through fiscal deficits, inflation and external debt accumulation. Hence, the new approach represented a fundamental break with the import substitution strategy of the earlier decades based on extensive State intervention, a policy which had appeared to have reached its limits in the second half of the 1970s.[1] A decade after the inception of the 'new economic strategy' we are now in a position to tackle a central interpretative issue: Is the pattern which emerged during the course of the 1980s consistent with the original aims of the programme? In other words, to what extent has Turkey become a more decentralized and market-oriented economy?

We ought to recognize at the outset that liberalization and privatization are now global phonomena. Hence, the Turkish experiment is not unique. Several countries have been undergoing similar types of transformation as part of a more general process in the restructuring of the world economy during the 1980s. The interesting puzzle is that essentially identical programmes of liberalization and privatization elicited highly dissimilar responses in different national settings. Countries have differed both in terms of the manner in which the programmes have been implemented, as measured by deviations from 'orthodox norms', as well as the degree of success achieved in terms of objective economic indicators. Both the differential *pattern* of liberalization and the contrast in the economic *performance* of countries undergoing programmes of liberalization almost simultaneously, emerge as serious issues for investigation.

The present study is motivated by and built around one assumption and one hypothesis. The assumption is that the analysis of 'domestic structures' and the specific

---

1 For a broad overview of the import-substitution strategy in Turkey and an analysis of the problems confronted by that strategy which led to its eventual demise in the second half of the 1970s, see Ziya Öniş, 'Inflation and Import Substituting Industrialization: An Interpretation of the Turkish Case', *Journal of Economics and Administrative Studies*, (Istanbul) 1 (1987):56-72; Ziya Öniş and Süleyman Özmucur, 'Supply-Side Origins of Macroeconomic Crises in Turkey', paper presented at the World Bank Conference, 'Macroeconomic Policies, Crisis and Growth in the Long-Run', Madrid, 14-18 May 1988.

manner whereby those structures interact with the international system, are crucial for explaining the dichotomy of the contrasting patterns that emerge in response to a 'common external shock', namely, an identical economic strategy. Domestic structures in turn should be investigated in terms of the structuration and interaction of the state and society. More specifically, we need to consider both the degree of centralization of the state as well as the degree of differentiation of the state from society.[2]

The hypothesis relates to the idea of 'retreating states and expanding societies' that one comes across in the recent social science literature.[3] We shall argue that the dichotomy of retreating states and expanding societies is rather superficial and misleading. In fact, what we observe in the aftermath of liberalization and privatization experiments in several contexts is not a retreat of the state, but a reconstruction of the state. In this respect, Andrew Gamble's recent work is highly illustrative.[4] Gamble's analysis is based on the U.K. experiment which hitherto has constituted one of the most ambitious and radical attempts in establishing a free market economy. Gamble demonstrates that the ability to implement the liberalization programme in Britain was facilitated by the creation of a strong state. The strong state in turn involved an increase in the coercive powers of the state as well as in the degree of centralization of the executive power, and thus the public policy-making process. The notion of a strong state, however, is problematic in the sense that there may not necessarily be a linear, one to one correspondence, between the degree of centralization of the state apparatus, on the one hand, and the extent of state strength, or capacity, on the other. There, we need to transcend Gamble's free market versus the strong state dichotomy, and provide a more subtle analysis of the changing nature of the state. The present chapter purports to undertake this exercise with a view to the post-1980 Turkish experience.

---

2 The framework for the present study has to some extent been inspired by Peter Katzenstein, ed., *Between Power and Plenty* (Madison, Wisconsin: University of Wisconsin Press, 1978).

3 The notion of 'state autonomy', the central concept of the state-centred paradigm, is defined as a situation where state actors may consistently have a set of preferences which are quite distinct from the views and interests of civil societal elements. See Peter Evans, Dietrich Rueschemeyer and Theda Skocpol, eds, *Bringing the State Back In* (New York: Cambridge University Press, 1985). Also relevant in the present context are Eric Nordlinger, *On the Autonomy of the Democratic State* (Cambridge: Harvard University Press, 1981); Ezra Suleiman, *Private Power and Centralization in France: The Notaires and the State* (Princeton: Princeton University Press, 1988); Jeff Frieden, 'The Third World Indebted Industrialization: International Finance and State Capitalism in Mexico, Brazil, Algeria, and South Korea', *International Organization*, 35 (1981): 407-31; Barbara Stallings, 'International Lending and the Relative Autonomy of the State: A Case Study of Twentieth Century Peru', *Politics and Society*, 14 (1985): 257-88. For a recent overview of the recent literature, see John Waterbury, 'State and Society in Contemporary Political Analysis', paper presented at the Conference, 'Dynamics of States and Societies in Middle East', Cairo, 17-19 June 1989. On Turkey's 'state tradition' and its ramifications, see Metin Heper, *The State Tradition in Turkey* (Walkington, England: The Eothen Press, 1985) and İlkay Sunar, *State and Society in the Politics of Turkey's Development* (Ankara: Ankara University Faculty of Political Science, 1974).

4 Andrew Gamble, *The Free Market Economy and the Strong State. The Politics of Thatcherism* (London: Macmillan, 1988).

Orthodox Aspects of the Turkish Adjustment Experience

For analytical convenience, it might be useful to distinguish between three subperiods of the 1980s:

- Phase I of stabilization and structural adjustment undertaken primarily by the government formed under the auspices of the military regime (January 1980 - November 1983).
- Phase II of liberalization and acceleration of growth, led by the public sector, following the return to parliamentary democracy (November 1983 - November 1987).
- Phase III of stabilization and slow growth following the 'mini-crisis' which developed in the aftermath of the November 1987 general elections (1988 and early 1989).

The initial steps in the direction of a market-oriented economy involved the deregulation of key relative prices. These prices, including the exchange rates, interest rates and the product prices of the state economic enterprises (SEEs), became flexible, and continuous real devaluations of the exchange rate as well as the transition to positive real rates of interest eliminated the bias against exports and private savings respectively, a bias which had become an endemic feature of the pre-1980 regime. In the 1980s, Turkey has emerged as a model in terms of the degree of *consistency* that the policy makers achieved with reference to the real exchange rate and real interest rate targets. Similarly, via flexible product prices, the SEEs started to report positive operating profits, again in stark contrast with the experience of the 1970s. Furthermore, pressures have been exerted on the SEEs to operate as autonomous commercial entities. The link between the SEEs' financial requirements on the one hand, and consolidated budget and the Central Bank on the other, have been substantially eliminated. [5] Yet price flexibility in the Turkish context should not be equated with price determination in a free market setting. In fact, what emerged is an 'intermediate regime' whereby the central government continued to exercise substantial leverage over the determination of key relative prices such as interest rates and the exchange rate.

The transition to a flexible price system constituted a profound transformation in the early 1980s. Another striking shift has involved the progressive withdrawal of the public sector from manufacturing into infrastructural activities such as transport, energy and communications. Hence, the role of the state as a direct producer of manufactured commodities was increasingly relegated into the background. Another significant change in the early 1980s involved the elimination of direct controls such as import quotas, which had been a salient feature of the pre-1980 economic regime.

The decisive shift in the direction of liberalization, however, occurred not during the first phase, but in the early months of the second phase. Both the trade regime and the capital account were substantially liberalized during the course of December

---

5 For detailed evidence, see Ziya Öniş and Süleyman Özmucur, 'The Role of the Financial System in the Creation and Resolution of Macroeconomic Crises in Turkey', paper presented to the World Bank Conference, 'Macroeconomic Policies, Crisis and Growth in the Long-Run', Madrid, 14-18 May 1988.

1983 and January 1984.[6] The degree of tariff protection on imports was reduced by a significant margin. Similarly, restrictions on capital flows and foreign exchange were substantially removed. The new measures enabled domestic residents to open deposit accounts denominated in foreign currency.

Foreign direct investment constitutes another sphere where a liberal regime has been established. Foreign investment in the pre-1980 period was extremely limited by international standards due to a host of restrictions and bureaucratic constraints. In the course of the 1980s, these restrictions were substantially eliminated. A single agency was created in the form of the Foreign Investment Department within the State Planning Organization which became responsible for foreign investment approvals, thereby alleviating the problems generated by the fragmented nature of the bureaucracy, which had characterized the pre-1980 regime. Furthermore, the foreign investment Code was made consistent with the Organization for Economic and Cultural Development (OECD) norms, in the sense that foreign investors became entitled to the same set of investment incentives and allowances as their domestic counterparts. Consequently, foreign and domestic investors became subject to equal treatment before Turkish Law. With the exception of domestic tax obligations, the new legislation also enabled foreign investors to transfer their profits abroad without any restrictions. An additional step to encourage foreign investors involved the establishment of free zones.

More recently, tentative steps have been taken in the direction of privatization. Privatization of state economic enterprises appeared on the government's agenda from 1984 onwards. Yet, it is interesting that the programme was not initiated until after the general elections of 1987. In fact, the first major case of privatization involving the sale of about half the public shares in the mixed telecommunications company, TELETAŞ, via the Stock Exchange, occurred only as late as February 1988. By 1990, only a few companies had been privatized.[7]

Wage flexibility constitutes yet another orthodox feature of the post-1980 adjustment process. Both real wages as well as the share of real wages in national income have been substantially reduced as part of the forced incomes policy, involving constitutional restrictions on strike activity and the bargaining power of trade unions. * The downward flexibility of real wages has undoubtedly contributed in the course of the 1980s to both Turkey's export drive and the increasing inflow of foreign investment.

In retrospect, the liberalization programme in Turkey has been a sequential affair. In contrast to many Southern Cone countries, liberalization in Turkey has been introduced on a step-by-step basis. While the scale of transformation has been quite extensive, the authorities have deliberately avoided introducing wholesale liberalization measures simultaneously.

---

6 For extensive empirical evidence concerning the dimensions of the trade and capital account liberalization which were realized in December 1983 and January 1984, respectively, see Sübidey Togan, Hasan Olgun, and Halis Akder, *Recent Developments in the External Economic Relations of Turkey* (Istanbul: Türk-Trade Publication, 1987).

7 See Ziya Öniş, 'Evolution of Privatization in Turkey: The Institutional Context of Public Enterprise Reform', paper presented at the Conference, 'Dynamics of States and Societies in the Middle East', Cairo, 17-19 June 1989.

* The restrictions in question are elaborated in chapter 4 in this volume (Editor's note).

Elements of Unorthodox Liberalism

The picture that we have presented so far is consistent with the liberal vision of retreating states and expanding societies. Yet, a closer examination of the Turkish experience in the 1980s reveals a more complex pattern. The steps taken in the direction of a market-oriented economy have been accompanied by a significant concentration of economic and political power.

Most observers of the Turkish economy would agree that export performance has been an outstanding success story, notably in the first half of the 1980s. For the orthodox, neo-classical economist the explanation is quite straightforward: the combination of import liberalization and appropriate exchange rates is sufficient to account for the transformation in export performance as compared with the pre-1980 period.

This explanation, however, is inadequate, or at least incomplete, in so far as it fails to take into account the organizational basis of Turkey's export drive in the 1980s. A major institutional innovation introduced in Turkey in the early 1980s involved the formation of foreign trade companies (FTCs). The legislation concerning the formation of these companies was directly influenced by the East Asian experiences, notably the cases of South Korea and Japan. The Act on Foreign Trade Companies stated that companies which surpassed a pre-specified export target would become eligible for export tax rebates. In fact, export tax rebates were established as a major instrument for export promotion, until they were eventually eliminated by the beginning of 1989.[8]

The explicit intention of the new legislation was to create a highly concentrated export sector based on a limited number of large-scale companies which would be in a position to exploit economies of scale, especially in marketing, and therefore be able to compete successfully in international markets. The foreign trade companies were also provided with additional incentives in the form of exclusive trading rights with specific countries, including the Eastern Europe and the Middle Eastern countries, with which trade has been conducted on a bilateral basis.

As a consequence of the special incentives provided, about twenty-five to thirty companies, many of which maintained organic links with large holding companies directed primarily towards the domestic market, steadily increased their share of Turkish exports, and accounted for about 50 per cent of Turkish exports by the second half of the 1980s. It would be inappropriate in the present context to provide a normative assessment of the contribution of these companies to Turkish export performance, or the extent to which they have actually managed to duplicate the Japanese and Korean models which they were designed to emulate. What is interesting for our purposes is that a model of export-oriented industrialization based on foreign trade companies is clearly in contradiction with the alleged aims of the creation of a liberal economy. In fact, to use Eric Nordlinger's terminology,[9] the creation of foreign trade compa-

[8] On the export tax system and the role of foreign trade companies, see Ziya Öniş, 'Organization of Export-Oriented Industrialization: The Turkish Foreign Trade Companies in a Comparative Perspective', mimeographed, Center of International Studies, Princeton University, 1989. The notorious case of 'fictitious exports' has constituted the most obvious form of abuse involving the export tax rebate system as well as an overt form of rent-seeking on the part of some of the foreign trade companies.

[9] Nordlinger, *On the Autonomy of the Democratic State*, passim.

nies can be conceived as a special case of 'state-engineered autonomy'. The State has consciously encouraged the formation of a group of companies directly dependent on a special set of incentives that it has provided. In retrospect, the creation of FTCs has encouraged export-oriented rent-seeking. The companies concerned competed for obtaining an additional share of tax rebates. Hence we observe an element of continuity with the earlier decades, although not on the scale of the pervasive rent-seeking behaviour under the import-substitution regime of the 1960s and 1970s. *

Turning our attention to the public sector itself, we observe several elements which again contrast sharply with the original objective involving the withdrawal of the state from economic affairs. First, public investment continued to be a dominant form of capital accumulation in the Turkish economy in spite of the fact that the composition of public investment has shifted dramatically from manufacturing into infrastructural activites. Throughout the 1980s, the public sector accounted for more than 50 per cent of total fixed capital formation. Secondly, in spite of a decline in the share of public sector in manufacturing production, the contribution of SEE's gross national product did not decrease during the post-1980 period. Thirdly, the public sector continued to dominate the financial system. The share of public banks in total bank deposits expanded during the 1980s. Furthermore, around 90 per cent of the securities issued on the Istanbul Stock Exchange, founded in 1986, has been public sector issues, showing the degree of control exercised by the public sector over the capital market.[10]

The continuing resilience of the public sector in the economic sphere has been accompanied by a parallel process involving an extension of central governmental, notably prime ministerial, power. The origins of this process can be traced to the Constitution of 1982, as a consequence of which the powers of the executive were significantly increased vis-à-vis the legislature.[11] Subsequently, in the post-1983 phase, a number of additional steps have been taken in the direction of strengthening and consolidating executive power, notably in conjunction with prime ministerial power in relation to the bureaucracy.[12]

The relative decline of parliament and the parallel expansion in executive power can be illustrated with reference to extra-budgetary funds (EBFs), which constitute one of the principal innovations of the period. [13] The original motive for the creation of EBFs lay in the government's inability to generate revenues from standard sources. The difficulties of raising revenues on an adequate scale compelled the government to resort increasingly to non-tax sources of revenue such as the 'exit fund' (read 'fee') paid by citizens travelling abroad. In addition to providing a solution to the revenue problem, the EBFs also embodied a critical advantage, namely that the revenues accumulated under the EBFs could be spent without prior parliamentary approval. Hence,

* Chapter 7 in this volume deals exclusively with the FTCs [Editor's note].

10 TÜSİAD, *1980 Sonrası Ekonomide Kamu-Özel Sektör Dengesi* (İstanbul: TÜSİAD, 1988). TÜSİAD is the Turkish acronym for the Turkish Industrialists' and Businessmen's Association (Editor's note).

11 Ergun Özbudun, *Türk Anayasa Hukuku* (Ankara: Yetkin, 1986).

12 Metin Heper, 'The Executive in the Third Turkish Republic, 1982-1989', *Governance*, 3(1990), pp. 299-319.

13 For an in-depth analysis of EBFs, see Oğuz Oyan and Ali Rıza Aydın, *İstikrar Programından Fon Ekonomisine* (Ankara: Verso, 1987).

the EBFs helped to provide considerable discretionary powers to the central government, and notably to the prime minister, in the allocation of revenues. For instance, in 1988, 11.2 per cent of public investment was financed from the EBFs.[14]

Finally, we ought to draw attention to two further aspects of centralization of government during the decade of the 1980s. The first dimension relates to the centralization of the bureaucratic apparatus. After 1983, new layers of bureaucracy were established. Two major examples of this process include the creation in 1984 of the [Board of] Mass Housing and Public Participation Fund ([B]MHPPF) under the direct control of the Prime Minister. This particular agency was assigned a wide range of responsibilities and powers, including the administration of the privatization programme. Similarly, the creation of a novel bureaucratic agency namely the Undersecretariat of Treasury and Foreign Trade (UTFT) led to a significant demise in the powers of the Ministry of Finance. The second dimension of centralization involved the creation of additional ministries of state with specific responsibilities. In fact, this trend pointed towards not only a decline in the powers of the legislature vis-à-vis the executive, but also those of the Cabinet itself relative to the office of the Prime Minister. The Prime Minister, surrounded by a limited number of ministers of state, special advisers and a number of high level bureaucrats, became the real locus of economic decision making.[15]

The underlying motive in the creation of new forms of bureaucracy such as [B]MHPPF and UTFT has been the concern with instituting a managerial bureaucracy in place of the traditional patrimonial bureaucracy. Installing such a bureaucracy in the form of a select group of technocrats, largely independent from both societal and intra-bureaucratic pressures, was seen as a necessary condition for the consistent implementation of the economic programme.

What is interesting for our purposes is the emergence of a complex pattern which a simple dichotomy such as 'retreating states and expanding societies' fails to capture. What has been happening is a significant restructuration of the State, that is, centralization of government as well as a (state-induced) concentration of private power, parallel to the steps taken in the direction of establishing a market-oriented economy.

A final example of the complexity of Turkey's recent political economy relates to the apparently contradictory trends involving centralization and decentralization simultaneously. The creation of the EBFs, for example, clearly implied an expansion in the discretionary powers available to the government. Yet, at the same time, there was a significant extension of the powers and financial means granted to the local authorities.[16] It is well to remember, however, that this was directly encouraged by the central government itself.[17] Thus, the fact that major local authorities, such as Istanbul, could emerge as significant borrowers in international financial markets was due to the explicit guarantees provided by the central government in the first place.

---

14 'Annual Report, 1988', by Ministry of Finance, Ankara.

15 For further consideration of this issue, see Metin Heper, 'The Motherland Party Governments and Bureaucracy in Turkey, 1983-1988', *Governance*, 2 (1989): 460-71 and Ayşe Öncü and Deniz Gökçe, in this volume.

16 See Metin Heper, ed., *Local Government in Turkey. Governing Greater Istanbul* (London: Routledge, 1989).

17 See Metin Heper,'Introduction', in *Democracy and Local Government. Istanbul in the 1980s*, Metin Heper, ed. (Walkington, England: The Eothen Press, 1987).

Hence, the increasing activity of local authorities is not necessarily synonymous with increased local government autonomy. In any case, towards the end of the decade, to central government took back some of the powers it had earlier granted the local government.[18]

Political Constraints and Policy Incoherence

The uneasy co-existence of tariff reform, opening up of the capital account and favourable incentives for foreign investment on the one hand, and growing macro-economic disequilibrium resulting from a public sector based on an expansionist strategy on the other, constituted a central paradox of the second phase, namely the 1983-1987 period. Data presented in Table 2.1 clearly illustrate the dimensions of macro-economic instability which emerged during the period.

Table 2.1 : Indicators of Macro-economic Instability, 1980-1988 (in percentages)

	GNP Growth	Inflation Rate*	Budget Deficit/GNP	External Debt/GNP
1980	-1.1	108.6	3.7	25.7
1981	4.1	36.7	1.0	28.4
1982	4.6	27.0	1.7	32.4
1983	3.3	30.5	2.5	35.6
1984	5.9	50.3	5.1	42.4
1985	5.1	43.2	2.8	47.4
1986	8.1	29.6	2.9	54.0
1987	7.4	32.0	4.0	60.5
1988	4.1	68.4	3.4	52.0

Source: State Institute of Statistics, Ministry of Finance and Central Bank.
* Based on the State Institute of Statistics wholesale price index.

The Özal government initially demonstrated a strong commitment to liberalization. A marked reduction in import tariffs and the associated opening up of the capital account were among the very first measures of the newly elected government. Yet, the re-establishment of multi-party democracy resulted in a significant shift of incentives for the political elites during the post-1983 period. The reform programme implemented between 1980-1983 had already resulted in a marked change in income distribution, with a number of socio-economic groups including wage earners and other fixed income groups, lower level bureaucrats and the farming community, emerging as the principal losers from this process.[19]

---

[18] See Metin Heper, 'Dynamics of Inter-Governmental Relations in post- 1983 Turkey', in *Structure of Local Politics in the Middle East*, Takeji Ino, ed. Tokyo: Institute of Developing Economies, 1991.

[19] See Süleyman Özmucur, *Türkiye'nin Milli Geliri* (İstanbul: İstanbul Ticaret Odası, 1987).

In the presence of electoral constraints, accentuated by the transformation of the distributional profile which occurred in the early 1980s, short-term 'political rationality' required the formation and consolidation of a broad coalition among groups with potentially conflicting interests. Hence, the government increasingly pressed for rapid growth based on the expansion of the public sector; the latter was utilized as the principal mechanism for constructing and consolidating a broad right-of-centre coalition.[20]

We need to consider at this juncture the interaction between governing parties and the State in Turkey, or more specifically the relationship between 'state autonomy' and 'party autonomy', which constitutes yet another key dimension in that country's complex political economy trajectory.[21] We need to recognize that the Motherland Party which emerged as the governing party in the 1983 general elections was a brand new party, although it was to some extent continuing in the footsteps of the Justice Party - the principal right-of-centre party of the 1960s and 1970s. The fact that Özal had been the architect of a successful adjustment programme, which had brought the country out of an acute phase of economic and political crisis, provided an obvious source of legitimacy for the newly instituted Motherland Party. In spite of this initial advantage, however, the party was confronted with several handicaps. Being a novel entity, the party was faced with the problem of developing and subsequently consolidating a solid electoral base. More significantly, the options available to the Justice Party during the previous two decades no longer presented themselves as feasible options in the context of the 1980s. During the 1960s, corresponding to the 'easy phase' of the import-substitution strategy, the Justice Party could rely on economic growth for incorporating major segments of the population in its electoral base via its populist strategy.[22] Rapid economic growth, based on extensive public sector participation ensured that all the major socio-economic groups would benefit in *absolute* terms. The 1980s, in contrast, constituted a period of adjustment which naturally signified that several groups in society would emerge as losers from this process. Hence, the context of the 1980s was not the positive-sum situation which had confronted the Justice party in the relatively problem-free decade of the 1960s.

A further complication was introduced by the fact that the Motherland Party itself was not a monolithic entity. The party elite itself has become divided into two separate segments in the form of a 'liberal wing' and a 'conservative wing', with the latter informed by an explicit Islamic view. The tension between these two segments of the party, although it was not immediately obvious, became increasingly more pronounced

---

20 For a detailed analysis of the mechanisms whereby right-of-centre parties tried to construct broad electoral coalitions in the post-1960 period, and especially in the context of the 1980s, see Ziya Öniş and James Riedel, 'The Political Economy of Macroeconomic Policies, Crises and Growth in Turkey', paper presented at the World Bank Conference, 'Macroeconomic Policies, Crisis and Growth in the Long-Run', Mexico City, 28 March - 1 April 1989, and John Waterbury, 'Coalition Building, Export-Led Growth and Public Sector in Turkey', paper presented at the Annual Conference of the Middle East Studies Association, Los Angeles, 5-8 November 1988.

21 On this matter, see Metin Heper, 'The State, Political Party and Society in post-1983 Turkey', *Opposition and Government*, 25 (1990): 321-33.

22 On the 'populist' nature of the economic strategy implemented in the 1960s by the Justice Party, see Korkut Boratav, *Türkiye İktisat Tarihi, 1908-1985* (Ankara: Gerçek Yayınevi, 1988). For an explicit attempt to compare the 1980s with the 1960s, see Ziya Öniş and James Riedel, 'The Political Economy of Macro Economic Policies, Crises and Growth in Turkey', typescript.

in the second half of the 1980s, especially as we entered the third phase. The conflict between the two groups also manifested itself in the context of the economic strategy pursued. The liberal wing, in close association with the new managerial elites, wished to proceed with the programme of liberalization while at the same time maintaining monetary and fiscal discipline. The conservative wing, in contrast, has been in favour of using the discretionary powers of the State as an instrument for broadening the electoral base of the party itself.

These sets of pressures help to illuminate why the government has increasingly relaxed fiscal discipline, and followed an expansionary strategy in the post-1983 phase. The result was the creation of a macro-economic environment, characterized by fiscal deficits and high loan rates of interest as well as by accelerating and volatile rates of inflation, which came into increasing conflict with the underlying objectives of liberalization and transition to a free market economy. High and volatile rates of inflation, for example, have retarded the development of capital markets which, in turn, placed a major restriction on both the pace and scale of the privatization programme. [23]

Furthermore, in the presence of high inflation, generating real devaluation and maintaining real interest rates on deposits at positive levels required frequent changes in the *nominal* values of the exchange rate and interest rates. The very frequency of the changes in nominal variables to achieve *real targets* under those circumstances generated great uncertainty on the part of economic agents, and led to considerable alienation on the part of some private sector groups from the government's economic programme.[24]

In retrospect, a basic contradiction emerged in the system in the second half of the 1980s. The government remained committed to its 'inflation tax' objective in order to finance its expansionist strategy, in the absence of an adequate tax base. Yet, at the same time, the economy has increasingly been transformed into an 'indexed economy' where various agents possessed avenues open to them to protect themselves against inflation. This apparent duality has progressively rendered the Turkish economy vulnerable to a potential macro-economic crisis.

Following the mini-crisis of 1987, the austerity measures introduced by the February Programme of 1988 were clearly intended to re-institute fiscal discipline. The immediate outcome of the programme was a reduction in the rate of economic growth, while the inflation rate still remained at very high levels. The decisive turning point was

---

23 See Ziya Öniş, 'Evolution of Privatization in Turkey: The Institutional Context of Public Enterprise Reform', paper presented at the Conference, 'Dynamics of States and Societies in the Middle East', Cairo, 17-19 June 1989.

24 For the case of the banking sector, see Ayşe Öncü and Deniz Gökçe 'Macro-Politics of De-Regulation and Micro-Politics of Banking', and, for the business community, see Ayşe Buğra, 'Political Sources of Uncertainty in Business Life in Turkey', both in this volume. A useful testimony to the criticisms voiced by the business community concerning the growing imbalances between the public and private sectors is from TÜSİAD itself. See TÜSİAD, *1980 Sonrası Ekonomide Kamu-Özel Sektör Dengesi*. Yet, there is an element of uni-directionality implicit in all these studies, namely that State-induced uncertainty has been responsible for the problems confronted by the business community. A more balanced analysis requires a consideration of the extent to which private sector has responded or, indeed, failed to respond to the opportunities provided in the context of the 1980s. This is particularly relevant to the privatization programme which is currently in progress.

reached in the local elections of March 1989, in which the Motherland Party could emerge as only the third party. From that point onwards, we observe a state of uncertainty concerning the route that the government will actually follow, given the pronounced weakening of its electoral base. In the late 1980s, two options were available: (1) a high growth-cum-redistribution strategy which could be politically rational in the short run but would nevertheless increase the risk of macro-economic crisis; (2) a slow growth-cum-liberalization strategy which would be unpopular in the short-run but whose benefits would accrue in the medium-term in the form of improved efficiency and growth performance.

From the perspective of the present study two broad conclusions might be drawn. Firstly, political rationality came increasingly into conflict with market rationality in the post-1983 period. Secondly, due to considerations of political rationality, the government has progressively undermined both its autonomy and also its ability to implement the long-term programme of liberalization and structural adjustment.

Impact of the International System

The Turkish experiment in the 1980s provides an interesting case for the study of the elusive triangle - the relationship between the state, society and the international system and the precise nature of their interaction at a particular point in time. We hypothesize, at the outset, that external influences have performed a crucial role in shaping the state and society and the manner of their interaction. Hence any attempt to investigate the dynamics of the state and society in a 'closed framework' is likely to generate a highly inadequate and misleading picture.

We have to recognize that in 1980 Turkey emerged as the test-case for the newly instituted World Bank-International Monetary Fund (IMF) joint programme involving 'cross-conditionality'.[25] In retrospect, several factors were responsible for the selection of Turkey as a test case. Firstly, the timing of the crisis was important. The crisis in Turkey occurred in the late 1970s, significantly prior to the emergence of the Latin American debt crisis. The second factor involved the strategic importance of Turkey as an integral part of the NATO alliance. Thirdly, a test-case would need to embody the ingredients of potential success. Compared to the vast majority of less developed countries (LDCs), Turkey possessed the infrastructure for successful adjustment. It was a middle income country with a highly developed industrial base and adequate administrative capacity as well as other location-specific advantages. Finally, there existed a bureaucratic elite which would identify itself with the new economic strategy

[25] For a detailed discussion and empirical evidence, see Colin Kirkpatrick and Ziya Öniş, 'Structural Adjustment Lending and Policy Reform in Turkey, 1980-1986', paper presented at the Annual conference of the U.K. Development Studies Association, Birmingham, 13-15 September 1988 and Peter Wolf, *Stabilization and Structural Adjustment in Turkey, 1980-1985* (Berlin: German Development Institute, 1987).

and would be committed to its implementation.[26]

During the 1980-1984 period, Turkey received five successive structural adjustment loans (SALs) from the World Bank - a record number. In addition to financial resources made directly available, the programme was instrumental in generating a significant flow of resources from official creditors, notably the governments of the OECD countries. Hence, the scale of the financial assistance provided to Turkey during the 1980s exceeded by a considerable margin the magnitude of resources made available elsewere under similar adjustment programmes.

Although structural adjustment in Turkey has involved, especially in the early stages, the collaboration of the World Bank with the IMF, the World Bank was unambiguously the principal actor in the post-1980 period.[27] The emphasis of the programme was clearly on structural adjustment as distinct from stabilization *per se*. In fact, 'stabilization' itself was achieved primarily from the supply-side via increased availability of imports and wage flexibility, as opposed to fiscal and monetary austerity.

By the end of 1984, the institutional limit on five successive SALs had been reached. Nevertheless, the relationship with the World Bank has continued after 1984 in the form of 'sectoral adjustment loans', with their associated conditionality requirements, a significant part of which could also be utilized for general balance of payments purposes.

The scale of resources channelled to Turkey as part of the SAL programme provided considerable freedom of action on the part of the policy makers, and consequently augmented the government's relative autonomy from societal pressures, in terms of its ability to implement the programme in a consistent fashion without any deviations from its targets. The favourable external environment enabled the technocratic elite, or rather Özal, to 'internalize' the policy package and to popularize it as the government's own strategy, as opposed to being a strategy imposed by an external agency. In fact, to its credit, the World Bank has always been in the background rather than being actively or openly involved in the policy formulation or implementation processes.

In retrospect, the Turkish case was clearly not a case of 'soft conditionality', in the sense that the programme would demand significant changes in a multitude of areas, and the initiation of the subsequent phase would be conditional upon realizing the

---

[26] A recent study by Stephen Haggard, 'The Politics of Adjustment: Lessons from the IMF's Extended Fund Facility' *International Organization*, 39(1985): 505-34 is highly illuminating in this context. On the basis of cross-country evidence, Haggard seeks to identify factors that are critical for the implementation and eventual success of IMF stabilization programmes. His principal conclusion is that the power, cohesion and ideological orientation of the technocrats is an important variable in explaining the fate of the IMF programmes. The existence of an IMF-sympathetic 'stabilizing cadre' within the state apparatus appears to be a prerequisite for programme success. Clearly, this type of argument would be equally applicable to the case of the SAL programmes undertaken in conjunction with the World Bank.

[27] We need to emphasize, however, that during the crisis period of 1977-1979 the IMF was the principal actor, and the World Bank was absent from the scene. Yet, the stand-by agreements concluded with the IMF ended in failure. The inability to conform to the conditions attached to the programmes resulted in their subsequent termination. For an overview of the relationship with the IMF in the 1970s, see Osman Okyar, 'Turkey and the IMF: A Review of Relations', in *IMF Conditionality*, John Williamson, ed. (Washington D.C.: Institute for International Economics, 1983).

changes required in the current phase. Yet, from a comparative perspective, the conditions imposed in the Turkish case were quite favourable in certain crucial respects. Firstly, a feature which is inherent in SAL conditionality, as opposed to IMF conditionality, was the emphasis on the *direction* of policy changes rather than the achievement of specific quantitative targets. Secondly, five successive SALs were provided in consecutive years rather than being distributed over a longer period. Thirdly, we may re-emphasize the obvious point concerning the magnitude of resources associated with SAL conditionality.

The World Bank, as well as the rest of the international financial community, were committed to the success of the Turkish experiment. Having already channelled a significant amount of resources, they clearly wished to demonstrate it as a model for the rest of the LDCs. Furthermore, the World Bank proceeded with the fourth and the fifth SALs immediately after the first three SALs to speed up the process of transition to democracy in Turkey. The acceleration of the process aimed at ensuring that the technocratic elites and especially Özal, who had been out of office after the 'Bankers Crisis' in 1982, would continue to implement their economic programme.

The fact that the institutional limit of five SALs was reached implied that the external constraint on government action was largely lifted by the end of 1984. This feature also explains the government's ability to relax fiscal discipline during the second phase of the 1980s. The World Bank and the international financial community, in general, continued to exercise an indirect influence during the post-1984 phase. For example, the practice of extra-budgetary funds and export tax rebates were subjected to strong criticism, resulting in a transfer of 30 per cent of revenues from the EBFs to the consolidated budget in 1986 and the eventual removal of the export tax rebate system by the end of 1988. Yet, the direct conditionality which had characterized the early 1980s has to a large extent been absent in the second half of the decade.

The key inference is that domestic political pressures increasingly substituted for external constraints in the context of the second phase. This trend, in turn, had significant ramifications in terms of the pattern of economic performance which emerged in the second half of the decade.

Conclusion

Turkey's political economy in the 1980s displayed a fundamental paradox. A series of measures in the direction of liberalizing the economy, especially in the context of the post-1983 period, was accompanied by an ambitious growth strategy based on the expansion of the public sector. Consequently, the projected retreat of the state did not materialize in the Turkish case, although a decisive shift occurred in the type of state intervention, plus a considerable reduction in the government's involvement in the price determination process. Instead of a retreat of the state, we observe a significant re-ordering and re-organization, as well as further centralization, of the state apparatus itself as compared with the previous pattern. Certain elements of the pre-1980 import-substitution regime, namely a large public sector and rent-seeking behaviour, albeit in novel and modified forms, continued to manifest themselves in spite of the profound shift in economic trajectory established in the post-1980 era.

The specific conditions in the 1980s, especially the international context which accompanied the adjustment programme, as well as the memories of the acute crisis of the late 1970s, helped to generate a considerable degree of State autonomy vis-à-vis domestic societal pressures and provided legitimacy for the new economic strategy. Yet, the emergence of domestic constraints created problems for the implementation of the underlying economic programme. Hence, government's autonomy, and the associated ability to proceed with its longer-term programme of liberalization, were undermined by the incoherent nature of the policies implemented during the post-1983 phase.

3

The Post-1980 Legal Framework for Interest Group Associations

Ergun Özbudun

Introduction

Perhaps the single most important difference between the Turkish Constitutions of 1961 and 1982 can be summarized as follows: the latter opted for a much less participant and pluralistic version of democracy compared to the former. One of the best vantage points from which this contrast can be studied is the different approaches of the two Constitutions to interest group politics. While even the 1961 Constitution, generally regarded as the most liberal constitution Turkey has ever had, did not adopt a totally liberal and pluralistic view of interest groups, its successor chose to put them under much stricter governmental controls.

Historically, Turkish interest groups have been regulated by three categories of legislation. One category applies to ordinary voluntary associations, *dernekler*. The second deals with 'professional organizations in the nature of public institutions', *kamu kurumu niteliğindeki meslek kuruluşları* (below, 'public professional organizations'). The third regulates trade unions. The National Security Council (NSC) rule in Turkey (1980-1983) brought about important changes not only in the constitutional status of such organizations via the 1982 Constitution, but also in their overall legal status by way of extremely detailed and comprehensive legislation.

Indeed, one of the generally observed characteristics of the NSC rule (especially compared to the earlier military intervention of 1960-1961) is its attempt to mould virtually the whole of Turkish society in accordance with a comprehensive social, economic, and political blueprint. The NSC passed 535 laws and 91 decree-laws *(kanun hükmünde kararname)* compared to 292 laws passed during the military rule of 1960-1961 (the National Unity Committee period). More important than numbers is the nature of the legislation passed by the NSC. They included (in addition to the Constitution, Electoral Law and Political Parties' Law) laws regulating almost all fundamental aspects of social, economic and political life in Turkey, such as laws pertaining to the judiciary, the police, martial law and emergency rule, municipal governments, universities, the Turkish Radio and Television Corporation, associations, public professional organizations, trade unions, collective bargaining and strikes, the press, the right to assembly, and the like.[1] This clearly contrasts with the pattern in 1960-1961, when the National Unity Committee and the House of Representatives (the civilian wing of

[1] Nurkut İnan and Cüneyt Ozansoy, 'Yasama Faaliyeti Açısından 12 Eylül', *Yapıt*, no. 14 (1986), pp. 3-43; Fazıl Sağlam, 'Türk Hukuk Yapısı Nasıl Değiştirildi? 12 Eylül Yasaları', *Cumhuriyet* (Istanbul daily), 9-13 November 1987.

the Constituent Assembly) limited themselves essentially to the making of the Constitution and the electoral law, and left the enactment of other fundamental legislation (in a sense, organic laws, although Turkish law does not distinguish between ordinary and organic laws) to the popularly elected legislative assemblies. The behaviour of the NSC, on the other hand, reflects a lack of confidence in civilian politicians and popularly elected organs.

A second characteristic of the NSC legislation is their excessively detailed and comprehensive nature. This is true both in regard to the Constitution and to ordinary legislation. Especially, the detailed provisions of the Constitution introduced a considerable element of inflexibility to the post-NSC Turkish political life, given the difficulty of amending the Constitution. Closely related to this is the Provisional Article 15 of the Constitution which bars the Constitutional Court from reviewing the constitutionality of the laws passed during the NSC period. This amounts to giving them a somewhat more exalted status than ordinary laws as they cannot be invalidated by the Constitutional Court, although they can, of course, be repealed or amended by the legislature. Thus, a leading constitutional law expert describes such NSC legislation as a 'bloc of constitutional norms', almost in the nature of a flexible constitution, or as a 'second and silent constitution' alongside the official one.[2] It may therefore be concluded that the NSC regime not only attempted to re-mould the entire Turkish society in accordance with a virtually comprehensive governmental-social blueprint but also to freeze these regulations as much as possible.

When we turn to the 'substance' of the NSC legislation on interest groups, we observe that they reflect a deep distrust of spontaneous and pluralistic development of associational life. In line with older Ottoman-Turkish political traditions, the present Constitution and relevant laws seem to give only limited legitimacy to pluralistic interest group life.[3] Although the 1982 Constitution recognizes basic associational freedoms (that is, the right to form associations and trade unions), such freedoms are hedged with so many qualifications that they can hardly be expected to permit a vigorous and truly pluralistic associational life.

A feature common to all three types of interest groups already noted is the constitutional ban on their 'political' activities. The makers of the 1982 Constitution did not envisage a model of pluralistic politics in which trade unions, voluntary associations, and public professional organizations play an open and active role in politics. This theme was clearly expressed by the then Head of State, Kenan Evren, in his speeches propagating the draft Constitution prior to the constitutional referendum of 7 November 1982. Thus, he stated that political activity should be carried on exclusively by political parties:

> The new Constitution lays down a principle valid for all institutions. Each institution, whether a party, a school, or a professional organization, should remain in its own functionally specified area. In other words, a party will function as a

---

2 Bülent Tanör, *İki Anayasa:1961-1982* (İstanbul: Beta, 1986), p. 113; also idem '1980 Sonrasının Bilançosu', *Yapıt*, no. 14 (1986), pp. 54-5.

3 For a good analysis of Ottoman-Turkish political traditions regarding interest group activities, see Robert Bianchi, *Interest Groups and Political Development in Turkey* (Princeton: Princeton University Press, 1984), chap. 3. Also see chapters 1 and 12 in this volume.

> party, an association as an association, a foundation as a foundation, and a trade union as a trade union. Political activity is reserved for political parties. No institution which is not organized as a political party may engage in political activity. On the other hand, political parties should not interfere in areas reserved for trade unions, associations, professional organizations, and foundations. Every institution will function within its own framework.[4]

This clear separation of political and associational spheres is reflected in many articles of the 1982 Constitution and of the relevant laws, as will be spelled out in greater detail below.

Voluntary Associations

The term 'voluntary associations' is used here as a generic term to include all kinds of private corporate bodies (legal personalities) governed by private law, that is, not only associations proper *(dernekler)* but also foundations *(vakıflar)* and business firms *(şirketler)*. Business firms will not be dealt with here, since their activities do not fall within the conventional scope of interest group politics. One possible exception is cooperative societies which in many countries play an important role in politics. Cooperatives are barred from political activity in Turkey by Article 171 of the Constitution which entrusts the State with the duty to promote the development of cooperatives, while stating that 'cooperatives shall be subject in all respects to the supervision and inspection of the State, and shall not engage in political activities and shall not cooperate with political parties'.

Associations and foundations differ from business firms on account of their non-profit orientation. The difference between the former two is that a foundation is formed by the allocation of a fund or property for a specified purpose. A donor of funds forms a foundation, and his intentions shape the organization and administration of the foundation. An association, on the other hand, is formed by a group of persons who pool their knowledge and engage in activities continuously for a non profit-sharing purpose.[5] Associations are governed by the Civil Code and the Law of Associations, while foundations are governed again by the Civil Code and by special legislation such as Act No. 2762 dated 1935, and Act No. 903 dated 1967. The foundations will be largely omitted from the present discussion because of their more specialized nature. In any case, the 1982 Constitution (Article 33, paragraph 8) states that the Constitutional provisions on associations shall apply equally to foundations and other organizations of the same nature. We shall take up here associations proper.

Associations are regulated by Article 33 of the 1982 Constitution and the Law of Associations No. 2908, dated 7 October 1983. The regulation of associations in the 1982 Constitution is considerably more detailed and less liberal than in the corresponding Article 29 of the 1961 Constitution. Previous constitutions recognized the basic right

---

4 *Türkiye Cumhuriyeti Devlet Başkanı Orgeneral Kenan Evren'in Yeni Anayasayı Devlet Adına Resmen Tanıtma Programı Gereğince Yaptıkları Konuşmalar (24 Ekim-5 Kasım 1982)* (Ankara: TBMM Basımevi, 1982), pp. 37-8, 41, 48, 56-8, 70-7, 128.

5 Tuğrul Ansay, 'Law of Persons', in *Introduction to Turkish Law*, Tuğrul Ansay and Don Wallace, Jr., eds. (Deventer: Kluver Law and Taxation Publishers, 1987), pp. 123-4.

to form associations without having to obtain prior permission. The 1982 Constitution, however, stipulates that an association is formed by submitting the necessary information and documents to the competent administrative authority, and if the information furnished and the documents submitted are not found in conformity with the law, the competent administrative authority (governor or district governor) may apply to the court for the suspension of activities or dissolution of the association involved (Article 33, paragraph 2).

The ban on the political activities of associations is regulated in paragraph 4 of Article 33, according to which associations are not allowed to pursue political aims, engage in political activities, receive support from or give support to political parties, or take joint action with trade unions, public professional organizations or foundations. The 1961 Constitution, in contrast, did not contain a general ban on political activities of associations. The Law of Associations No. 1630 dated 1972, however, banned associations from engaging in certain kinds of political activities. Thus, Article 35 of the Act stipulated that 'associations may not organize meetings or publish materials with the purpose of praising a political party, a corporate personality, a community, a dead or living person whose aims or activities have been put under ban by law on account of their regimes, doctrines, or ideologies'. The apparent intention of this article was to protect democratic political order by preventing the spreading of totalitarian ideologies through associational activities. However, the rather ambiguous wording of the article was criticized as constituting 'the sword of Damocles' over associations.[6] The present ban on political activities is much more comprehensive, prohibiting associations from engaging in any kind of political activity even if such activities are supportive of democratic political order or consistent with the declared aims of the association. For example, if a human rights association circulates a statement criticizing the government for some human rights abuses, it is not clear whether such an activity would be considered 'political' and lead to the dissolution of the association.

The Law of Associations (Article 5) provides further details of the ban on political activities. Thus, associations are forbidden to engage in all kinds of political activity, including providing support for a any political party or to work against it; to ensure collaboration among political parties; to support or campaign against a political party or a candidate thereof, or an independent candidate in the elections for the Turkish Grand National Assembly, local government elections and elections for village or neighbourhood headmen and Council of Elders; nor can they collaborate with trade unions, public professional organizations and foundations in pursuit of a political aim.

The Constitution also states that the activities of associations shall not be in violation of the general grounds of restrictions for basic rights and freedoms as stipulated by Article 13 of the Constitution, according to which 'fundamental rights and freedoms may be restricted by law, in conformity with the letter and spirit of the Constitution, with the aim of safeguarding the indivisible integrity of the State with its territory and nation, national sovereignty, the Republic, national security, public order, general peace, public interest, public morals and public health, and also for specific reasons set forth in the relevant articles of the Constitution'.

---

6 Ergun Özsunay, *Medeni Hukukumuzda Tüzel Kişiler* (İstanbul: İstanbul Üniversitesi Hukuk Fakültesi, 1982), pp. 295-6.

These bans were further clarified by Article 5 of the Law of Associations dated 7 October 1983. Thus, no association can be formed with the aim of destroying the national and territorial integrity of the State; of endangering the existence of the Turkish Republic as defined by the Constitution, by manipulating linguistic, ethnic, class, religious and sectarian differences; of abolishing basic rights and liberties as stipulated by the Constitution; of carrying out activities in violation of national sovereignty, national security, public peace and order, public interest, public morals, and public health; of taking action on the basis of regionalism, ethnicity, social class, religion and sect; of promoting rights for ethnic, religious, sectarian, cultural, and linguistic minorities, or of claiming the existence of such minorities; of establishing the hegemony of one social class over others, or eliminating a social class, or creating a personal dictatorship, or overthrowing the established economic, social, political, and legal order of the country; of exploiting or manipulating religion or religious feelings with the purpose of gaining personal or political influence, or of basing the fundamental social, economic, political, and legal order of the state on religious principles; of advocating the repeal of the reform laws of Kemal Atatürk as referred to by Article 174 of the Constitution; of demeaning Atatürk's personality, principles, works, and memories; of belittling the corporate personality of the Turkish state; of inciting to commit crimes, etc.

Further restrictions on the right to form associations were brought by paragraph 7 of Article 33 of the Constitution, which states that 'provisions of the first paragraph of this Article shall not prevent imposition of restrictions on the rights of armed forces and security forces officials and civil servants to form associations, or the prohibition of the exercise of this right'. Based on this constitutional permission Article 4 of the Law of Associations forbids the following categories of persons to form associations: judges and public prosecutors; personnel of provincial administrations; members of the armed forces and the security forces; teachers of the public and private, middle and high schools; middle and high school students, etc. However, members of some of these categories may become members in already established associations with the permission of authorities specified by law. Such authority is the Ministry of Justice for judges and public prosecutors, and the appropriate ministers for other public personnel (Article 16). Clearly, the Law of Associations restricts the rights of government employees to form or join associations to a degree unheard of in liberal democracies.

The Law of Associations also introduced strict governmental controls over associations. Under Article 45 of the Act, associations are supervised by the Ministry of Interior. The Ministry or its agents are entitled to temporarily remove from office those association executives (presidents and the members of the executive committee) who obstruct such supervision or whose records show fraudulent behaviour. As for the dissolution of associations, the 1982 Constitution (Article 33, paragraph 6) stipulated that associations may be dissolved by decision of judge in cases prescribed by law. They may be suspended from activity by the competent authority designated by law pending a court decision in cases where delay endangers the indivisible integrity of the State with its territory and nation, national security or sovereignty, public order, the protection of the rights and freedom of others, or the prevention of crime. This system is similar to the one adopted by the 1961 Constitution as amended in 1971. The corresponding Article 29 of the 1961 Constitution had stated that 'associations may be dissolved by a decision of the court in cases specified by law. They may be suspended from activity by the competent authority designated by law pending a court decision in cases where delay endangers the indivisible integrity of the State with its territory and nation, national security, public order and public morality. The main difference between the two articles is that the 1982 Constitution enlarged the scope of exceptional circumstances permitting the temporary suspension of an association by administrative authorities.

Public Professional Organizations

Public professional organizations, some of which date back to the late Ottoman period,[7] were first given constitutional recognition and status by the 1961 Constitution (Article 122). This article stated that 'public professional organizations are established by law; their bodies are elected by themselves from among their own members. Administrative authorities may not remove from office or temporarily suspend their elected bodies without a court decision. The regulations, administration and activities of professional organizations may not be against democratic principles'. The 1982 Constitution (Article 135) gave a more detailed definition of such organizations: 'Public professional organizations and their unions are public corporate bodies established by law with the objectives of meeting the common needs of the members of a given profession, of facilitating their professional activities, of ensuring the development of the profession in keeping with public interest, of safeguarding professional discipline and ethics in order to ensure integrity and trust in relations among its members and with the public. Their bodies shall be elected by their own members by secret ballot in accordance with the procedure set forth in the law and under judicial supervision'.

As a consequence, public professional organizations in Turkey have a 'hybrid', if not a *sui generis*, nature. On the one hand, their structuring brings together members of certain professions to promote their professional interests; their members do not normally work for the government, and their functions as organizations are essentially non-governmental; they elect their own bodies from among their members without any interference by governmental authorities. On the other hand, they are created by law; membership in them is obligatory in the sense that nobody may practise his/her profession without becoming a member of the relevant professional organization except those regularly employed in public corporations; they exercise certain regulatory and disciplinary powers that are derived from public law; like other decentralized administrative bodies (local governments and public corporations) they are subject to the administrative tutelage and supervision of central administrative authorities; again like other administrative agencies, their acts and actions are subject to judicial review not by general courts but by administrative courts. For all these reasons, there is no doubt that their 'public' character predominates, and that they are public cor-

[7] For example, the first Chamber of Commerce was established in Istanbul in 1882 based on a regulation issued in 1880. Similarly, the first Bar Association was established in Istanbul in 1878 based on a regulation dated 1876. See Harun Çetintemel, 'Kamu Kurumu Niteliğindeki Meslek Kuruluşları' (unpublished manuscript, available at the Council of State *(Danıştay)* Library, Ankara, 1976, pp. 3, 12.

porate bodies. Even the rather awkward name given to them by the Constitution, i.e., 'professional organizations in the nature of public institutions' *(kamu kurumu niteliğindeki meslek kuruluşları)* attests to the legally problematic, *sui generis* nature of such organizations.[8] Although their constitutional recognition came only with the 1961 Constitution, many of these organizations have existed for a much longer time. At the moment, ten categories of such organizations exist: (1) Chambers of Commerce and Industry, Chambers of Commerce, Chambers of Industry, Chambers of Maritime Trade, Trade Exchanges, and the Turkish Union of Chambers of Commerce, Industry, Maritime Trade, and Trade Exchange;[9] (2) Chambers of Agriculture, and the Union of Chambers of Agriculture;[10] (3) Associations of Small Traders and Artisans, their federations and confederations;[11] (4) Bar Associations, and the Turkish Union of Bar Associations;[12] (5) Medical Associations, and the Turkish Union of Medical Associations;[13] (6) Associations of Veterinarians, and the Turkish Union of Veterinary Medicine;[14] (7) Associations of Dentists, and the Turkish Union of Dentistry;[15] (8) Associations of Pharmacologists, and the Turkish Union of Pharmacologists;[16] (9) Chambers of Engineers and Architects, and the Turkish Union of the Chambers of Engineers and Architects;[17] (10) Chambers of Notary Publics and the Turkish Union of Notary Publics.[18]

The 1982 Constitution imposed upon public professional organizations the same kind of bans on political activities as apply to voluntary associations. Thus, under paragraph 3 and 4 of Article 135, 'public professional organizations shall not engage in activities or take joint action with political parties, trade unions or associations. Political parties, trade unions and their higher bodies shall not nominate candidates in elections for the bodies of public professional organizations or their higher bodies, nor shall they engage in activities or propaganda for or against particular candidates'.

---

8 Ibid., pp. 17-46.

9 Regulated by Act No. 5590 dated 8 March 1950, as amended by the Decree-Law No. 63 dated 5 August 1983. For a good sociological analysis of the chambers of industry and their role in overall State-industry relations, see Ayşe Öncü, 'Chambers of Industry in Turkey: An Inquiry into State-Industry Relations as a Distributive Domain', in *The Political Economy of Income Distribution in Turkey*, Ergun Özbudun and Aydın Ulusan, eds. (New York: Holmes and Meier, 1980).

10 Regulated by Act No. 6964 dated 6 May 1957, as amended by the Decree-Law No. 67 dated 5 August 1983.

11 Regulated by Act No. 507 dated 17 July 1964, as amended by Decree-Law No. 62 dated 5 August 1983.

12 Regulated by Act No. 1136 dated 19 March 1969, as amended by Decree-Law No. 54 dated 5 August 1983.

13 Regulated by Act No. 6023 dated 23 January 1953, as amended by Decree-Law No. 65 dated 5 August 1983.

14 Regulated by Act No. 6243 dated 9 March 1954, as amended by Decree-Law No. 68 dated 5 August 1983.

15 Regulated by Act No. 3244 dated 7 June 1985.

16 Regulated by Act No. 6643 dated 25 January 1956, as amended by Ordinance No. 69 dated 5 August 1983.

17 Regulated by Act No. 6235 dated 27 January 1954, as amended by Ordinance No. 66 dated 5 August 1983.

18 Regulated by Act No. 1512 dated 18 January 1972, as amended by Ordinance No. 55 dated 5 August 1983.

Such a ban on political activity should not, of course, be construed in a way to restrict the rights of these organizations to issue statements and take other appropriate action within their legally prescribed areas of activity - supporting or criticizing certain public policies. In fact, public professional organizations have often continued to get involved in such activities after the adoption of the 1982 Constitution, and especially after the re-transition to multi-party politics towards the end of 1983.

As public corporate bodies, public professional organizations are subject to the tutelage of central administration. Administrative tutelage *(idari vesayet)*, as distinct from hierarchical supervision that is exercised *within* each administrative agency, can be defined as follows: 'The organs, decisions, contracts, budgets, and by-laws of local and functionally decentralized agencies are controlled *a posteriori* by central authorities explicitly designated by law, such as ministers, Council of Ministers, Council of State, governors and sub-governors, in a manner which is known as "administrative tutelage". This control, in very exceptional cases, can be used in an *a priori* manner or in the form of action on behalf of the decentralized agencies'.[19] Although Article 122 of the 1961 Constitution was silent on the tutelary powers of central administrative agencies over public professional organizations, there was no doubt in the juridical doctrine and the court decisions that the exercise of such powers was permitted by the Constitution, since these organizations were, after all, public corporate bodies. This point was made more explicit by paragraph 5 of Article 135 of the 1982 Constitution which stipulates that 'public professional organizations shall be subject to administrative and financial supervision of the State as prescribed by law'. Legislation on public professional organizations specifies the central administrative agency entitled to exercise tutelary supervision over each professional organization, as well as the ways in which such supervision is exercised. The tutelary control agency for the Bar Associations and the Notary Public Associations is the Ministry of Justice; for the Chambers of Commerce and Industry and the Associations of Small Traders and Artisans, the Ministry of Commerce; for the Medical, Pharmacological and Dentistry Associations, the Ministry of Health and Social Welfare; for the Chambers of Agriculture and the Veterinarians' Associations, the Ministry of Agriculture; and for the Chambers of Engineers and Architects, the Ministry of Reconstruction and Resettlement.

The 1982 Constitution preserved the rule of its predecessor to the effect that the elected bodies of public professional organizations may not be removed from office by central administrative authorities without a court decision. Thus, paragraph 6 of Article 135 states that 'the responsible bodies of public professional organizations which engage in activities beyond their objectives or in political activities, shall be dissolved by a court decision at the request of the authority designated by law, and new bodies shall be elected in their place'. However, paragraphs 7 and 8 of the same Article allowed exceptions to this rule, permitting central administrative authorities to take direct action in urgent cases. The Constitution stipulates that 'the highest administrative official at the localities may temporarily remove from office these bodies where delay is deemed prejudicial to the existence and independence of the Turkish state, the indivisible integrity of the State with its territory and nation, social peace, and the pre-

[19] Sait Güran, 'Administrative Law', in *Introduction to Turkish Law*, Ansay and Wallace, eds., p. 96.

vention of activities threatening the fundamental characteristics of the state as defined by the Constitution. The decision to remove from office shall be communicated to the court within three days. The court shall decide within ten days at the latest whether the decision of removal from office is justified'. These provisions of the Constitution endanger the autonomy of public professional organizations which constitute, together with trade unions, the most important organized interest groups in Turkey.

The restrictions on the autonomy of public professional organizations stem not only from the 1982 Constitution itself but also, and perhaps to a greater extent, from a series of decree-laws laws issued by the Council of Ministers during the NSC rule, based on the enabling Act No. 2767 dated 28 December 1982. Nine such ordinances, all passed on 5 August 1983, specified and greatly increased the tutelary powers of the relevant ministries over professional organizations. Since under Turkish law tutelary powers can be exercised only in cases explicitly specified by law, such detailed legislation put professional organizations under highly restrictive central governmental controls. To give a few examples, the participation in international conferences of the representatives of public professional organizations is subject to the permission of the relevant ministry. The Ministry of Justice supervises the bodies of the Bar Associations to ensure that they perform their duties in accordance with law, and whether their financial records are kept in accordance with the relevant regulations (Decree-Act No.54, Additional Article 4). The criteria for the right to vote in the elections for the bodies of the Chambers of Commerce as well as the rules for eligibility are determined by the Ministry of Commerce by a regulation (Decree-Act No. 63, Article 3). In case of the temporary or permanent abrogation of the bodies of the Chambers of Commerce, their functions are performed by a committee appointed by the Ministry of Commerce pending new elections (Decree-Act No.63, Additional Article 5).

As already noted, for all the restrictions imposed upon professional organizations by the 1982 Constitution and the relevant legislation, a positive aspect seems to be that elections should be held by secret ballot and under judicial supervision. A related constitutional provision stipulates that political parties shall not nominate candidates in such elections, nor shall they engage in propaganda for or against a particular candidate. These two constitutional rules make it somewhat difficult for political parties (especially the government party) to manipulate elections and to colonize public professional organizations as they often attempted to do in the pre-1980 period.

Trade Unions

A third major type of interest group is trade unions. Legally speaking, trade unions are, like voluntary associations, private corporate bodies. Because of their highly special characteristics, however, they are regulated by separate legislation such as the Trade Unions Act No. 2821 dated 5 May 1983, and the Collective Bargaining, Strike and Lockout Act No. 2822 dated 5 May 1983. Under the 1982 Constitution (Article 51), 'workers and employers have the right to form trade unions and employers' associations and their higher bodies without having to obtain prior permission in order to protect and promote the economic and social rights and interests of their members in industrial relations'. Thus, the Constitution, unlike Article 46 of its predecessor, attempted to give a definition of trade unions, and limited their field of activities strictly to 'industrial'. Together with the ban on their political activites to be discussed below, this clause seems to hinder the development of political unionism. It should be pointed out, however, that Article 47 of the 1961 Constitution used similar language in recognizing the right to strike and collective bargaining: 'Workers have the right to collective bargaining and strike in their relations with employers in order to protect and improve their economic and social conditions'.

The procedure to be followed in the formation of trade unions is described in paragraph 2 of Article 51 of the Constitution: 'In order to form unions and their higher bodies, it shall suffice to submit the information and documents prescribed by law to the competent authority designated by law. If this information and documentation is not in conformity with law, the competent authority shall apply to the appropriate court for the suspension of activities or the dissolution of the union or the higher body.' Thus, no prior authorization is required for the formation of trade unions. The Constitution did not specify the kinds and levels of 'higher bodies', or federations, that trade unions can establish among themselves. Under the existing legislation, however, only one such level, namely confederation, is allowed. Similarly, although the Constitution did not specify the organizational basis of trade unions, the Trade Unions Act of 1983 has forbidden the formation of unions on the basis of workplace *(iş yeri)*, as well as 'profession' (trade). Therefore, unions can be formed only on the basis of work branch *(işkolu)* (Trade Unions Act, Article 3). This ban on workplace-based unionism is generally seen as a positive change, preventing the spread of 'yellow unionism'.[20]

The 1982 Constitution mentions the right to form trade unions by 'workers', but not unlike its predecessor (1961) as amended in 1971, does not contain an explicit ban (Article 119) on the unionization of civil servants. To put it differently, the Constitution remains silent on the subject. Therefore, the right to form trade unions can be extended to civil servants by ordinary legislation, although the present laws do not recognize such a right.

The right to unionize has both an individual and a collective aspect. As it pertains to individuals, it includes the rights to form trade unions, to become or not to become a member thereof, to terminate one's union membership at will, and to freely choose one's union. These individual aspects of the right to unionize are regulated in paragraphs 3, 4, 5, 6 of Article 51 of the Constitution: 'Everyone shall be free to become a member of or withdraw from membership in a union. No one shall be compelled to become a member, remain a member, or withdraw from membership of a union. Workers ... cannot hold concurrent membership in more than one trade union or refrain being a member of a trade union.'

The freedom to choose one's union implies a multiplicity of unions in any work branch. This is explicitly stated by Article 3 of the Trade Unions Act: 'More than one trade union may be formed in any work branch.' However, a union must represent at least ten per cent of the total work force in its work branch in order to have the right to conduct collective bargaining (Act No. 2822, Article 12). The right to choose

---

[20] Nuri Çelik, *İş Hukuku Dersleri* (İstanbul: Marmara Üniversitesi Eğitim ve Yardım Vakfı, 1986). pp. 282, 321- 2.

one's union also implies the rejection of 'closed-shop' and 'union-shop' clauses. Thus, as noted, employment may not be conditional upon workers joining or not joining a particular union and maintaining one's membership. Collective agreements may not carry clauses in violation of this rule; if they do, such clauses are considered null and void. Employers may not discriminate in any way among workers on account of their union affiliation or the absence thereof. More specifically, employers may not fire or discriminate against a worker for his union activities in the workplace outside working hours, or with the permission of the employer within such hours (Trade Unions Act, Article 31).

As for the executive officers of a trade union, the Constitution stipulates that in order to become eligible for such office they should have held the status of a worker for at least ten years (Article 51, paragraph 7). Also, holding an executive office in a trade union is incompatible with membership in the Turkish Grand National Assembly (Article 82).

In its collective aspect, the right to unionize implies the freedom of trade unions to take any legal action in order to protect and promote the socio-economic rights and interests of their members. In liberal democracies, such a freedom clearly includes the right to take appropriate political action, ranging from establishing organic links with a political party to supporting or working against a particular candidate. Any involvement in politics by trade unions is strictly forbidden, however, by the 1982 Constitution in line with its attempt to de-politicize voluntary associations and public professional organizations. Thus, the Constitution stipulates that, 'unions, in addition to being subject to the general grounds for restrictions set forth in Article 13, shall not pursue a political cause, engage in political activity, receive support from political parties or give support to them; nor shall they take joint action with associations, public professional organizations and foundations to promote such aims'.

Thus, as compared to the pre-1980 period, the present ban on the political activities of trade unions is clearly much more comprehensive. The 1961 Constitution did not contain a ban on political activities, but the Trade Union Act of 1963 (No. 274) banned the unions from establishing organizational links with political parties, as well as giving to or receiving financial support from them (Article 16). The same law did not hinder them, however, from supporting a political party or a particular candidate in elections, or urging its members not to vote for a particular party or candidate. Given the explicit language of the present Constitution, now no such political action seems to be allowed. In fact, Article 37 of the Trade Unions Act of 1983 went even further than the Constitution by making it illegal for the unions 'to co-operate or take any kind of joint action with political parties'. If a union official is elected or appointed to an executive post in a political party, his union office will be automatically terminated. If he becomes a candidate in national or local government elections, his union office will be suspended and, upon election, terminated. On the other hand, the same Article states that 'those professional activities of trade unions and their confederations pursued exclusively with the purpose of protecting and promoting the socio-economic rights and interests of their members shall not be considered as political activity'. Taking advantage of this qualification unions have often issued statements, especially after the transition to multi-party politics in 1983, severely criticizing economic and social policies of the government, sometimes by forcing the limits of the law.[21] Given the essentially political aspects of trade union activities, it seems very difficult to maintain in a liberal democratic regime such excessive restrictions, some of which have already become unenforceable in practice.

Another major area of difference between the 1961 and 1982 Constitutions with regard to union activities is to be found in the articles on the right to strike. The 1961 Constitution (Article 47) simply stated that, 'Workers have the rights to collective bargaining and strike in their relations with employers in order to protect and improve their economic and social conditions. The manner in which the right to strike is exercised, its exceptions, and the rights of employers shall be regulated by law'. In contrast, the 1982 Constitution regulated (and limited) the right to strike in a much more comprehensive manner. Article 54 of the Constitution states:

> Workers have the right to strike if a dispute arises during the collective bargaining process. The procedures and conditions governing the exercise of this right and the employer's recourse to lockout, and the scope of both actions and their exceptions shall be regulated by law.
>
> The right to strike and lockout shall not be exercised in a manner contrary to the principle of goodwill, to the detriment of society, and in a manner damaging national wealth.
>
> During a strike, the trade union is liable for any material damage caused in a workplace where the strike takes place, as a result of deliberate negligence by the workers and the trade union.
>
> The circumstances and places in which strikes and lockouts may be prohibited or postponed shall be regulated by law. In cases where a strike or lockout is prohibited or postponed, the dispute shall be settled by the Supreme Board of Arbitration....The disputing parties may apply to the Supreme Board of Arbitration by mutual agreement at any stage of the dispute.
>
> The decisions of the Supreme Board of Arbitration shall be final, and have the same force as a collective agreement.
>
> The organization and functions of the Supreme Board of Arbitration shall be regulated by law.
>
> Politically motivated strikes and lockouts, solidarity strikes and lockouts, occupation of work premises, work slowdowns, production decreases and other forms of obstruction are prohibited.
>
> Those who refuse to go on strike shall in no way be barred by strikers from working at their workplaces.

Based on a comparison between the two Constitutions and the relevant legislation (the Collective Bargaining, Strikes and Lockouts Act of 1963, No. 275, and of 1983, No. 2822), two points are worth noting.

---

[21] In the constitutional referendums of 1987 and 1988, *Türk- İş*, the largest workers' confederation in Turkey, called on its members to vote against the position of the Motherland Party government. A more recent example is provided by the statement of Mustafa Başoğlu, the education secretary of *Türk-İş*, against the possible presidential candidacy of the then Prime Minister Turgut Özal *(Milliyet*, Istanbul daily, 17 September 1989).

The 1982 Constitution and Act No. 2822 limited the right to strike to 'interest disputes', that is, those arising out of the collective bargaining process and pertaining to the economic and social conditions of workers. What is known as 'rights strike' *(hak grevi)* arising out of the violation by the employers of a previously concluded collective agreement, which was considered legal under the old system, is not permitted by the present legislation. However, certain other types of strike (such as politically motivated strikes, solidarity or sympathy strikes, protest or warning strikes, work slowdowns) that are explicitly prohibited by the 1982 Constitution and Act No. 2822, were also considered illegal by the previous legislation.[22]

Act No. 2822 on Collective Bargainings, Strikes and Lockouts (Articles 29, 30) increased the number of work branches where strikes are totally prohibited. The new additions include coal and petroleum production and distribution, health and banking services, educational institutions, and the like. In addition, the Council of Ministers may postpone a strike for a period of sixty days on account of national security or public health (Article 33). Such a possibility of postponement also existed in the previous law which permitted strikes only at the end of the postponement period. Under the present system, in cases where a strike is prohibited or postponed, the dispute will be settled by the Supreme Board of Arbitration as mentioned above (Article 34). The present law retains the provision of its predecessor which permits the judicial review of the Council of Ministers' postponement decrees by the Council of State; the Council of State is also entitled to issue a stay order with respect to those postponement decrees (Article 33, paragraph 2).

---

22 Turhan Esener, *İş Hukuku* (Ankara: Ankara Üniversitesi Hukuk Fakültesi, 1978), pp. 592-6, 601-5; Çelik, *İş Hukuku Dersleri*, pp. 470-1.

Part Three

THE STATE AND ECONOMIC INTEREST GROUPS

4

Labour: The Battered Community

Ümit Cizre Sakallıoğlu

Background

The 1960s and 1970s formed the extraordinary background for the emergence after 1980 of the particular patterns of relationship between the State and labour in Turkey. True enough, the Turkish labour movement has a long and not insignificant historical past, harking back to the Ottoman period. Until the 1960s, however, the 'labour question' was easily dealt with. Since a distinct industrial working class had not yet fully emerged, the State elites incorporated the popular sector by controlling the genesis and development of potential for militancy on the part of labour without much difficulty. The 1961-1980 period, on the other hand, turned out to be problematic. The troublesome features of the decade ultimately paved the way to the 1980 military intervention and the radical re-organization of the sector.

Both the 1961 Constitution, with its emphasis on liberal pluralist freedoms and social and economic rights and duties, and the ensuing labour legislation enacted in 1963,[1] were marked by a concern for diffusing power in the polity. Both encouraged the emergence of new power centres in the form of interest group associations over a broad range of ideological, economic and social issues. This particular orientation as well as the adoption of the idea of a 'social welfare state' were prompted by the progress of the Turkish polity to a certain stage of socio-economic development, and by a further differentation and activation of social class interests. Still, there were also developments in the same period working in other directions.

First, as regards labour, until the formation of the Confederation of Revolutionary Trade Unions (DİSK) in 1967, there was only one major confederation - the Confederation of Turkish Trade Unions (Türk-İş), formed in 1952. Throughout the period, Türk-İş was legally aided by the State in its efforts at 'centralization'[2] and consolidation of its power, and thus was granted a representational monopoly at the national level, undermining its rivals even in those areas where the latter had already organized the greatest number of workers.[3] Secondly, the role of the State in tempering the demands of Türk-İş and its internal governance and leadership selection did not decrease. As

[1] Trade Unions Act, No. 274, and Collective Bargaining, Strike and Lockouts Act, No. 275, both enacted on 24 July 1963.

[2] See in this regard Act No. 1317 which was passed in 1970 to amend the 1963 Trade Unions Act, No. 274, on the grounds of 'union inflation' caused by the legal possibility of forming several unions competing with each other in the same work branch. Act No. 1317, by stipulating a representational threshold for unions (one third of workers in the work branch), effectively cut down their numbers.

[3] See Robert Bianchi, *Interest Groups and Political Development in Turkey* (Princeton: Princeton University Press, 1984), p. 126.

Ergun Özbudun shows in this volume, unions in general were also legally barred from forming any links with political parties; they were subjected to the financial auditing of the Ministry of Labour; and their applications for membership in international organizations had to be approved by the same Ministry.

On the other hand, Türk-İş was given a place on mixed consultative boards and regulatory commissions in the public sector as the sole representative of labour. The end result was a labour sector which was co-opted, controlled and induced to stay out of high politics, and which gave priority to job-unionism.

The 1970s, however, was a period of polarization and radicalization of political forces on the Right and Left. Although the chief representational cartel, the Türk-İş, was constrained and dependent on the State, some unions were able to break their ties with Türk-İş and establish politically autonomous, radical, and class-based political unions. The latter rejected the representational monopoly of Türk-İş. In the process, the labour movement was divided into different groups: (1) Social Democratic unions within Türk-İş supporting left-of-centre policies of the Republican People's Party; (2) the unionists within Türk-İş who had sympathies towards the Turkish Workers Party (formed in 1961), and who later established the DİSK in 1967; (3) those who formed the Confederation of Nationalist Trade Unions (MISK), hankering after the ultra-nationalist ideology of the Nationalist Action Party (formed in 1970); and (4) the unionists, who set up in 1976 the religiously-oriented Confederation of 'Justice Seekers' Trade Unions (Hak-İş). All these were after obtaining some autonomy from the State, and had a stake in accentuating their differences with the 'non-political' Türk-İş, in order to bid for the workers' support in the same arena.

These then were briefly the main features of the development of Turkish trade unionism between the two military interventions of 1960 and 1980. Although the model of pluralist interest group politics was pervasive in the minds of the State elites who made the 1961 Constitution, the project that emerged in the field of labour corresponded to neither a purely pluralist interest representation nor a neo-corporatist intermediation: there was a colossal degree of state leverage over the 'peak' organization Türk-İş. It is true that Türk-İş had official recognition and monopoly of representation; it was entitled to state subsidy; and it was favoured against the rival confederation DİSK. All this was, however, at the expense of its being subjected to state-imposed constraints on its demand-making, leadership selection, and internal governance, a point already made. The intent was to produce on the part of the Türk-İş a docility towards and 'good' relations with the employers' interest group associations and the state. However, this mode of incorporation of labour into the political system did not lead to the adoption of policies characteristic of neo-corporatism such as 'incomes policy', 'wage-restraint' and 'social contracts', notwithstanding the futile and short-lived experience of the 1978 'Social Contract'. Nor were relations with the employers and the state highly institutionalized.

Industrial relations, however, have not taken place within the context of an authoritarian or coercive State. What the politics of labour incorporation served to secure was union quiescence and compliance in maintaining social peace, by simultaneous enforcement of legal and de facto constraints on one hand, and material inducements on the other.

As already noted, outside the co-opted Türk-İş, which was 'loyal' to the state, this period of incorporation ended with fragmentation of labour into competing confederations, all of which had close relations with different political parties. The consequence was '...division and a reduction in the strength of the movement as a whole, which simply served the interests of the business sector'.[4] One outcome of the fragmentation and radicalization of labour was the rising perception in the minds of the general public that by its political unionism organized labour was responsible for the high level of inflation. Türk-İş, which carefully tried to avoid such unionism and gave priority to securing wage increases and welfare benefits, could not escape this accusation, too. This was because it failed to achieve organizational cohesiveness and strength, and act as an effective counterweight to the rival confederations.

Post-1980 Developments: The Micro Bias of the New Order

As should be apparent from the preceding discussion, on the eve of the 12 September 1980 military intervention Turkey was in the grip of a serious political crisis caused by intense fragmentation and polarization of the polity. Superimposed on this state of affairs was a fiscal crisis. These problems were interrelated. Balance of payments deficits since the mid-1970s showed the failure of the export sector to develop, which endangered the inward-oriented strategy of import substitution where state economic enterprises played a significant role. High rates of inflation revealed the inability of the governments to resist the demands made upon them. The stabilization policies were bound to be vehemently resisted, especially by labour, since those policies would have imposed particularly heavy costs on that sector. The disrupting effects of the political and economic crises were also felt in the investment and productivity levels in industry and agriculture. The problems were cumulative: they could no longer be dealt with in a 'piecemeal' fashion; success or failure in one area would have had significant repercussions for the economy as a whole.

Thus, the post-intervention tasks of the military government, which stayed in power until the general elections on 6 November 1983, were two-fold: providing for order and stability, and laying the foundation for a shift to an alternative growth model. In this 'holistic' and 'interrelated' approach, monetarist policies constituted the new panacea: 'The [s]tate's function...[was] reduced to providing the system [with] a blue print',[5] since the objective was a free market economy without state intervention in the market. Reducing the size of the public sector would remove the basis for pressures coming from private sector firms for concessions from the government; opening the economy to free trade would provide the means for growth without state protection for uncompetitive sectors; allowing the market forces to regulate wage rates would undermine

---

4 This view was expressed by Kaya Özdemir, the then Secretary-General of Türk-İş responsible for membership education and a former long-term member of the National Executive Committee, and later political adviser to the leader of Türk-İş, in a personal interview on 3 May 1989. The same point of view is shared by Fehmi Işıklar, the then Secretary-General of DİSK, later a member of Parliament for the Social Democratic Populist Party, in another personal interview on 9 May 1989.

5 Udo Steinbach, 'Turkey's Third Republic', *Aussen Politik*, 3 (1989), p.243.

the political bargaining strength of labour. All these measures, combined with flexible foreign exchange rate policy, would eliminate inflation.

In what spheres of the political system was restructuring needed? It was necessary vis-à-vis the Constitution, the party system and interest group associations. Reconstruction was to be carried out through political authoritarianism; the definitions such as '...democracy with narrow limits',[6] '...a well-corseted framework... for the conduct of political competition by civilians',[7] '...disciplining' or 'depoliticization' of public life...and the strengthening of the president's position', [8] delineated the contours of the emerging regime. Social peace, political consensus and above all a powerful executive were to be instrumental in political as well as economic restructuration. It was hoped that the old forms of political allegiance would disappear and new forms, harmonious and directed by national interest, would evolve.

The post-1980 developments concerning labour, including multi-party rule which began in 1983, can be fully grasped only if they are viewed from this particular perspective. A variety of adjectives has been used - all with the prefix 'de' - to account for the changing place of labour during the decade of the 1980s: 'de-politicization', 'de-mobilization', 'de-radicalization', and 'de-unionization'. To understand these new trends and patterns, however, one must go back to the earlier mode of incorporation of labour into the political system, which set the parameters for the new order.

Here, two points need to be made. First, the strange blend of interest group politics of the post-1960 period was hardly congruent with the prerequisites of economic orthodoxy introduced after 1980. Since the more politicized segments within the main representative cartel, Türk-İş, had split off and formed their own unions largely autonomous from the State, the situation posed difficulties for 'economic performance' and, therefore, for 'governability'. Thus, not surprisingly, the designers of the new system opted for neither of these past forms of associability. However, the strategy preferred was not outright repression of all unions. Second, and more important, the new labour regime was a product of elite consensus. When in the 1960s labour was still an integral part of import-substitution industrialization, Türk-İş was offered inducements as well as subjected to constraints. With the changing priorities and policy goals of the 1980s summarized above, the image of labour as being responsible for market distortions through political unionism, found a broad acceptance both inside and outside the country. Thus, the new labour regime was adopted and implemented with such vehemence, coherence and dedication that this era represented an authentic 'crisis' for organized labour. The scope of attack included both the material well being and the right of labour to organize.

One of the first measures of the military upon assuming power was to close down all

---

6 İlkay Sunar and Sabri Sayarı, 'Democracy in Turkey: Problems and Prospects', in *Transitions from Authoritarian Rule. Southern Europe*, Guillermo O'Donnell, Philippe Schmitter and Alan Whitehead, eds., (Baltimore and London: The Johns Hopkins University Press, 1986), p. 186.

7 Nicholas S. Ludington and James W. Spain, 'Dateline Turkey: The Case for Patience', *Foreign Policy*, 50 (1983), p. 161.

8 Steinbach, 'Turkey's Third Republic', p. 239.

three union confederations (DİSK, Hak-İş, and MİSK) outside Türk-İş,[9] and to ban all strikes (as well as lockouts) until further notice. The next step was to lay the bases for the new industrial relations system in line with the prevailing notions of political and economic order. Since the legal restructuration of the sector has been taken up in chapter three in this volume, it will suffice to delineate here some major changes and their implications.

The new system sought to erase the 'unionist malaise' of the 1960s and 1970s, which had manifested itself as proliferation of unions, the infiltration of ideological unionism at the leadership level and lack of trade union leadership capable of restraining the membership. Accordingly, trade unions were prohibited from pursuing a political cause and engaging in political activity, if these did not directly relate to their (socio-economic) interests. The trade unions were also barred from receiving or giving support to political parties. It is interesting to note in this regard that even Türk-İş was against this last provision, on the grounds that it amounted to a restriction on the activities of the unions on the basis of a rather vague concept of 'political'. As it has been aptly put, '... independence from political parties does not imply non-political action....Such provisions are irreconcilable with the freedom of unions.... The activities of unions cannot be isolated from politics'.[10]

In addition, a system of inspection was set up. This led to a close, day-to-day supervision of the activities of the unions and, in the process, to an outright campaign against Türk-İş. Türk-İş at one point protested that the allegations of misappropriation of funds were not true.[11] Gradually, such controls were discontinued.

The most serious restrictions in the new Labour Code, however, were those on the right to strike, so much so that the fashionable debate until 1987 was whether or not the right to strike was a viable option.[12] First, the conditions under which strikes could occur were so narrowed down that they became practically impossible. Secondly, the legislation limited the nature of the disputes that could end in strikes only to those arising from the collective bargaining process itself. Türk-İş, at its most intense moments of opposition, claimed that since in the pre-1980 period the number of strikes emanating from violations of collective agreements did not exceed five, this particular provision was nothing but a product of hostility towards unions.[13] Finally, in cases of deadlock in the collective bargaining process, and where a strike or a lockout was pro-

---

9 Hak-İş and MİSK were reinstated in February 1981 and May 1984, respectively, leaving DİSK as the only confederation excluded from the system by legal proceedings which today (1990) have not yet been concluded.

10 'Türk- İş Çalışma Raporu 1983', pp. 172-3.

11 See *Türk-İş* (the monthly publication of Türk- İş), no. 191 (July 1985), pp. 20-5; also interview with Mustafa Başoğlu, the leader of Sağlık-İş (Health Workers Union) in *Yeni Gündem* (Istanbul fortnightly), 16-30 June 1984, p.18.

12 The statistics for 1984, the first year when collective agreements were signed after the 1980 military takeover, show that there were only 4 strikes in 4 work-places; in 1985 and 1986 the number rose to 21; in 1987, the peak year, to 307. The top union officials (as expressed by Kaya Özdemir in a personal interview) did not favour a high incidence of strikes, seemingly on the grounds that the outcomes demonstrated that they were not worth the trouble. Furthermore, they created the false impression abroad that the strike weapon was still effectively utilized in Turkey (figures from *Petrol-İş Yearbook for 1987*, p. 149).

13 'Türk-İş Çalışma Raporu, 1983', p. 162.

hibited or postponed, the dispute was to be settled by a new body called the Supreme Board of Arbitration.[14]

The Supreme Board of Arbitration has been a matter of much controversy. As an arm of the public bureaucracy, the Board exercised close supervision over industrial relations, and interfered in collective bargaining negotiations, an area of jurisdiction that throughout the 1960s and 1970s had been jealously guarded by trade unions as their own preserve.

Before concluding this section two further problematic issues deserve mention. One is to do with the structuration of the relationships between capital and labour at the summit organizations. The most remarkable development here has been the emergence of the State as the arch-employer, to the extent of overshadowing the role of the main representative bodies for employers - Turkish Confederation of Employers' Association (TİSK), and the Turkish Industrialists' and Businessmen's Association (TÜSİAD). The state, acting in its role as the employer of around 600,000 workers in the state economic enterprises, and making and enforcing critical economic decisions, moved further to centre stage by setting up the State Collective Agreement Coordination Committee in 1984, whose functions were transferred in 1986 to the Public Employers' Association (PEA), affiliated with TİSK. TİSK and PEA have since been formulating the 'framework of principles', which in effect sets the 'ceilings' for the wage demands of organized labour in the private as well as public sector. Reflecting the extraordinary consensus of the ruling elite concerning the 'labour problem', this insurmountable show of strength has led to a real impasse for the unions. In the words of a Türk-İş union leader, 'With this odd body [PEA], which is staffed entirely by public employees, there is no bargaining to speak of; there is only the imposition of the terms and conditions which the government itself sets'.[15] Türk-İş leaders believe that the sole and ultimate decision-maker and 'principle-setter' for PEA as well as TİSK, which work hand-in-hand, has been the Prime Minister himself. If he decides a pay rise of not more than 19 per cent, nobody in the private or public sector offers more than 19 per cent. Nobody stepped out of line until mid-1987, when rapidly rising inflation forced labour to stage unorganized strikes'.[16]

Another source of distress for organized labour in the post-1980 period has been the de-unionization policy of the government in the public sector, which was put into effect by a circular letter of the Prime Minister's office in 1985. The policy was based on the recruitment of public sector employees on the basis of contracts. This mechanism, by offering higher wages and better working conditions to the new employees, aimed at reducing the attraction of unionization and, in the final analysis, at eliminating the effectiveness of unions.[17]

---

14 The number of such collective agreements finalized by the Supreme Board of Arbitration shows a rising trend since 1984. See, ibid., p. 127.

15 See the speech by Şevket Yılmaz, the Leader of Türk-İş, at the summit meeting with the government on 29 April 1989, as quoted in *Türk-İş*, no. 188 (1985), pp. 13-6; *Petrol-İş* (monthly publication of Petrol-İş), no.s 55-6 (May-June 1985), pp. 12-3; *Petrol-İş Year Book 1984*, pp. 151-5; 'Petrol-İş Year Book 1987', p.308; 'Türk-İş Çalışma Raporu', 22-28 December 1986, pp. 23-31.

16 Personal interview with Kaya Özdemir (3 May, 1989). For the rise of unofficial strikes in 1987, see 'Petrol-İş Year Book 1987', pp. 149-60; and Şükran Ketenci, 'Grevler Nasıl Yürüyor?', *Cumhuriyet* (Istanbul daily), 14 May 1987.

Labour and Government during the 1980s

With this most dramatic legal restructuring, the subordination of one of the critical social groups in civil society - labour - via its single most important association - Türk-İş - was completed. The civilian governments of Turgut Özal (1983-1989) proceeded with full vigour to implement the Labour Code with little or no deviation from its original version. How did Türk-İş react to the repressive measures in question? Türk-İş openly supported the 1980 military intervention and the ensuing military government on the grounds that although the legislation by the military restricted trade union freedoms, '...Turkish unionists, led by Türk-İş, harboured the hope that once democracy was re-installed the restrictions would be lifted and unions... would then act freely'.[18] It is for this reason that Türk-İş threw its full weight behind the acceptance of the new constitution in the 1982 referendum, and concomitantly for the election of the leader of the military intervention, General Kenan Evren, as the new president. However, before long, an upsurge of resentment was bound to emerge. Indeed, with the publication of the first draft of the new Labour Code, which did not incorporate their views, the Türk-İş leadership devised an action plan which comprised the following:[19] (1) carrying out various activities for the protection of rights and freedoms of workers, (2) collaboration with the International Labour Organization (ILO),[20] (3) improving work conditions, and (4) trying to have a series of summit meetings with the government.

The major line of attack by Türk-İş on all these four levels was based on the allegation that the labour regime devised by the military intervenors had been an 'exact replica' of the explicit demands that TİSK had made in 1982 concerning industrial relations in Turkey.[21] The latter were based on the following view that TİSK had formulated still earlier, that is, during the 1970s. TİSK had argued: 'It is a well-known fact that the predominant idea in the past with regard to the relationship between labour and the employers was that workers needed protection. The invalidity of assertions to the effect that labour is repressed and exploited is now quite evident. The welfare level that workers have reached go far beyond that of civil service employees. If we also take into account the existence of nearly 3 million unemployed, it is possible to claim that workers in our country form a happy minority.'[22]

Throughout its counter offensive, however, Türk-İş followed a cautious strategy of keeping within the confines of 'legality'. There was no attempt to incite the workers to wide-spread strikes; in fact, as noted Türk-İş leaders had been involved in the academic debate on whether or not the 'strike' was still an effective weapon. Also,

---

17 The Constitutional Court annulled the Decree in December 1988.

18 *Türk-İş*, 191 (July 1985), p. 12.

19 'Türk-İş Çalışma Raporu, 1983.'

20 One basic theme running through the opposition to the legal restructuring of labour unions was lack of observance of international legal norms, notably Agreement No.87 of ILO.

21 See 'Türk-İş Çalışma Raporu, 1983', pp. 77-100. This section of the report discloses and itemizes the demands of the TİSK which later were turned into the articles of the new Constitution and the new Acts on Labour.

22 Ibid., pp. 78-9.

there was no change of vision concerning its mission, which was stated as being to improve the economic and socal rights of the members. There were also no attempts at creating a grass-roots movement in the work-place. Neither were top union officials replaced when the opportunity arose in 1986, in the Fourteenth General Congress of the Confederation.[23] Türk-İş, in short, limited its efforts to 'correcting', or 'normalizing', the tight corset it had been forced to wear. As a result, both the Labour Code and the union structure remained intact, giving rise to the commonly held assumption among some circles that Türk-İş had followed the line of least resistance against the anti-labour restructuration of the period.

The case for inter-union opposition by some recalcitrant Social Democracy-oriented union leaders and their followers against the Türk-İş leadership, was based on both the substance and the form of the Türk-İş policy response to the government - its reliance on its traditional policy of 'dialogue' with the government, and its failure to resort to the 'strike weapon' as often as desired to support those who were on strike. In other words, Türk-İş was accused of following the 'degrading' policy of begging for 'dialogue' with a government which turned a deaf ear.[24] The reluctance of the government to enter into a dialogue with Türk-İş in the post-1980 period, was most evident in 1986 when the number of such contacts was reduced to a minimum despite the urgings of Türk-İş. In an effort to placate the disquiet emerging within the unions, Türk-İş organized in İzmir on 22 February 1986 its sixth open-air meeting in its thirty-four years of history, under its traditional slogan of 'Bread-Peace-Freedom'. However, neither this nor similar meetings in other provinces (still others also planned were banned by the government), seemed to produce the desired outcome: No changes were made in the Labour Code. As should be expected, dissident voices within Türk-İş and the press remained unsatisfied. A stream of criticism was directed at Türk-İş. It was accused of being reduced to a powerless association at the mercy of the government.

The ineffectiveness of the response of Türk-İş to the post-1980 emasculating legal provisions had much to do with the history of the genesis and development of Turkish trade unionism, both during the early Republican and the multi-party period prior to the military takeover in 1980. The Türk-İş, the largest confederation of labour in Turkey, had been a product of 'legalism' as opposed to being a spontaneous association formed from 'below'. The confederation, therefore, relied on the State's benevolent support - in return for political restraint - for consolidating its power. This endemic source of weakness, which in the past had manifested itself in the form of divisions in its ranks, re-surfaced in the post-1980 period in its campaign against the Labour Code. Initially, Türk-İş hoped to bolster its organizational strength through certain provisions of the new Code which aimed at eliminating multiple unions in one work place. One top Türk-İş official, while strongly criticizing the anti-unionist stance of the new measures, admitted that he 'likes the 10 per cent and 51 per cent thresholds introduced for the authorization of unions'.[25] It is therefore difficult not to agree with the leader of 'Otomobil-İş', an independent union not affiliated with Türk-İş, that '...during both

[23] In this Congress, Şevket Yılmaz who had been elected as leader in 1982, was re-elected for his last term.

[24] Interview with Cevdet Selvi (the leader of Petrol-İş) in *Nokta* (Istanbul fortnightly), 4 August 1985.

[25] Kaya Özdemir, personal Interview, 3 May 1989.

the drafting and implementation of these legislation Türk-İş leaders did not make much clamour, ...its voice came alive only when their interests were adversely affected'.[26]

The Türk-İş leaders have always had harmonious relations with the employers and the State. And their staunch support for Atatürkism, the official ideology of the Republic, also led to the deeply rooted belief among Türk-İş top-cadre that the role of the confederation in labour affairs would never be minimized. In a sense, this illusion was related to the failure of Türk-İş to fully grasp the implications of the dynamics of the new economic growth model in post-1980 Turkey, which involved pushing back trade union strength by means other than compromises and agreements.[27] Strong domestic labour pressure was detrimental both to the logic of opening up the economy to the outside (which necessitated competitive pricing of export goods), and to bringing inflation under control. In fact, exactly the opposite claim was voiced by at least one Türk-İş leader: 'There are those who assert that for the 24 January policies to reach their goals, the sphere of unions had to be regulated the way it is now. But I don't share this view. I am not sure if such a causality existed.'[28]

Perhaps one final cause for the ineffectiveness of the counter-strategy of Türk-İş on the 'rights and freedoms of unions' issue, had to do with the weakness of its internal democracy. There had been an absence of organic links between the mass of the working-class and the union leadership. The historical legalism surrounding Türk-İş had not been helpful for democratic structures at the work-place and thus enable the rank and file to impinge on top cadres. Combined with the general de-politicising climate, this last factor must have played some part in pushing the labour movement - as distinct from its central organization - back into the same state of immobilism it had evinced before 1960.

The strategy that had been pursued by the Türk-İş against the government underwent an important transformation in 1987, due to the spontaneous resurgence of the labour movement as a response to the drastic decline in the purchasing power of the workers brought about by skyrocketing inflation. Statistics compiled by various groups,

---

26 Interview with Aydın Özeren, *Yeni Gündem*, 16-31 August 1984.

27 On 24 January 1980, the last pre-coup coalition government led by the Justice party adopted a new policy package which represented a transition from the strategy of import-substitution industrialization, which until then was the dominant mode, to a qualitatively different one. In this new model for economic growth - popularly known in the literature as 'export-led' or 'outward-oriented' model - the defining principles were to open up the economy, liberalize the markets and promote exports. The abandonment of government protection for the indigenous industries and producers and letting the market have a free hand, had behind it the rationale of promoting an export sector of competitive manufactured goods and the establishment of domestic capital goods industries. The full implementation of the programme, however, was precluded by the crisis situation that the country faced. The last coalition government, like its predecessors, proved to be unable to produce a climate of stability, let alone fully employ the policy instruments needed to bring about fundamental shift in the economic model.

28 Interview with the leader of Sağlık-İş, Mustafa Başoğlu, who is also a long standing-member of the National Executive Committee of Türk-İş, in *Yeni Gündem*, 16-30 June 1984; the same view was shared by Kaya Özdemir (personal interview, 3 May 1989). Muzaffer Saraç, who rescinded his leadership of Yol-İş to be founding member of Social Democratic Populist Party in 1983, expressed a contrary view: 'There is no place for unions in the model which is applied now. Türk-İş must first diagnose this. It should then attack it.' (*Yankı*) (Ankara weekly), 14-20 May 1984, p.16.

including those of the TİSK, revealed that since 1980 the rate of decline in real wages (both daily and monthly) was worst in 1987. Taking the year 1983 as the base year, the TİSK data showed that in 1987 the fall in real wages was 14 per cent. The 1988 Annual Programme prepared by the State Planning Organization in turn indicated that the fall in real wages amounted to 25.7 per cent in the public sector and 14.8 per cent in the private sector.[29] According to Şevket Yılmaz, the leader of Türk-İş, real average wages fell around 50 per cent between 1980 and 1987,[30] and according to some, in 1987 it was at its lowest level for 25 years.[31] While both real average wages and minimum wages decreased, in reality the gap between these two had been closing. What this meant for average wage earners was that their living standards were declining to the same level as those of minimum wage-earners, who were socially and economically at the bottom bracket amongst the employed.[32]

When other data such as the share of wages and salaries in the national income over the years are considered, the emerging picture was again that of an extremely unequal distribution of income for the wage/salary earners.[33] The main culprit for this state of affairs was the uncontrollable rate of inflation.[34] The plan devised by the government was that of introducing annual percentage wage increases. The increases in question were decided by trying to figure out the inflation that would materialize the following year, which always proved to be a gross underestimation of the real figure. The final decision-maker being the Prime Minister himself, the percentage wage increase so determined was scrupulously implemented by PEA as well as by TİSK, which was only too happy to go by it in the private sector.

Under the circumstances, the Türk-İş leaders could no longer ignore the massive rank-and-file pressure. Wage grievances in 1987 were qualitatively more important than other problems, that is, the protection of union rights and freedoms. Since Türk-İş trade unionism was traditionally based on bread-and-butter issues to the exclusion of other grievances, Türk-İş was obliged, at the expense of slipping into that gray area between legality and illegality, to prevent the erosion of the confidence of its rank-and-file members and to hold the cohesion and unity of the union intact. The rise in the number of strikes that year organized not only by Türk-İş, but by independent unions and the Confederation on the religious right, Hak-İş, as well as those occurring spontaneously, were de facto developments to which Türk-İş had to lend its support. At this point, factors outside the labour sector were also favourable. There was a growing agitation against the economic policies of the government coming from all quarters; they included the widely publicised views of economic experts that the role of wages in the

---

29 *The Turkish Economy*, 1988 (publication of the Turkish Industrialists' and Businessmen's Association).

30 *Türk-İş*, no: 218 (1987), p.92.

31 *Petrol-İş Year Book 1987*, p.92.

32 Ibid., pp. 100-1; *Petrol-İş Year Book 1985*, pp. 159-62; *Petrol-İş Year Book 1986*, pp.98-105; Kenan Mortan, 'Asgari', *Sabah* (Istanbul daily), 13 October 1985.

33 See *Petrol-İş Year Book 1986*, p. 49.

34 There are many statistics of annual rate of inflation in Turkey with often contradictory data. *The Year Book of Petrol-İş 1987*, however, quotes an inflation rate of 50.4 per cent, which is much lower than those that had been quoted by some newspapers.

high levels of inflation was negligible, and, therefore, there was room for improvement.[35]

Given this widely-shared consciousness about the need for a change in government policies concerning labour, the vital question that Türk-İş faced was whether or not a wage-struggle should be complemented by an anti-government stance. It was on this particular question that the year proved to be a turning point for the Türk-İş. Having had three summit meetings with the government between 1983-1987 with no tangible results, and being constantly pressurized by the rank-and-file, Türk-İş was forced to change its traditional stand on this issue. In a strategic move to increase its leverage over the government it withdrew its support from the ruling Motherland Party (MP) on three different occasions: (1) the by-elections of 1986, (2) the referendum on 14 September 1987, for the reinstatement of the political rights of the pre-1980 political leaders, and (3) the 29 November 1987 general elections. Since the MP suffered losses on all three occasions, Türk-İş could claim 'victory' in each case.[36] First, it could claim to have demonstrated by its campaign against the MP that it was an efficient and vigorous source of opposition to be taken into account especially in the industrialized metropoles, and that in that sense it could still 'make' or 'break' governments. Secondly, by this 'dissensus' politics, its leaders thought they proved their political strength as an organization capable of taking independent political action to the potential inter-union groupings increasingly critical of its passive, if not collaborationist image, and to their disaffected workers. Finally, this political stand provided the Türk-İş leadership with a ready-made opportunity to claim that it was fighting for Western pluralist democracy with full rights for the unions. When the then Minister of Labour threatened Türk-İş with legal proceedings for being actively involved in 'politics', Mr Şevket Yılmaz, the leader of Türk-İş, retorted: '... politics in Turkey will be monopolized by a handful of capitalists and their allies; the economically poor majority will be excluded from politics; associations representing the latter will be intimidated by threats and repression; and this state of affairs will be called democracy.... Who would believe that? Where on earth can this happen?'[37]

This new line of political activity against the ruling party continued prior to the 6 September 1988 referendum, and the 26 March 1989 local elections, both of which again yielded unnerving results for the incumbent party, the MP. These setbacks for and demoralization of the ruling party spurred a new round of activism in the trade union movement, starting in April 1989. The breakthrough came with the deadlock in the collective bargaining negotiations which had been going on since December 1988 in the public sector, with the PEA. The PEA's delaying tactics which jeopardized the wage increases for around 600,000 workers in the public sector, and coincided with the postponement by the Council of Ministers of a strike by independent Iron-and-Steel Workers Union (not affiliated with Türk-İş), opened up a new vista for workers in this sector. In a public sector-wide movement, the workers began to get round the technical-

35 For instance, see Erdoğan Alkin, 'Bırakın Ücretler Yükselsin', *Milliyet* (Istanbul daily), 20 March 1985; Osman Ulagay, 'Enflasyon Bahanesiyle Ücret Sınırlanmasına Hayır', *Cumhuriyet*, 23 May 1986; Teoman Erel,'Vahim Ama Ciddi Değil', *Milliyet*, 24 January 1986; Yavuz Donat, 'Birbuçuk Saatlik Bir Macera', *Tercüman* (Istanbul daily), 25 March 1987; Nazlı Ilıcak, 'Türk-İş ve Hükümet', *Tercüman*, 24 December 1986.

36 *Türk-İş*, no.217 (1987), pp. 1-2.

37 Ibid., p.3.

ity of not being legally on strike, by non-violent, 'new' forms of resistance: boycotting the meals, slowing down the work, growing beards, not working for over-time, paying collective medical visits to doctors, walking to work bare-footed, and the like.

Even more significantly, Türk-İş rose to the occasion by not only planning and coordinating this line of activity but also promoting and publicly supporting them solidly. In fact, this largest resistance movement in Turkish union history was presented by Türk-İş as its own feat.[38] The force of this showdown seemed to have caught the government by surprise. The Prime Minister himself, as the chief engineer of the government's policies with regards to labour, came up with the promise that the workers would be paid back the percentage lost in the official rate of wage increases.

The general political climate of the country and the employers' favouring the workers' demands for wage increases [39] contributed to the change of attitude on the part of the government. Still, Türk-İş's past record prevents us from predicting that Türk-İş-government relations reached a critical point of no return, and that in the future Türk-İş would not give in completely to the dictates of the government.[40]

Conclusion

The structural and relational ties between the main organizational spokesman for labour - the Türk-İş - and the State in the pre-1980 period, had not ended up in the complete incorporation of labour into the state apparatus. If that had been the case, there would have been no need for the rigid state controls introduced in the period under consideration.

Nevertheless, the legacy of the past has inflicted Türk-İş with two congenital weaknesses which, together with the incapacitating impact of the new Labour Code, have impeded its functioning as an effective instrument of labour in the post-1980 period as well - absence of internal democracy and its dependence on the state for obtaining economic favours for its members in return for political restraint.

The post-1980 concern for economic liberalism necessitated ensuring political stability through close integration of the economic, political and moral forces of trade unions into an 'holistic' system, though not through granting them an autonomous area of interest representation. The economic liberalism of the MP governments did not imply a weak State; it was simply opposed to extensive bureaucratic meddling in 'efficient', 'technical', 'rational' functioning of the market. The cost of doing this was, however, considerable interference with the rights and freedoms of unions.

There are some paradoxical consequences of this arrangement. Unless totally liquidated, no trade union can accept a subordinate role to the state and to the employers indefinitely, without trying to represent its members' immediate interests. If it does

[38] Kaya Özdemir, one of the top officials in Türk-İş, claimed (in a personal interview) that all was being directed from the corridors and meeting rooms of Türk-İş.

[39] *Cumhuriyet*, 31 March 1989 and 29 April 1989; *Hürriyet*, 31 March 1989.

[40] After protracted meetings, a pay agreement was finally struck on 17 May 1989, between the Prime Minister and Türk-İş, on a level below the offer Türk-İş had made, but above that of the government's. Politically the most important collective bargaining negotiation Türk-İş had entered into throughout its history ended with its implications open to interpretation.

not, it signs its own death warrant, since soon incipient rival unions would develop. Neo-corporatism, in this sense, is an attempt to solve this dilemma. Unions accept periods of wage and other restraints only on condition of receiving certain other benefits for their members (via social welfare legislation, for instance), and for their own organizations (privileged representational status), and a share in the making of economic policy. By this token, the post-1980 arrangements were not neo-corporatist. Also, they could hardly be called pluralist. The State's intention was to de-activate, re-organize and then to exclude the present unions from the political sphere. Any gains that unions could make always remained precarious.

5

Agriculture: The Forgotten Sector

Üstün Ergüder

Introduction

Perhaps the most interesting problem that Turkey faced during the past forty years was the development of democratic political institutions styled on the Western parliamentary model in a predominantly agricultural country. However, between 1945 and 1988, along with the experimentation in democratic political institutions, the country has also become less agricultural and rural. In 1950, 84 per cent of the population was living in rural areas while in 1988 the same figure was around 40 per cent. The share of agriculture in the Turkish gross domestic product (GDP) fell from about a half in the 1940s to a quarter in the early 1980s, a trend which is still continuing (1990). Turkish exports are no longer dominated by agricultural goods, with the share of agriculture declining during the 1980s to around 23 per cent of the total.

Also, the proportion of the labour force employed in the agricultural sector declined from 80 per cent in the 1950s to 57 per cent during the latter period. Despite the fact that Turkey became one of seven countries in the world to be entirely self-sufficient in food with an annual agricultural growth of around 3.5 per cent in the 1962-1980 period, productivity remained low, landlessness increased with a corresponding rise in share cropping and absentee landlords, and land relations in sections of southeast Anatolia remained socially backward with a few families owning most villages.[1]

The performance of the agricultural sector may be considered a success story if self-sufficiency and the relative lost cost of food in Turkey are taken as yardsticks. On the other hand, the low productivity of labour in general, the continuing and abundant supply of labour in the agricultural sector, an increasing re-distribution of land and the emergence of small plots, make up the gloomier side of the picture.

Still, one of the salient features of the development of Turkish democracy since 1950 has been the very important role that the agricultural sector played in that process. In turn, the democratic experiment left a very important mark on Turkish agriculture. The present author had earlier noted that a unique feature of Turkish agriculture was its domination by vast numbers of small, and often non-economic, land-holdings. This is a legacy of the arrangements in the Ottoman Empire concerning land, including the Islamic inheritance codes and traditions.[2] In Turkey, Latin American *latifundia* types of holdings had been the exception rather than the rule, and had been confined to such regions as the southeast. Although one could come across market-oriented large

---

1 Mina Toksöz, 'Turkey to 1992: Missing Another Chance?', The Economist Intelligence Unit, Special Report No. 1136, p. 30.

2 Üstün Ergüder, 'Politics of Agricultural Taxation in Turkey', unpublished Ph.D. dissertation, Syracuse University, U.S.A., 1969, passim.

landholdings in the west and the southeast Mediterranean region, these were not the dominant forms of ownership in those regions.

The 'rural vote' shaped by small landholdings thus played a very important role in the development of Turkish democracy. All elected governments had to take into account the grievances against a State that in the past had treated the 'peasant' heavy-handedly, and the demands for higher incomes and a better life. Consequently, with democratization, party organizations became highly sensitive to the excesses of the public bureaucracy in the countryside;[3] tax reforms were not meaningfully extended into agricultural incomes - a result of bureaucratic difficulties and the resistance of large landowning interests;[4] the land tax remained at token levels, as any substantive hike would have to cover both large and small land holdings;[5] agricultural subsidies and price support policies were also aimed at winning the support of small producers. Especially price support policies were highly sensitive to electoral competition, with higher prices expected at election times.[6]

One of the most important consequences of the democratic experience in Turkey has been to integrate the countryside into the political system and accelerate resource transfer to the agricultural sector. Elections and party competition have figured prominently in that process. In contrast, agriculture-based interest groups have had very little impact in the making of those policies. Elections, local party congresses, party organizations, and direct contact with party leaders have served as vehicles for articulation of demands emanating from the agricultural sector. In short, 'the party' has served as the vehicle of interest articulation in this sector.[7]

The pre-1980 Period

The most important era in terms of interest group activity in the agricultural sector was the 1960-1980 period. The agricultural interest groups active in the early 1960s were the peak associations of the Turkish Union of Chambers of Agriculture (TUCA) and the Turkish Union of Chambers of Agricultural Experts (TUCAE). These were chambers organized as public professional organizations to facilitate control and management of agricultural affairs by the state.

An interesting aspect of interest group activity in this sector at the time was the formation and the activities of the Turkish Federation of Farmers (TFF), a voluntary organization set up by farmers mainly from southern (Mediterranean) and western (Aegean) regions of Turkey. Unlike the south-eastern region where a 'semi-feudal' landownership pattern exists, the southern and western regions, from the 1950s onwards, moved into modern and capitalist forms of farming through mechanization. The TFF was based on the Farmers' Unions, which already existed in certain locali-

---

3 Ibid., pp. 418-24.

4 Ibid.

5 Ibid.

6 Üstün Ergüder, 'Politics of Agricultural Price Policy in Turkey', in *The Political Economy of Income Distribution in Turkey*, Ed. by Ergun Özbudun and Aydın Ulusan (New York: Holmes and Meier, 1980), pp. 169-97.

7 Ibid.

ties. The main force behind the Federation was the prosperous cotton farmers of the Aegean and the Mediterranean regions, who ploughed large tracts of land. The formation of the TFF was prompted mainly for three reasons:[8] (1) increasing pressure for land reform that was coming from the intellectual-bureaucratic elites after they had gained the upper hand once again during the military interlude of 1960-1961; (2) the attempts to extend agricultural income taxation to the agricultural sector as well as to increase the overall tax burden of the sector; (3) the critical attitudes of the press and various urban groups towards the agricultural sector. (It was thought that the economic policies of the *Demokrat* Party between 1950-1960 had unfairly favoured the large farmers. Unequal distribution of land and rather light tax burden of the farmers were the main issues.)

The political parties, although sympathetic to agricultural interests, responded favourably to pressures for an agricultural income tax and land reform coming from the intellectuals and the civil bureaucracy. Although action on land reform looked remote, it became a major issue of political debate, and every coalition government of the early 1960s prepared its own version of a land reform programme. It was the salience of these issues that motivated the establishment of the TFF in 1962 as a voluntary association.

The TFF was not aligned with any one political party. However, its leadership was dominated by supporters of both the Republican Peoples' Party (RPP) and the Justice Party (JP). This was perhaps a deliberate strategy on the part of the TFF to have open channels of communication to the leadership of the two major political parties.

It is rather significant that the TFF did not adopt positions on agricultural income taxation and land reform different from those of the TUCA. In fact, the TFF was dominated by farmers who were also very active in the TUCA.

It must also be noted in passing that the Turkish Association of Agriculturalists (TAA) also preceded the TFF. It was not, however, a very active association. In any case, the membership of the TAA had not been exclusively made up of farmers. In 1986, only 1,000 of a membership of 15,000 were farmers. The rest were predominantly agricultural technicians, 'agricultural engineers' and home economics experts.[9] The TAA had been formed in 1946, and acquired in 1952 the status of an 'association in the public interest', entitling it to financial support from public funds.

The TUCAE had been the least farmer-oriented organization of the group. Associated with the Chambers of Engineers, it mainly represented university-trained agricultural experts. The members of the TUCAE were well aware of the farmer's problems. Nonetheless, the closeness of this organization to the academic and the intellectual-bureaucratic elite resulted in its rather indifferent attitude towards the taxation of the agricultural sector. For example, in a report published in 1965 by a commission set up by the Union, the inclusion of agricultural incomes within the coverage of income taxation was defended.[10]

---

8 Ergüder, 'Politics of Agricultural Taxation in Turkey', pp. 337-8.

9 Data provided by Professor Binnaz Toprak of Boğaziçi University which she obtained at an interview with Mr İbrahim Yetkin, the President of the TAA. According to Toprak, 8,500 members of TUCAE were agricultural technicians, 2,500 were home economics experts, and 1,500 were agricultural engineers.

10 See 'Türkiye'de Zirai Vergiler', Ziraat Odası Mühendisleri Yayınları, No.22, 1965.

In addition to the TFF, TAA and the Chambers, various cooperatives in the agricultural sector need to be mentioned: Agricultural Credit Cooperatives and their Unions, Agricultural Sales Cooperatives and their Unions, and Village Development Cooperatives. Some of these dated back to the pre-World War II days. A common characteristic of the cooperatives is that they had been very much dependent on governmental financial institutions. Similarly, many of them had been affiliated to the various government agencies and, thus, had been under close governmental tutelage.

The post-1980 Period

The impact of the State vis-à-vis the agricultural interest associations increased during the 1980s. For instance, the Motherland Party (MP) governments relied on the agricultural credit and sales cooperatives in the distribution of credits and in the purchase of subsidized agricultural products. Our interviews with the officials and founders of *Trakya Birlik* (Thrace Union) indicated that these cooperatives did not exhibit any systematic pattern of interest articulation by the producers. The cooperatives and their unions have functioned more like state economic enterprises.[11] Only the Village Development Cooperatives were relatively autonomous from governmental control.[12]

As already noted, the episode of the TFF and the land reform and taxation issues reveal that in the 1960s there was an attempt to organize the agricultural sector along voluntary lines. The important question concerning the 1980s is to what extent a similar action by agriculture-based groups took place within the framework of the 'liberal economic revolution' of Turkey. During the 1980s, the old issues of land reform and taxation were no longer on the political agenda. Yet, important problems of a more significant nature plagued the Turkish agricultural sector.

A criticism levelled at the Motherland Party governments is that they have had a pro-urban bias, leading to a virtually total neglect of the agricultural sector. In fact, one of the major differences between the JP, a party of the centre-right, which was in power either by itself or as a leading partner of coalitions during most of the 1960s and 1970s, and the MP, a party of the centre-right of the 1980s, concerns their constituencies .The JP derived its strength mainly from the countryside of the west and the coastal areas of Turkey, where modern agricultural production constitutes the dominant pattern. In contrast, electoral support for the MP has been more evenly distributed in the countryside while the party has a strong base in the major urban

---

11 The Agricultural Credit Cooperatives and Unions were re-organized in 1984 through a Decree-Act (No.237). Their elected officials were replaced by government-appointed personnel. Similarly, Agricultural Sale Cooperatives and Unions were re-organized in 1985 (Act No.3186) and the power of the Ministry of Industry and Commerce was considerably increased over them. Now the Directors-General of the Unions are also appointed by the Ministry, and all decisions of the General Council of the Unions and the Cooperatives take effect only upon official approval.

12 See M. Talim, T. Güneş, A. Çıkın, İ.H. İnan and N. Bektöre, 'Tarımda Teşkilatlanma', T.C. Tarım ve Orman Bakanlığı Türkiye II. Tarım Kongresi (Ankara: Tarım ve Orman Bakanlığı, 1981), pp. 493-511.

areas, too.[13] Its emphasis on urban development is one of its features that distinguishes it from the JP.

The policies of the pre-1980 governments were characterized by import subsidies, low interest credit, tax exemption, large scale irrigation projects and tariff protection. Low land tax and income tax rates were maintained, while generous agricultural price supports were a hallmark of governmental policies during that period. Although agricultural support policy dates back to the 1930s, it was in the 1950s that it became a major policy instrument through which the agricultural sector was subsidized. Although initially only six crops were subject to price supports, by 1965 the scheme was extended to cover eleven items. The policy, by guaranteeing a base price for produce, attempted to protect the producer from the vagaries of weather conditions as well as from the whims of price movements in the market place.

This situation underwent a significant transformation during the 1980s. Interviews conducted with representatives of agriculture-based organizations and producers revealed that the farmers were very critical of the MP, and of its leader Turgut Özal (1983-1989) in particular. Some of the critical problems of the agricultural sector that had existed before were salient during the 1980s, too. Two of them were low productivity, due to the failure to extend irrigation through canals despite the emphasis on macro irrigation projects, and a lack of emphasis on agricultural training and extension services. Another important problem related to productivity was the fact that over 55 per cent of the labour force was still employed in the agricultural sector. What this meant in absolute terms, according to Mr Erol Baras,[14] the President of the Chamber of Agriculture of Marmara region, was that in 1989 the sector was employing roughly 27.5 million people compared to 16 million in 1950, when close to 80 per cent of the population lived off the land. Mr Baras argued that a figure of 25 per cent earning a living in the agricultural sector could produce the same amount. Towards the end of the 1980s, maldistribution of land, too, was a problem in the southeastern region of Turkey, while in the west the division of land into small plots stemming from local inheritance customs continued to lead to low levels of productivity.

During the decade in question, inflation was by far the most important problem that the Turkish farmer faced. Critical of the agricultural price support policy of the 1960s and the 1970s, Toksöz had noted:

> In theory, price support should function to signal priorities in the choice of crops. But in Turkey until 1973 official prices would be set at harvest time after the sowing decisions had been made. Even after this had changed to sowing time, it made little difference since small farmers would sell most of their crops to middlemen in advance....Yet, because of the high rates of inflation, the official prices announced half a year ahead of marketing, would fall below market prices at harvest time, rendering the policy ineffective. The government was too inflexible to adjust prices automatically in line with inflation. Furthermore, the support price payments reached such proportions that in some years their total sum surpassed

13 Üstün Ergüder and Richard I. Hofferbert, 'Restoration of Democracy in Turkey? Political Reforms and the Elections of 1983', in *Elections in the Middle East. Implications of Recent Trends*, Linda L. Layne, ed. (Boulder, Colorado: Westview Press, 1987), pp. 19-47.

14 Personal interview.

the money supply (M1). This, of course, further fuelled inflation.[15]

The same problems persisted during the 1980s as well, but with a new twist; inflation was running at much higher rates, and never went below 40 per cent and was, at the end of the decade, running as high as 70 per cent. Moreover, the price support policy did not show the same flexibility as it did in the 1960s and 1970s to political events such as elections. Mr Osman Özbek, the President of the TUCA, stated that Özal's concentration on exports, cities, and the like necessitated an agricultural price policy oriented towards 'economic rationality' rather than a political one. Mr Özbek also argued that before 1980 thirty two agricultural products received subsidies, whereas after 1980 only eight products were supported.[16] Moreover, during this period, there were no meetings and consultations with the leaders of the chambers and the other interested associations on the problems of the agricultural sector. Inputs from the representatives of the sector were not welcome; policy formulation was simply a technocratic affair. With reference to the impact of inflation on the agricultural sector a common complaint of those interviewed may be summarized as follows: 'In this sector, it is impossible for us to adjust to changing prices. We buy throughout the year [reference to inputs], but sell only once a year [reference to their produce]. The Motherland Party has forgotten this sector.'

The attitude of the government, however, appeared to revert to the pre-1980 pattern with increasing party competition between 1986 and 1987, when the restrictions imposed by the military, barring former political leaders from competition for power, were lifted through a popular referendum. The referendum itself in September 1987, and the early general elections that followed in late November 1987, brought the new political forces, then Prime Minister Turgut Özal and the MP, of Turkish politics face to face against the old, such as Süleyman Demirel and his True Path Party (TPP),[17] the Social Democratic Populist Party (SDPP) under the leadership of Erdal İnönü,[18] and Bülent Ecevit and his Democratic Left Party (DLP)[19] in an atmosphere of stiff political competition. In addition, the return to politics of Necmettin Erbakan leading the Prosperity Party, and Alparslan Türkeş heading the National Work Party, both leaders of pre-1980 minor parties, made competition on the right of the political spectrum even more interesting.[20]

Within this political environment, and during the general elections of 1987, better support prices were announced, especially in tobacco growing provinces such as Manisa, where the competition for votes between the MP and the TPP was very keen. The complaints of the producers did not end, however. A common grievance was that even

---

15 Toksöz, 'Turkey to 1992: Missing Another Chance?' p.33.

16 Personal interview.

17 The TPP claims to be the inheritor of the mantle of the old JP.

18 Although Erdal İnönü is a post-1980 leader, the SDPP had the strongest claim to be a successor to the RPP, which was dissolved by the military after September 1980.

19 Bülent Ecevit was the leader of the RPP before 1980. He, however, tried to divorce the DLP from the leading members of the RPP, and founded the new party with a 'grass roots' approach.

20 Necmettin Erbakan was the leader of the National Salvation Party, a religious fundamentalist party. Alparslan Türkeş led the Nationalist Action Party, an ultra-rightist party. Both parties played an important role in Turkish politics in the 1970s as they were able to hold the balance in the Grand National Assembly when none of the major parties were able to form a government by themselves.

though better support prices may have been given, payments to the producers were actually made in instalments. In an inflationary environment this forced the producers to sell their produce to buyers in the private sector at prices lower than the public support prices.

In sum, during the 1980s, despite the lack of an issue like land reform that prompted interest group activity, there were important problems that the agricultural sector faced. Yet organized action from the agricultural sector to put these issues on the political agenda was not extensive. Our survey of the press revealed that the attention of the media to issues that concerned the agricultural sector was minimal compared with the space that the associations of the industrial and commercial sectors received.

In fact, voluntary associations such as the TFF were eventually disbanded by their membership. The TAA was still around, but it lost some of its organizational vitality following the military intervention of 1980 when some of its provincial offices were closed, limiting its provincial organizations to 24 out of 67 provinces in 1986. Also, the TAA did not receive any public funds after 1980. Most of the staff and the consultants of the Union happened to be former Ministry of Agriculture bureaucrats, and it functioned more like an appendage of the Ministry. One further problem plagued the effectiveness of the TUCA vis-à-vis the government - the identification of the leadership and most local chambers with the opposition TPP of Süleyman Demirel.

The ruling MP of Turgut Özal did not make any attempt to capture or colonize chambers and unions as Süleyman Demirel and the JP had done in the pre-1980 days. There were several reasons: (a) the impact of post-1980 attempts to depoliticize voluntary associations and chambers played a role; (b) the MP had its own organizational problems as a new party, and did not pay attention to placing sympathizers in positions of leadership in interest group associations, and (c) 'economic rationality' in policy formation meant, for the MP leaders, integration of 'experts' into the policy process rather than 'interest representatives'. This attitude of the MP, according to Osman Özbek, changed after the 1987 general elections. He argued that the MP now tried to capture local chambers and mobilize them against the Union (TUCA).[21]

When the diffuse and intricate nature of the post-1980 issues is coupled with the structure of the agricultural sector in Turkey, which is largely based on a small and fragmented pattern of ownership, associational activity did not seem to be very likely, despite the fact that Turkey was said to be on the throes of a liberal revolution.

One further point must be mentioned here: political parties played a very important role in the agricultural sector during the 1960s and 1970s. Interest representation was more party-centred rather than being based upon interest group associations. Only those interest group associations, which had been colonized by a political party played a role in interest articulation during the pre-1980 period. TUCA was a case in point.

It is worth reiterating the striking difference between the former JP of Süleyman Demirel and the MP of Turgut Özal as political parties of the centre-right, concerning their approach to interest group associations. The JP always attempted to place party faithful or sympathizers in the ruling committees of those associations. This approach was particularly marked in the agricultural sector. For instance, TUCA leadership

---

21 Interview with Özbek.

has always been associated with the Justice party. The tradition has continued; the present leadership under Mr Osman Özbek is close to the TPP, the successor to the JP. In contrast, the MP under Özal has not made an effort to establish links with the agricultural sector. The loss of a party channel accounts for the common complaints of those interviewed about being excluded from the policy formulation process.

6

Commercial Groups: Love-Hate Relationship with the State

Ersin Kalaycıoğlu

Commercial interests are organized in different patterns in different countries. Cultural, historical and legal reasons are often mentioned as the main factors which determine how interest groups operate, organize and relate with the state.[1] A brief scrutiny of these conditions in Turkey will enable us to understand some of the basic features of the current commercial interest representation in that country. It is also in order to mention the market conditions of traders in Turkey and how these affect their organizational ability and contacts with the state.

Pre-1980 Period

Under the influence of growth-oriented economic policies that postponed welfare programmes, and the political crises of the 1960 -1980 period, the interest group system in Turkey functioned to fuel conventional and protest forms of participation in politics.[2]

The state desperately tried to cope with heightened interest group activity. The Justice Party governments attempted to create monopolistic associations in various sectors of the economy, covering all industrialists and traders on the one hand, and the labour, on the other. Robert Bianchi, has argued that, since their origin in the Young Turk period, modern business associations have grown more and more to fit the corporatist paradigm of a semiofficial, unitary, compulsory, hierarchical structure joined in a fairly secure and mutually beneficial clientelistic relationship with the major economic ministries. The Turkish Union of Chambers and Stock Exchanges (Türkiye Odalar ve Borsalar Birliği) (TOBB) is recognized officially as the most authoritative spokesman for 'free enterprise', and tries to represent the interests of all merchants, industrialists, and commodities brokers simultaneously.[3]

---

1 Gabriel A. Almond and G. Bingham Powell, Jr., *Comparative Politics. Process and Policy*, 2nd edition (Boston, Mass.: Little, Brown and Co., 1978); William D. Coleman, 'State Construction Industry', in *Organized Interests and the State. Studies in Meso-Corporatism*, Alan Cawson, ed. (London, etc.: Sage, 1985); Gabriel A. Almond, 'Corporatism, Pluralism and Professional Memory', *World Politics*, 35 (1983), pp. 245-60; and Henry W. Ehrmann, *Interest Groups on Four Continents* (Westport, Conn.: Greenwood Press, 1958).

2 Ergun Özbudun, *Social Change and Political Participation in Turkey* (Princeton: Princeton University Press, 1976), passim; Ersin Kalaycıoğlu, *Karşılaştırmalı Siyasal Katılma* (İstanbul: İstanbul Üniversitesi Siyasal Bilimler Fakültesi, 1983), chap. 11; and Robert Bianchi, *Interest Groups and Political Development in Turkey* (Princeton: Princeton University Press, 1984), pp. 142-5.

3 Bianchi, *Interest Groups and Political Development in Turkey*, p. 251.

Although there was a distinct inclination towards bringing some kind of order to the representation of commercial interests in the 1960-1980 period, it was not possible to bridge the increasing gap between the conflicting interests of commerce and industry. 'The common interests of free enterprise', as it was termed, was more of an aspiration than a reflection of reality. Conflicts arising either between the small and large firms or the commercial and industrial interests could not be bridged even in the 1970s, when severe political and economic crises were unfolding.[4]

In the event, there was a tendency towards pluralist interest representation. Industrialists founded two voluntary associations of their own: the Turkish Confederation of Employers' Association (TISK) and the Turkish Industrialists' and Businessmen's Association (TÜSİAD). This was the upshot of their dissatisfaction with their under-representation within the TOBB.[5]

Post-1980 Developments

As Ergun Özbudun in this volume has shown, the regime set up by the 1982 Constitution in Turkey was one of strict control by the state of the activities of public professional organizations. The overall aim had been that of preventing the recurrence of the pre-1980 'dysfunctional politicization' of the interest groups. It was, for instance, possible for the government to request the dissolution of a chamber of commerce on the grounds that its criticisms of the government's economic policy was itself a political activity.

A second motive at the back of the minds of the designers of the post-1982 regime was that of inhibiting the development of *interest* groups into *pressure* groups. Their role in the polity was to be restricted to one of 'pleading' from the 'sublime State' for some aid from the 'sublime State' to assist their members. At the same time, they were expected to regulate the behaviour of their members so that the latter would not employ any pressure tactics against the government, such as wildcat strikes, illegal rallies, picketing, and the like. No interest association could be permitted to wield any veto power over the government's policies. The designers of the post-1982 political regime wished interest groups to act in a docile manner, and thus be 'loyal' groups 'minding their own business', and expressing the views of their members on matters that directly pertained to their particular domain of activity.[6] They were saddled with the responsibility of explaining the benevolence associated with the policies of the government to their members, and persuading them to act in line with those policies. All this suggests a particular perception of national interest: what is good as espoused by the party government is also good for Turkey, and there is 'a public good' that is dissociated from and elevated above the interests of economic (as well as social) groups.

As in the pre-1980 period, so in the post-1980 period, too, commercial interests were encouraged to be represented through hierarchically organized bodies of public

---

4 Ibid., pp. 251-9.

5 Ibid., pp. 270-4.

6 Series of articles in *Milliyet* (Istanbul daily), 15 April-15 June 1982.

professional associations (PPOs). * Not only the government but the TOBB itself often declared that public professional organizations were the sole and legitimate representatives of the commercial and business interests in Turkey.[7] Illustrative here were the declarations of the TOBB Chairman, Mr Ali Coşkun, that only TOBB had the right to (legitimately) represent the interests of the commercial and industrial sectors, and no other association had the authority to speak as representative of any group or sector. The TOBB and the individual chambers of commerce representatives went so far as to argue that voluntary interest associations, such as TÜSİAD, could not criticize government policies; such activities constituted 'involvement in politics', and thus violated the laws, and they should be punished accordingly.[8] Nine (governmental) resolutions were adopted by the military government of the 1980- 1983 period, which further weakened the status of the TOBB and also put all the PPOs, including the TOBB, under the close tutelage of different ministries. However, there have been limits to the efforts of the state to directly control commercial and industrial interests. TİSK and TÜSIAD, which are employers' and businessmen's and industrialists'associations, respectively, are two prominent examples of effective voluntary interest associations, which also represent the interests of the major trading companies of Turkey. The pluralistic tendencies of big business spill over to other levels of the commercial sector.

On the other hand, the subjection of commerce to political decisions and the governments' ability to influence elections to the higher bodies of the TOBB and the individual chambers of commerce, continued during the 1980s. Commerce has always been a major concern of the Turkish governments. In fact, the commercial sector often depended on governmental support to survive, let alone thrive. For instance, industrialists argued that 'since the days of the Ottoman Empire, the Turkish private sector has always been nurtured by the state and obtained its power and nectar from the state. Even today a businessman is under the command of the bureaucrats of Ankara'.[9] Despite claims to the contrary,[10] spokesmen of business interests continue to assert with some exaggeration that the public bureaucracy is still in command of the Turkish economy, and that it even possesses a de facto veto power over government policies.[11]

During the 1960s and 1970s, import substitution policies and import quotas were major sources of state influence on the commercial sector.[12] Chambers of commerce issued import licenses for importers, and they were instrumental in determining who obtained permission to export commodities which were not freely exportable out of Turkey.[13] In the post-1983 period, export promotion gained particular importance in Turkey's foreign economic relations. During this period, export promotion premiums

---

* On PPOs, see Ergun Özbudun in this volume (Editor's note).

7 For instance, see *Cumhuriyet* (Istanbul daily), 20 May 1986.

8 *Güneş* (Istanbul daily), 20 January 1988.

9 Quoted in *Milliyet*, 9 October 1987.

10 Dankwart A. Rustow, 'Turkey's Liberal Revolution', *Middle East Review*, 17 (1985), pp. 5-11.

11 See series of articles in *Milliyet*, 5-8 May 1988. Elsewhere in this volume (chapter 12) it is shown that during the 1980s, responsibility for making critical decisions concerning the economy passed from the bureaucracy to the ruling party (Editor's note).

12 Bianchi, *Interest Groups and Political Development in Turkey*, pp. 251-9.

13 Cem Kozlu, *Uluslararası Pazarlama* (İstanbul: İş Bankası, 1982).

and tax rebates for export items began to function as a major means of government influence on the 'rising' groups of traders, namely the exporters. Skirmishes among exporters over the premiums and tax rebates were rife. This author was able to find 78 oral or written questions (approximately 4 per cent of all oral and written questions of that period), posed by deputies of the parliamentary opposition parties to Cabinet ministers between 1986 and 1989 concerning corruption associated with illegal exportation of commodities from Turkey.

In the post-1983 period, being on good terms with the government has been a more effective strategy for commercial groups than setting up their autonomous associations to confront it. The dependence of the commercial groups (among others) on the decisions of government and the public bureaucracy is well documented. A businessman publicly declared that, 'Most Turkish businessmen make more money from the decisions of Ankara than they do by production of some items.... Regardless of the circumstances, the business community must be on very good terms with the government. Because they always need the support and protection of the State'.[14]

In turn, the pro-business attitudes of the Motherland Party (MP) governments (1983 to the present) * has made life easy for commercial interest groups. The chairman of the Istanbul Chamber of Commerce declared: 'We have a very good dialogue with the government.... We appreciate a government that believes in the merits of the private sector'.[15]

Finally, big trading firms were (and are) either extensions of industrial holdings, or affiliates in partnership. Commercial interests were thus able to find a means of additional representation via the voluntary businessmen associations, without endangering their TOBB connections.[16]

Have commercial groups played a role in the making of economic decisions? As Üstün Ergüder in this volume has shown, during the 1980s, the state continued to have a major impact on commodity prices through its determination of support prices of agricultural commodities, such as cotton, tobacco, sunflower, sugar beet, etc., which are major trade items either in the domestic or international markets. Government also interfered in the quantities to be traded with other countries. Turkish exports, on the other hand, often ran up against some quotas determined by treaties signed with member states of the European Community, the United States, and the Eastern European countries. Oil and petroleum derivatives, which continued to be major items among Turkish imports, were usually purchased by barter and clearing deals with the

14 Quoted in *Milliyet*, 27 July 1986. My translation.

* 'The present' here signifies 1990 (Editor's note).

15 Quoted in *Milliyet*, 12 July 1988. My translation.

16 It is almost impossible to differentiate between the members of commercial and industrial interest groups. Furthermore, multiple membership of businessmen or corporations in different Chambers, both of Commerce and Industry, is a fact. In most cases, this author found it very difficult to judge where a private sector representative acts as the representative of a business interest, an industrial interest, or a commercial interest. From time to time, the same group of people play different roles as representatives of commercial and industrial interests. Every major holding company is involved in both production and marketing activities of the same commodities. The owners of corporations belong to both commercial and industrial interest groups. Therefore, it is not possible to avoid referring to industry when one writes about commercial interests in Turkey.

Arab oil states. Those countries, too, imposed certain limits and restrictions on the list of exportable items. Chambers of commerce played some role in domestic and international negotiations over the quota limits and the prices of commodities to be traded. In the process, a new type of businessman, namely 'businessman as diplomat', emerged in the post-1983 era.[17]

One should not, however, be misled by the participation of the representatives of chambers of commerce in the foreign economic contacts of the Turkish government, or by the occasional meetings of Prime Minister Turgut Özal with the representatives of major commercial (as well as other interest) groups to discuss economic matters. The tone and style of Mr Özal's talks at these meetings, and his public speeches, indicate that he was more inclined to *instruct* interest groups than *exchange* views with them. The role of commercial interest groups in the economic policy-making process of the government is either minimal or non-existent. The major decisions concerning the economy, and even the structure and status of the TOBB, were made without prior dialogue between the TOBB representatives and the government. The Chairman of the Ankara Chamber of Commerce once retorted: 'It is time to halt the thinking of "I do it, so will it be". We will get involved in politics and sever our ties with the government.'[18]

During the decade of the 1980s, the pattern of Turkish commercial interest representation was such that a limited number of non-competitive and compulsory associations were established by the state as representatives of the major commercial interests. They were organized in the form of a federation; each chamber was functionally connected with another of superior jurisdiction and authority.[19]

All the chambers were placed under the authority of the TOBB. Chambers themselves were also put under the tutelage of the public bureaucracy (by summer 1983), and the governors of the provinces were endowed with the authority to remove the chairpersons of the chambers from office under certain circumstances.[20] It follows that there were no routine and formalized procedures that governments would use in consulting, negotiating, and/or accommodating commercial interests in economic policy making.

On 8 August 1989, the government promulgated a new series of radical policy changes concerning the convertibility of the Turkish lira and export-import regime. The Decree-Law in question was duly approved by the President, and published in the Official Gazette on 11 August 1989. Import tariffs on consumer goods, such as electrical and electronic kitchenware, TV, VCR, casette players and even automobiles were lowered. For the first time, every Turkish citizen was permitted to buy foreign currencies up to 3000 U.S. dollars at banks without showing an intent for travel to foreign countries. Other measures which encouraged free movement of capital in and out of Turkey up to 25 million U.S. dollars were also made operational by the same decree. Exporters were given greater leeway in depositing part of their foreign exchange earnings outside of the country. Thus, a drastic change took place in the export and import regimes of

---

17 *Güneş*, 29 July 1987.

18 Quoted in *Milliyet*, 19 April 1987. My translation.

19 Şerafettin Gökalp, *Açıklamalı Dernekler Kanunu ve İlgili Mevzuat* (İstanbul: Yetkin, 1986).

20 *Nokta* (Istanbul weekly), 15 August 1983.

Turkey by what was called a 'shock decision' personally made by the Prime Minister.[21]

The decision was made without even consulting and, in fact, over the objections of the technocrats, such as the Head of the Central Bank and the Undersecretary (Director) of the State Planning Organization; for a while the latter even considered resigning.[22]

The reactions of the commercial interest group representatives to this policy move confirmed that no previous consultations, negotiations, or bargaining took place between them and the government, or with Mr Özal. They all disagreed over the timing of the measures.[23] Editorials in the daily newspapers hinted that the timing of the decree was based on 'political' considerations, that is, Mr Özal's ambition to run for the Presidency.

The chambers may be expected to be involved in policy-implementation, if not policy-making. In fact, chambers did pay attention to some matters concerning policy implementation. A most common form was to remind the traders that there would be a crackdown on tax evaders if tax revenues of the state remained low. However, nothing seems to have come of such threats. Thus, it seems the 'I do it, so will it be' approach of the State continued to be the pattern of the interface between the commercial interest groups and the State. During the 1980s, the role of voluntary associations was, in fact, further diminished in such areas as collective bargaining, commercial policy-making and implementation. The post-1983 governments discouraged voluntary associations from interacting within and across sectors without the control or license of the state. The public employers' unions, which were under the influence of the government, set the norm for agreement over the wages of all salaried personnel within both the public and private sector corporations. Private sector employers' unions did not raise wages beyond the level that the public sector employers' unions settled for.[24] Hence, the state, as the public sector employer, determined the outcome of 'free collective bargaining' between the employers and the work force. *

To be sure, voluntary associations to represent commercial interests still exist. Their activities, however, consist of voicing grievances and demands of commercial groups often *after* the implementation of economic policies. Commercial economic interests have been of necessity quite successful in *adapting* to government policies.

Despite the fact that the Prime Minister personally declared that not too much was to be expected from the state in the form of guidance and support, because 'if we take the State as a "father figure" he may catch and beat us',[25] some businessmen still cherished the idea that governmental support was essential to the performance of Turkish industry and commerce.[26] Some even pointed to the importance of having good relations with Mr Özal.[27] Intra-group relations and competition, under the auspices of the state and with a distinct feature of clientelistic networks tied personally to the Prime

---

21 *Milliyet*, 11 August 1989.
22 *Milliyet*, 11 and 12 August 1989.
23 *Cumhuriyet*, 10 August 1989.
24 *Milliyet*, 2 February 1987.
* On this matter also see chapter 4 in this volume (Editor's note).
25 Quoted in *Milliyet*, 17 November 1986.
26 *Milliyet*, 13 March 1987.
27 *Milliyet*, 9 October 1987.

Minister, characterized the post-1983 regime.

This does not constitute a major break with the recent past. In the post-1983 period, the economic regime of the country per se has not on the whole been a contentious issue. Conversely, during the 1970s the capitalist nature of the Turkish economy was constantly debated, and arguments about the 'merits of socialism' were repeatedly made by various groups and political parties on both the right and left of the political spectrum. Both the religious and the ultra-nationalist political parties had promoted the idea that capitalism was not suitable for Turkey. The Republican People's Party (RPP) and the National Salvation Party had formed a coalition government in 1973, although the former was a secularist and the latter a religious party, and thus did not see eye to eye on many issues. On the other hand, the leading figures of both political parties had declared that they had a common platform - that of changing the economic order.[28] Under the circumstances, from time to time, the business community could not help but feel threatened that their clientelistic links with the government were in danger. In spite of the threat in question, it was not possible to promote unity among traders and businessmen, a point made above.

During the 1980s, pro-business governments have been in power. Furthermore, none of the opposition groups and parties have taken a strong anti-capitalist position. In contrast to its predecessor RPP, the largest political opposition party - the Social Democratic Populist Party (SDPP) - has tried to project the image that it does not seek to 'change the economic order'.[29] Consequently, the likelihood of the development of a feeling of unity among the traders and the businessmen is much less than it was during the 1961-1980 period. The intra-group conflicts in question and the emerging diversification of interests across the commercial and industrial circles have led to increasing intensity of conflict among sectoral interests, and caused the relative importance of conflicts with other groups to diminish.

The overall consequence of this development has been the increasing importance of sectoral interest groups and their voluntary associations. Thus, instead of commercial interests being represented by rallying around a political party or the TOBB, as they had done during the 1970s, they have tended to concentrate their efforts on promoting their sectoral (meso) or company (micro) interests.[30]

In fact, Mr Mehmet Yazar, Minister of State, in a speech he delivered at the annual convention of TÜSİAD in January 1988, argued that as long as it remains divided the business community will not be effective in articulating its interests; if united and disciplined, it will be much better at receiving 'benefits' from the government.[31]

All in all, during the 1980s, the relationship between the State and commercial interests emerged as an elaborate network of clientelistic ties between sectoral and even company interests on the one hand, and the political and bureaucratic elites including the mayors and other municipal authorities on the other. The relations between single firms or commercial interest associations and the state have been developing along the lines of direct contacts with the top-level officials of the public bureaucracy and/or

---

28 Series of articles in *Milliyet*, 1-15 November 1973.

29 Series of articles in *Milliyet*, 2-7 December 1988.

30 *Hürriyet* (Istanbul daily), 29 October 1985.

31 *Milliyet*, 20 January 1988.

ministries, and sometimes with the Prime Minister himself. No other political groups or institutions, such as the ruling party and/or the Parliament, emerged as mediating agents between the executive branch of government and the commercial interest groups.

In surveys I conducted in 1984 and 1988 in the Turkish Grand National Assembly (TGNA), one issue that the deputies repeatedly kept referring to was their minimal role in the policy-making process. Almost without exception, all of the 125 deputies in 1984 and 225 deputies in 1988 who were interviewed, argued that they were overburdened with the particularistic demands of their relatively less powerful local constituents. About 80 per cent of the deputies interviewed reported that they never received demands from the sectoral commercial interest groups; the latter preferred to deal directly with the ministries, rather than the TGNA and/or the ruling party.[32]

It may be suggested, in Joseph LaPalombara's terminology, that in the decade of the 1980s commercial interest groups tried to set up clientala relations with the state. They always wished to work through such agencies as the State Planning Organization, Ministry of Industry and Commerce, and especially the Prime Ministry. Governments, on their part, had always been keen on keeping a close eye on who were elected to the executive boards of the TOBB. Governments always tried to work with people who agreed with their economic policies.

The system of interest representation as delineated above has been considered by the members of the business community as functional. A study conducted in Istanbul in the autumn of 1987 found that almost no corporation executive mentioned any problems with their public professional associations.[33]

The authors of that study safely omitted interest representation through PPOs as a main concern on the part of the business community of Istanbul. The contacts between the corporate interests and the government at the national or municipal levels were considered to be so smooth by the businessmen that more than 95 per cent of the firm owners and/or managers interviewed failed to register any complaints from the central or the municipal government.[34] Relatively strike-free labour and business relations during the 1980s created favourable conditions for commercial activities. However, it is not known whether the present structuring of interest group activity could work when and if the Social Democrats come to power. The events of the 1970s, from basic commodity shortages to TÜSİAD's anti-government advertisements in the major daily newspapers (when clientelistic approaches were not successful), may be taken as indicators of possible reactions of the commercial as well as business sectors to governments that promote and/or implement economic policies they are not sympathetic to.

---

32 The findings are reported in Ersin Kalaycıoğlu, 'Türk Yasama Sistemi ve Siyasal Temsil', in *Türk Siyasal Hayatının Gelişimi*, Ersin Kalaycıoğlu and Ali Yaşar Sarıbay, eds. (İstanbul: Beta, 1986).

33 Yılmaz Esmer, Hamit Fişek, Ersin Kalaycıoğlu and Süleyman Özmucur, *İş Dünyasının Sorunları. Öncelikler, Beklentiler ve Sorunlar* (İstanbul: TÜSİAD, 1988), p.12.

34 Ibid., pp. 55-6.

Conclusion

The current system of commercial interest representation in Turkey is a product of the reaction of the state to the mounting class conflicts of the 1970s. The 1982 Constitution and related laws were precautions taken to prevent the resurrection of similar, unconstrained socio-political conflict in Turkey. The primary measure adopted for preventing socio-political conflict from becoming overtly dysfunctional has been outright control by the state of interest group activities. Both voluntary associations and public professional organizations are controlled by rules that inhibit them from 'engaging in politics'. The system imposed by the state promoted clientelistic relations between the political authorities in charge of the economy and the representatives of commercial interests.

7

Exporters: Favoured Dependency

Selim İlkin

Introduction

The major problem of the Turkish economy between 1960 and 1980 was the difficulty in securing its foreign exchange requirements.[1] Attracting investments foreseen by the Development Plans in that period depended, to a great extent, on the solution of this problem. This was the case for both infrastructure investments and industrial investments.

Throughout this period, the government, in order to increase exports, expanded incentives given to this sector of the economy, which was essential because of the fixed exchange rate policy. Some increases in exports could be achieved, but these were not enough to overcome the foreign exchange bottleneck.

Business circles were in an intense competition to obtain a share of imports rather than exports. Imports created significant rents for both importers and import-substituting industrialists. An extensive study carried out for 1968 shows that rents from 'import licences' had reached 10 to 15 per cent of GNP.[2] There were not any policy changes between 1968 and 1980 that could lower this ratio significantly. The fact that business circles and some interest groups wished to have a share from 'imports', also shows that this kind of rent persisted. Therefore, it was hardly likely that a strong interest group of exporters could to be formed in the 1960-1980 period.

Then, by the beginning of 1980, many people in government and business circles realized that the Turkish economy had reached a bottleneck and that it was almost impossible to bring the economy back into equilibrium with existing policies. A programme consisting of radical policy changes was prepared by the Justice Party government in 1979. * This programme, made public on 24 January 1980, was shaped according to the suggestions of international institutions such as the IMF and the World Bank.[3]

The goals of this programme, consolidated by supplementary economic measures over a short period of time, were achieving domestic and foreign equilibrium, expanding free market practices, and achieving outward orientation of the Turkish economy.

In the transformation of the economy along the lines outlined here, exports were

---

1 For an elaboration on this period, see William Hale, *The Political and Economic Development of Modern Turkey* (London: Croom Helm, 1981), 117-69.

2 Anne D. Krueger, *Foreign Trade Regimes and Economic Development. Turkey* (New York: Columbia University Press, 1974); idem, 'The Political Economy of Rent-Seeking Society', *American Economic Review*, 64 (1974), pp. 291- 303.

* On the new economic policy discussed here, also see Öniş in this volume (Editor's note).

3 Peter Wolff, *Stabilization Policy and Structural Adjustment in Turkey, 1980-1985* (Berlin: German Development Institute, 1987).

ascribed the largest role. Policy proposals regarding foreign payments under this stability programme were, to a large extent, aimed at increasing exports. Policies such as contracting domestic demand and lowering wages, with the goal of reaching domestic equilibrium, were essentially policies that would pave the way for more exports.

The 24 January 1980 programme provided incentives for promoting exports. Some of the measures taken were as follows:

Initially, a substantial devaluation was carried out. Later, in May 1981, a system by which the exchange rate was adjusted on a daily basis was put into effect;

Most of the subsidies were removed and high incentives for various export goods were introduced;

Some of the redtape regarding export regulations were removed.

The military regime which seized power on 12 September 1980 not only continued to implement the 24 January 1980 programme, but it also brought Mr Turgut Özal, an architect of that policy package as Undersecretary in the Prime Ministry, to the post of vice premier. Özal served in this post in the 1980-1983 period, except for a short break.

He became Prime Minister when the Motherland Party (MP), of which he was the founder, won the general elections of 6 November 1983. Thus, the economic policies initiated on 24 January 1980 were maintained in the post-1983 period, too.

The role of exports in an outward-oriented economy was clear, and for Özal the country's future essentially depended on exports.[4] According to the Prime Minister, this was crucial also for the consolidation of the democratic system in Turkey. He argued: 'If you study Turkey's economy since 1950 you will encounter a balance of payments crisis every ten years, and a military coup that follows it. Therefore, we took up this [export] problem as soon as we came to power. Our purpose was not only to increase exports but also to transform a large part of them into industrial exports.' [5]

Shortages caused by the lack of foreign currency prior to 1980, long queues formed for buying sugar, margarine and other staples, and the increase in foreign exchange earnings after 1980, became some of the political themes that the Motherland Party used extensively.[6]

Emergence of Foreign Trade Capital Companies

Turkey tried to make use of the experiences of countries which had earlier adopted export-oriented development strategies and had become important industrial goods exporters. This was an economic model that gave more incentives to large exporters (or export capital companies) in comparison to small exporters. This model, first practiced in Japan under the name of *Sogo Shosha*, was later adopted by many late

4 *Milliyet* (Istanbul daily), 9 January 1984.
5 *Cumhuriyet* (Istanbul daily), 23 January 1988. My translation.
6 See the brochure published by the MP about the situation in the pre-1980 period: 'Dünü Nasıl Unuttular?', Ankara, 1988, typescript.

industrializers, from South Korea to Brazil.[7]

Some of the advantages of the model are as follows:

Competition among a large number of small exporters leads to lower prices in foreign markets. When exportation is carried out by large, specialized firms these disadvantages are reduced;

Only the large export companies can reduce to a minimum commercial and political risks that are greater in foreign trade than in domestic trade;

Exportation necessitates specialization. Extensive organization is essential for carrying out exportation effectively. This can only be done by large export companies that enjoy economies of scale. Large volumes of operations allow economy in the costs - especially marginal costs - of many services, from the setting up of information networks to transportation;

Large export companies can obtain more domestic and foreign loans and on better terms.

Thus, effectiveness is achieved in each phase of operations from sales to production.[8] The Decree-Law of 18 July 1980, issued with the objective of encouraging export companies, envisaged the development of foreign trade companies in Turkey. This Decree-Law, stated that for a firm to become an 'export capital company' it must have reached a certain size and it should fulfil certain conditions. The most important requirements were that the export company should not be a manufacturing firm; its paid capital must at least be TL 50 million; the volume of its annual exports must be at least US $ 15 million and at least 50 per cent of the exports must be industrial or mining goods; and its annual exports must have increased by at least 10 per cent every year. As the volume of trade expanded, the figures in the said conditions were raised in order to limit the number of export capital firms; consequently the system remained selective.[9]

Some import rights were granted to selected firms in 1984, and the 'export capital companies' were turned into 'foreign trade capital companies' (FTCC). There were seven FTCCs in 1981; their number rose to 28 in 1984, and to 38 in 1988.[10] The increase in the number of FTCCs resulted from the significant rise in exports. The implementation of a method called 'by-pass' also contributed to this increase. 'By-pass' is a practice whereby a medium- or small-sized export and/or manufacturing company, that is excluded from the incentive scheme, records its exports through a financing firm with the marketing and risks remaining its own responsibility. Here, all that the FTCC scheme provides is passive mediation. This system, although it later led to a conflict of interests (to be discussed later), initially played a role in the increase in the number of FTCCs.[11] As the number of FTCCs rose, their overseas offices and foreign

---

7 Mustafa Özel, *Dış Ticarette Sermaye Şirketleri*, (Ankara: Türk-Trade, 1988); Ali Niyazi Gürcan, *Dış Ticaret Sermaye Şirketleri* (Ankara: İş Bankası, 1986); Ziya Öniş, 'Organization of Export-Oriented-Industrialization: The Turkish Foreign Trade Companies in Comparative Perspective', Istanbul, 1989, typescript.

8 Gürcan, *Dış Ticaret Sermaye Şirketleri*, pp. 61-2; Bülent Varlık, 'Dış Ticaret Sermaye Şirketleri', Ankara, 1989, typescript.

9 Gürcan, *Dış Ticaret Sermaye Şirketleri*, pp. 63-71; Kadir Eser, *Dış Ticaret Sermaye Şirketleri* (Ankara: İş Bankası, 1989), pp. 40-2.

10 In publications about the FTCCs, there are significant differences in these figures.

11 Eser, *Dış Ticaret Sermaye Şirketleri*, pp. 19-20.

subsidiaries also increased. As of the end of 1987, FTCCs had formed nearly 50 foreign offices and subsidiaries, and they had a big part in the organization of foreign trade.[12]

Establishment of Turkish Foreign Trade Association

Export capital firms organized themselves into an association in the mid-1983, the 'Exporters Association'. Its name was turned into 'Foreign Trade Association' in 1984 in accordance with relevant legal changes. In 1986, its name became the Turkish Foreign Trade Association (Türk-Trade).

Türk-Trade's objectives were to take measures that would allow Turkey's exports to reach their highest levels by means of bringing together Turkish exporters and providing exchange of information, coordination and solidarity among them. In addition to finding out what the problems of exporters were and carrying out related research, Türk-Trade was to monitor and evaluate existing and future laws, decrees, regulations and official bulletins, development plans and programmes, and convey the Association's views and proposals to the relevant authorities. It had to maintain contacts with authorities, organizations, commissions, institutions and committees in the field of its operations.[13]

The requirements for a firm to become a FTCC were altered over time. Consequently, the number of FTCCs changed from one year to another. The changing trade performances of the companies also played a role here. Almost all FTCCs have become members of Türk-Trade.[14] Thus, Türk-Trade has gained the status of the most important institution representing and protecting the interests of the private sector FTCCs.

Research that Türk-Trade carried out in 1988 has shown that 21 (out of 22) FTCCs have been set up as the exporting subsidiaries of some of Turkey's largest business conglomerates. FTCCs were formed by each of the following:

Large industrial holding companies (7);
Large construction companies (4);
Iron-steel works groups (5);
Textile manufacturing groups (3);
General trade and industry groups (3).

Although the FTCCs were administratively independent, they maintained organic links with their parent companies. This structure allowed Türk-Trade to operate effectively. But the same structure led to conflicts between Türk-Trade and other interest groups, which will be discussed below.

Türk-Trade took part in the formation of the Foreign Economic Relations Board (FERB). Thus, it was able to have close contacts with other members of FERB such as the Turkish Union of Chambers and Stock Exchanges, the Turkish Industrialists' and Businessmen's Association, and the Foreign Capital Association. Morever, Türk-Trade

12 *Söz* (Istanbul daily; no longer published), 17 January 1988; *Dünya* (Istanbul daily), 20 January 1987.

13 Türk-Trade, *Ana Tüzük* (İstanbul: Türk-Trade, 1985); idem *Türkiye'de Dış Ticaret Derneği Nedir?* (İstanbul: Türk-Trade, 1986).

14 Quoted from the interviews made by this author with the directors of Türk- Trade.

became a member of the Confederation of International Trading Houses Association in 1987, and thus it began to represent the export sector abroad.

Türk-Trade promoted itself and tried to expand its influence by means of a journal (*Dış Ticarette Durum*), numerous studies, conferences and seminars at which prominent politicians and higher civil servants took part.

Türk-Trade's most important contribution has without doubt been that of ensuring that incentives to the FTCCs be expanded or at least kept at certain levels. For the FTCCs' formation depended on the support given to exporters; these incentives were in a sense the *raison d'etre* of the FTCC. In this setting, Türk-Trade leaders frequently visited the relevant ministers, undersecretaries and directors-general, and conveyed to these officials their work reports, decisions and demands.[15] When problems regarding exportation became acute, governmental officials were invited to the Türk-Trade centre in Istanbul to discuss possible solutions.[16] A comparison of 'wishes' in one annual Türk-Trade report with the 'developments' in the report of the following year, made by this author, has shown the parallels between the demands of the Association and the decisions of the government. A report in the daily *Hürriyet* in late 1987 also claimed that Türk-Trade had a significant influence on the State Planning Organization and the Undersecretariat of Foreign Trade and Treasury.[17] When the period is evaluated as a whole, Türk-Trade - at least in the beginning - seems to have been an important representative of the FTCCs and a vital instrument of the post-1980 export-oriented policies.

Changing Fortunes of FTCCS

Initially, the FTCC's exports had increased rapidly and reached a significant percentage of total exports. The most important factor behind the success of the FTCCs was, no doubt, the numerous incentives provided to them. Yet, although exports had a priority for the government, there were certain limits to the incentives given to the FTCCs. The expansion of the system based on incentives made it necessary to impose some limitations. Therefore, governments in different periods expanded or contracted the incentives.

In the period between 1980 and 1984, exports were strongly encouraged by using various instruments. The decree-law that enabled the establishment of the FTCCs in 1980 listed the incentives then granted to them as follows:

> Exporters were provided with one-year term loans with low interest rates from the Export Incentive Fund, amounting to 90 per cent of the value of industrial-mining exports guaranteed by the firms;
>
> Whether or not they themselves were engaged in manufacturing, exporters were

[15] 1983- 1984 Board of Directors Decisions, 1989-90 Annual Work Reports, and reports containing Türk-Trade's formal demands regarding the foreign trade regime from the Undersecretariat of Foreign Trade and the Treasury.

[16] Türk-Trade's most recent General Council Report contains an illuminating chapter on the Association's relations with the bureaucracy: Türk-Trade, 'VI, Olağan Genel Kurul Raporu', Istanbul, 1990, typescript.

[17] *Hürriyet* (Istanbul daily), 18 November 1987.

given priority in the procurement of imported inputs (raw materials, intermediate manufactures and packaging material) related to the products they exported;

Exporters were provided with seven-year term investment and three-year term management to assist in expanding exports (packaging, storing, transportation, and the like).[18]

At the beginning of 1983, a new and important incentive was added in the form of a ten per cent additional tax refund to exports exceeding US $ 30 million.

The MP government, after having come to power on 6 November 1983, rapidly put into effect a series of new incentives for the FTCCs. These incentives were to a great extent in line with the demands of Türk-Trade. The most important one was the exclusive right to import from countries whose foreign trade was controlled by the state. This privilege was conferred on FTCCs with export revenues over US $ 50 million.[19] In the second half of 1984, the government decreased the rates of tax refunds twice in response to reactions both in external and internal circles. On the other hand, during the same period, some new incentives were granted to the FTCCs. They were as follows:

Obtaining loans from abroad;

The right to keep a part of foreign currency earnings abroad to meet import requirements;

Lowering the import deposit requirements.

By the end of 1984, the subsidy effect of all these incentives reached 54.9 per cent of export values. [20] The FTCCs' export performance in this period can be outlined as follows. Between 1980 and 1984, there was a steady and big increase in exports in general, and in FTCC exports in particular. During this period, total exports rose by 52 per cent, whereas exports by the private sector FTCCs rose by 580 per cent - a six-fold difference. The share of the private FTCC exports in total exports rose to 40.4 per cent in 1984 - up from 9 per cent in 1981. When we add the public sector FTCCs' exports to those of the private FTCCs, that ratio goes up from 3 to 6 per cent. All of these help to explain the crucial role played by the FTCCs in promoting exports. That during the period under consideration there was a major leap forward in exports in Turkey is beyond doubt. Foreign circles, too, often praised this success, and even called it a 'miracle'.[21]

However, the social costs and the contradictions it created were often overlooked.[22] Thus, excessively optimistic scenarios regarding the future of Turkish exports were mentioned. During this period, Türk-Trade was never heard of in public. This was only to be expected; at the time, the government's policies coincided with the interests of the FTCCs.

---

18 Unless otherwise stated, this section draws upon Gürcan, *Dış Ticaret Sermaye Şirketleri*, pp. 62-7.

19 *Cumhuriyet* (Istanbul daily), 29 December 1983.

20 *Milliyet* (Istanbul daily), 20 June 1985.

21 İsmail Arslan and Sweder van Wijnbergen, 'Turkey: Export Miracle or Accounting Trick?', Washington, D.C.: The World Bank Working Papers, April, 1990.

22 As one of the rare discussions of this topic, see, 'Dışsatımda Patlamanın Maliyeti Tartışılıyor', *Cumhuriyet*, 5 February 1982.

There was a dramatic reduction in the number of incentives granted to the FTCCs in 1985 and the first half of 1986. The reasons behind the government's decision to do so were mainly the following: In the first place, there was the 'Subsidy Code' agreed between Turkey and the GATT following the reactions to a tax refund scheme. Under this code, reductions in incentives began at the end of 1985 and continued intermittently. Secondly, the government wished to lower public deficits. The contraction of incentives was part of the drive to shrink the deficits in question. Although not overtly stated, a third factor was the negative reaction to ghost exports in the public eye.[23] Under such circumstances, the government was forced to be more cautious regarding incentives.

As a consequence of these developments the government decreased all the incentives earlier accorded to exports, including the additional incentives that had been given to the FTCCs. The most important of the changes in question were:

The freezing of low-interest loans from the export incentive fund;

A continual reduction of the rate of tax refunds;

Limitations on the right to import from countries where foreign trade was handled by the state, also to those companies which only had investment incentive documents.

This contraction in incentives lowered the increase in total exports in 1985. And the increase in the exports of the FTCCs were less than the increase in total exports.

But a decree-law issued in the last days of 1985 re-defined an FTCC; the requirement that an FTCC should increase its exports by 10 per cent annually in order to qualify for incentives was removed. Many FTCCs were saved from losing the rights to incentives under this decree, an amendment which had been demanded by Türk-Trade, too. Later, FTCCs were also allowed to make 'portfolio' investments. As the shrinking of incentives continued in the first half of 1986, tax refund rates were lowered and some monetary incentives were first decreased and then frozen.[24]

Around 25 to 30 per cent of Turkey's exports after 1980 were directed to Iran and Iraq. As these then warring nations were adversely affected by the fall in oil prices in international markets in the second half of 1986, they, but especially Iraq, ran into trouble regarding payment for exports. More than 50 per cent of exports to these countries were from the FTCCs. Türk-Trade, which frequently made public statements concerning the difficulties faced by the FTCCs, pointed out that the companies were 'stuck between contracting markets and falling incentives', and warned that 'the export drive could recede'.[25]

The government was thus compelled to search for new policies. Meanwhile, in a two-day meeting in Istanbul, senior officials from Türk-Trade and the Undersecretariat for Foreign Trade and Treasury, the Ministry of Finance, the State Planning Organization

---

[23] What came to be popularly called 'fictitious exports' was also experienced before the 1980s. But it expanded after 1980. These were illegal transactions aimed at taking advantage of incentives - especially tax refunds - for exports. Some of these were registering commercially worthless goods as goods eligible for incentives, recording export prices higher than the actual price, even alleging falsely to have exported goods while in fact nothing was exported.

[24] *Cumhuriyet*, 27 December 1985.

[25] *Güneş* (Istanbul daily), 13 May, 1986.

and the Central Bank discussed a report prepared by Türk-Trade.[26] Shortly after this meeting a number of measures were announced, some of which brought back incentives to exporters and especially to the FTCCs. The incentives, which were in line with the report prepared by Türk-Trade, were the following:

Abolition of VAT when a company exported goods that it had purchased from a manufacturing firm;

Putting back into effect tax refunds for exports, except textiles and ready-wear (4 per cent tax refund for exports with a value of US $ 30 million to $ 50 million, and 6 per cent tax refund for exports with a value greater than US $ 50 million);

Payment of premiums for some goods on the basis of quantity;

Providing low-interest (38 per cent) loans to the FTCCs.[27]

But Türk-Trade was not satisfied with this scheme, although the incentives in question were dubbed as 'super incentives' by the press.[28] The Association was of the opinion that the funds earmarked for loans to exporters were too small in volume and the interest rates on them were too high. Türk-Trade argued that an interest rate almost twice the targeted annual inflation rate of 20 per cent was in fact a disincentive, and it demanded that the government pay back to the exporters the difference, in case the actual inflation rate was less than the interest rate.[29]

As tax refunds and other monetary incentives were constantly lowered and were to be totally removed by the end of 1988, there arose a need for new incentives.[30] Towards this end, the government set up the Export Credit Bank (EXIMBANK), and the bank started its operations at the beginning of 1988. EXIMBANK provided the FTCCs with new loan facilities through its own or other banks' funds. It also introduced an export insurance scheme. The most important incentive to the FTCCs, introduced by the EXIMBANK, was a low-interest loan amounting to 5 per cent of the FOB value of exports of companies whose annual export earnings exceeded US $ 100 million.[31]

Türk-Trade was dissatisfied with the EXIMBANK's loan scheme, too, and pointed out that it was far from being suitable to replace tax refunds. Some FTCCs even termed the scheme a punishment rather than an incentive. Türk-Trade officials began to press for a different system of incentives that would exclusively focus on the FTCCs.[32] That the EXIMBANK's loan scheme covered only the biggest companies (with an annual export revenue exceeding US $ 100 million) led to reactions by other export companies which stressed that it was unfair that only about 20 FTCCs were eligible for the incentives, which they called the 'cream of exports'.[33]

---

26 *Milliyet*, 19 October 1986.

27 Regarding this report, see *Cumhuriyet*, 25 January 1986 and 1 February 1986.

28 *Cumhuriyet*, 5 December 1986; *Milliyet*, 4 December 1986.

29 *Cumhuriyet*, 16 November 1986.

30 Unless otherwise stated, incentives after 1986 are summarized from Eser, *Dış Ticaret Sermaye Şirketleri*, pp. 42- 3.

31 C. Tayyar Sadıklar, 'İhracat Destekleri Yön Değiştirirken', *Hürriyet*, 16 May 1988.

32 *Tempo* (Istanbul weekly), 30 October 1988, pp. 36-7; *Kapital* (Istanbul monthly), May 1988, pp. 38-41; *Milliyet*, 30 April 1988.

33 *Hürriyet*, 7 April 1988.

As the bottleneck in the Iraqi market persisted during the second half of 1988, the government felt it necessary to increase the funds allocated to this credit scheme. Towards the end of 1988, the government lowered the required minimum value of exports, in order for a FTCC to qualify for loans, to US $ 50 million.[34]

Exports continued to rise in 1988 although at a slower pace than the previous year. The FTCCs' exports rose faster, and reached 48 per cent of total exports. The main factor behind this increase was the devaluation of the lira, the value of which had reached its lowest level against the major currencies since 1980. Thus, the exchange rate policy more than compensated for the effect of the reduction in incentives.[35]

It must be noted in passing that the rise in the cost of incentives, brought about by the increasing volume of exports, prompted reaction in public opinion, too.[36] When the ruling Motherland Party government lost votes in the March 1989 local elections, this was, in fact, linked to the government's failure to bring down inflation.

Although, starting in 1989, monetary incentives were totally lifted, the government showed restraint in introducing new incentives in order to control public deficits and ameliorate other interest groups' reactions. This was denounced by Türk- Trade officials: 'The government has been influenced by false suggestions and pressure of public opinion. An impression has been created as if all incentives and subsidies went into the hands of the FTCCs. In fact, the amount remaining in the FTCCs hands is expressed in the peanuts.'[37] Türk-Trade called on the government to introduce new incentives 'bravely' and without being influenced by the unfavourable opinions in question. But government officials warned the Association not to wait 'in vain' for a new incentive scheme.

All of these developments led to a further deterioration in relations between the government and exporters. Complaints from both sides regarding incentives to exporters became widespread. The government was urged to take some steps when figures for the first quarter of 1989 showed that export revenues were falling.[38] And some new incentives - although limited - were introduced for exportation. These measures were meant to protect the small- and medium-scale exporters. The EXIMBANK's new scheme for extension of credits before shipment of export goods was an indicator of this tendency.[39] In mid-1989, the government made it more difficult to form FTCCs by raising the value of minimum required capital to TL 5 billion and that of annual exports to US $ 100 million. This measure was followed by the introduction of two new incentives:[40]

Payment of a 2 per cent performance premium;

Supply of discount credits (planned to replace the afore-mentioned EXIMBANK loans).

---

34 Reactions came from industrialists who did not own export companies. See *Hürriyet*, 20 July 1988 and 10 October 1988.

35 Süleyman Uysal, 'Türkiye'de Teşvik Sistemi ve Etkinliği', Türkiye İhracat Kredi Bankası, Ankara, 1989, typescript.

36 *Hürriyet*, 14 August 1988.

37 *Hürriyet*, 19 February 1990. My translation.

38 *Dünya*, 12 April and 12 September 1989 and *Milliyet*, 15 May 1989.

39 *Dünya*, 18 November 1989; *Milliyet*, 1 August 1989.

40 *Dünya*, 28 July 1989.

But this new scheme was deferred until the end of 1989. Exporters could not secure an adjustment in the exchange rate levels equal to or above the rate of inflation realised in 1989.[41] The incentives provided to the FTCCs receded to 19 per cent of the value of their exports. As a result, in 1989, total exports fell. But the decrease in the FTCCs' exports was greater than that in total exports; the ratio of the FTCCs' exports to total exports dropped to 42.6 per cent.[42] These negative developments in 1989 led many FTCCs to withdraw from the market. This was considered to be the total collapse of the FTCC system. A system fed by wide-ranging incentives for nearly 10 years could not stand on its own feet.[43]

Conclusion

Türk-Trade became an interest group as governments granted many incentives to the FTCCs after 1980. Türk-Trade can be said to have had an influence on government in the 1984-1987 period. There were significant parallels between the government's decisions and Türk-Trade's demands.

After 1987, there was a decline in the Association's effectiveness. The rising cost of incentives because of the expansion in exports, reactions by other interest groups to the privileges of the FTCCs, changing of priorities on the government's part, and the pressures exerted by some international organizations contributed to the fall in Türk-Trade's influence.

The inadequacy of the FTCC model was voiced very frequently, and there was talk of the need for a new model. Then a draft bill was proposed by the government. It was not, however, enacted. That seemed to be the upshot of a lack of agreement on the new incentive system that would replace the existing one.

In the meantime, the small- and medium-sized exporters had been demanding that associations that represent exporters should come under a single umbrella. The voices behind these demands assumed that interests related to incentives constituted a zero-sum model. But in essence, incentives made up a system of interests that reflected *political* choices and, was, therefore, not a zero-sum model. Thus, the fortunes of the FTCCs as well as that of the Türk-Trade was closely tied to the government's preferences.

---

41 Mustafa Somersan, 'DTSŞ Penceresinden İhracatımızın Görüntüsü', *Dünya*, 27-29 December 1989.

42 *Barometre* (Istanbul weekly), 25 December 1989.

43 Hayri Kozanoğlu, 'İhracatı Teşvik Sistemini Değerlendirme', EXIMBANK, Ankara, 1989, typescript.

8

Macro-Politics of De-Regulation and Micro-Politics of Banks

Ayşe Öncü and Deniz Gökçe

Introduction

'Free market economy', 'opening to the outside', 'removing bureaucratic barriers', have become key phrases in the official discourse and political lexicon of the 1980s' decade in Turkey. Faith in the efficiency of the spontaneous and self-adjusting order of 'market forces' appears to have displaced the traditional imagery of justice and welfare as emanating from the State. It is now competition in a free market that is expected to reward productivity and efficiency rather than a patrimonial State deciding the distribution of spoils. No longer is a powerful bureaucracy seen as the *sine qua non* of economic development; it is perceived as an obstacle to be removed to allow for unfettered operation of a 'free market'. Once cumbersome State regulations are dismantled, both 'hidden local capital' and the flow of foreign capital - patiently awaiting a favourable political climate - will enable Turkish society to 'skip a century', to quote Prime Minister Turgut Özal's phrase.

For all the polemics of Turkish liberalizers against the State, the question of whether and in what direction the state is changing remains controversial. Is the state now in 'retreat' before an expanding 'civil society'?[1] How does a state, often described in terms of an ancient tradition of centralization and autonomy, 'retreat'? Is it simply that the 'public sector' of yesterday is becoming the 'private sector' of today? Is the state 'disengaging' itself from the economy?[2] If so, does this mean it is becoming more open to societal pressures over policy-making, and hence losing its alleged 'autonomy'? Or does it mean that state policies are becoming increasingly constrained by exigencies of international finance, such that the state is losing its capacity for autonomous action in the organization of the domestic economy? Perhaps the growing power of the international financial community has had paradoxical effects on state agencies. Is it possible that the increased availability of international finance has helped place state agencies in a central position vis-à-vis the organization of the domestic economy, thereby actually strengthening state capacity?[3]

---

1 'Retreating States and Expanding Societies' was the organizing theme of the JCNME/SSRC conference at Aix-en-Provence, 25-27 March 1988.

2 See, for instance, Victor Azarya and Naomi Chazan, 'Disengagement from the State in Africa: Reflections on the Experience of Ghana and Guinea', *Comparative Studies in Society and History*, 29 (1987), pp. 106-31.

3 As suggested, for instance, by Barbara Stallings, 'International Lending and the Relative Autonomy of the State: A Case Study of Twentieth-Century Peru', *Politics and Society*, 14 (1985): 257-88.

The present essay is an attempt to probe these questions at the sectoral level, from the ground up. Specifically, it aims to look at the evolving relations between state agencies and banks in post-1980 Turkey, under an official policy of de-regulation of financial markets.

Our initial premise is that it is misleading to conceptualize the changing role of the state in Turkish financial markets along a continuum of polar opposites, ranging from 'tight controls' to 'full de-regulation'. Change need not be 'directional' in this sense. The Turkish financial system, like most other financial systems, has always been, and continues to be, neither totally regulated, nor fully liberalized, but somewhere in between. Thus, to try to capture change in terms of 'degree of state regulation' is to confuse the issue. The question is not more or less state regulation but *what* the state seeks to regulate and *how*. The dynamics of change in Turkish financial markets in the 1980s' decade has to be sought in the logic and mode of state intervention rather than in its 'degree'.

Below, we try to develop and elaborate a series of specific points with regard to changing state-financial sector relations in the 1983-1988 period in Turkey.[4] The Turkish experiment with liberalization of financial markets has been accompanied by a progressive insulation of actual policy-making and implementation within an inner circle of technocrats directly attached to the Prime Ministry. In terms of state-financial sector relations, this has resulted in the atrophy of traditional associational and bureaucratic channels as well as the truncation of political channels of influence through party networks.

Banks, the oligopolistic giants of the Turkish financial system, have found themselves targeted for major restructural reforms, after decades of 'riskless' or 'comfortable' profits, nurtured through interest ceilings well below inflation rates and isolated from international markets through currency regulations. Deemed old fashioned, noncompetitive and complacent, the Turkish banking sector has been foremost among the strategic priority areas marked for reform in line with the requirements of an internationalized economy.

The general strategy of 'liberalization of financial markets' has been applied into a rapid succession of policy moves, inevitably fraught with inconsistencies, delays, periodic readjustments and unexpected developments in the sequencing and application of actual policy measures. Decisions with regard to the timing as well as the particular mix of such discrete and rapid policy shifts have emanated from the 'inner circle of technocrats' at the centre.

Since banks have been excluded from this so-called 'fine tuning' process, the oscillation between different types and degrees of regulation and de-regulation according to the administrative-technical imperatives of the new strategy has meant overwhelming uncertainty and instability for the sector as a whole. Thus, from the point of view of the banking sector, economic policies of liberalization have amounted to 'arbitrary'

---

[4] Our analysis is primarily based upon information gathered through focused interviews with top ranking executives of banks during the summer of 1988. A variety of sources which provide news on current financial-cum-economic events, published trend reports, round-table proceedings, commentaries by leading figures from the world of finance and politics were used to obtain supplementary information on changes between 1983-1988.

state intervention; arbitrary, because the insulation of policy-making from social processes, from politics and from the bureaucratic State tradition as well, has rendered the rapid strategy shifts emanating from the inner-circle of technocrat-planners totally unpredictable.

The Turkish banking sector has nevertheless remained politically quiescent, refraining from any public challenge and continuing its support of the incumbent centre-right coalition in government. In other words, the much publicized 'crisis' of the Turkish banking sector has not, as late as the end of 1990, translated itself into overt political opposition. The oligopolistic giants of the Turkish economy, trembling under 'shocks' administered by swift policy shifts over the past decade, would appear to have been reduced to political impotence.

The Turkish banking sector has been both unable, and unwilling, to challenge the prevailing pattern of policy insulation; unable, due to the close links between the state, banks and industry and the strong state influence over the banking sector itself, and unwilling, because Turkish banks have found the new era of 'liberalism' very profitable in the short run. Riding on a wave of economic expansion based on external and internal borrowing, they have been reluctant to seriously challenge their isolation from policy-making. Thus, continued economic expansion has been the necessary candition for the policy of exclusion that has characterized state-banking sector relations in the post-1983 period in Turkey.

In the following sections of this chapter, we elaborate each of the points above, introducing the necessary qualifications and modifications to the arguments, which entail gross crudities when stated in synopsis form. Our aim in stating these points from the very beginning is simply to give the reader a sense of direction in following through the compartmentalized sub-sections which attempt to capture, separately, what in reality constitutes a changing totality.

Political Dynamics of Policy Insulation

The political dynamics of increasing policy insulation in the post-1983 period in Turkey can best be understood in terms of the fundamental dilemmas of a narrowly based centre-right 'coalition' government, attempting to reconcile the strategic priorities of its economic restructuration programme with the vagaries of populist politics.

Turkey's pursuit of export markets and foreign capital since 1983, have been politically managed by a centre-right coalition of interests under the umbrella of the Motherland Party (MP). The party itself was formed six months prior to the restoration of contested elections in November 1983.[5]

The MP's minimal winning coalition - in the range of 35-40 per cent of all validly cast votes - brought under a single umbrella elements of the centre-right, which had earlier been fragmented among the Justice (liberal centre-right), National Salvation (religious right) and Nationalist Action (nationalist right) parties prior to the military intervention of 1980.[6] In the restricted political arena of the 1983 general elections, with former political parties closed down and their leaders banned from politics, the MP's architect, Mr Özal, successfully projected himself as the only leader capable of managing inflation, the export drive and continued economic expansion. With trade unions, voluntary associations, the universities, the press and the media effectively brought under control through the 1982 Constitution and subsequent legislation, the MP government faced little challenge from non-parliamentary organizations.[7] Broad political exclusion, that is, political demobilization through restrictions upon the activities of autonomously-organized social and political groups, had already been accomplished through legislation enacted by the military regime.

Yet broad political closure was only one aspect of Mr Özal's ability to effect a rapid and coherent strategy of economic restructuration. A second very important precondition was the exclusion of different groups within the MP's coalition umbrella from the actual economic policy-making processes. In other words, the government's strategic capacity to pursue the technocratic rationality of its developmental model pre-supposed, at least initially, a substantial degree of autonomy from 'coalitional' challenges and compromises. Political closure in the narrower sense, that is, the insulation of technocratic planning and implementation from the need to reconcile conflicts of interest and calculations of political feasibility among coalition partners, offered a short-run resolution to this dilemma. Short-run, because its effectiveness threatened to undermine the alliance in the long term, portending to unglue the constituent wings of the party. As the attendant outcomes of 'successful' economic restructuration such as declining social expenditures, reductions in state subsidies and worsening income distribution became increasingly apparent, the danger resided in the erosion of the

5 The founder of MP, Mr Turgut Özal, served as the Vice Prime Minister, with full and sole responsibility for economic affairs between 1980-1982, during part of the military rule of 1980-1983. In terms of its economic policies, the MP espoused continued liberalization and deregulation (initially introduced by the Süleyman Demirel government in January 1980, and subsequently put into effect by the military), as well as reduced public spending, public sector reform and privatization, upon which the support of the international financial community, the European Economic Community, multi-national agencies and the like remained contingent. In terms of domestic political alliances, the MP represented a precarious coalition, forged under the special circumstances of the 1983 general elections.

6 On the dissolution of existing political parties during the military rule and the new parties of the post-1983 period in general, see Birol Yeşilada, 'New Political Parties and the Problems of Development in Turkey', *New Perspectives on Turkey* 1 (1987), pp. 35-62, and İlter Turan, 'Political Parties and the Party System in post-1983 Turkey', in *State, Democracy and the Military: Turkey in the 1980s*, Metin Heper and Ahmet Evin, eds. (Berlin and New York: Walter deGruyter, 1988). On the Motherland Party, see Üstün Ergüder, 'The Motherland Party, 1983-1989', in *Political Parties and Democracy in Turkey*, Metin Heper and Jacob Landau, eds., (London and New York: I.B. Tauris, 1991).

7 For a review of this legislation, see Taha Parla and Ayşe Öncü, 'Militarism and Corporatism in Turkey', 1986, typescript, and Ergun Özbudun in this volume.

MP's narrow electoral majority, and hence the disintegration of its coalition bases.

A broader discussion on the dilemmas of an elected government involved in a balancing act between demands of international financial agencies for structural reform on the one hand, and pressures from divergent interests among its own constituent wings on the other, while attempting to maintain its slim majority at the polls, extends beyond the scope of the present chapter. Suffice it to underline that the emergent trend towards increasing insulation of decisional and operational authority on strategy-relevant issues within the confines of an 'inner circle' directly attached to the Prime Minister, needs to be couched in the context of these dilemmas. *

Institutional Underpinnings of Policy Insulation

The creation of an 'inner circle', insulated from the bureaucratic apparatus of the centralized ministries as well as political bodies of the incumbent coalition government, has entailed a series of organizational changes in the scope and responsibilities of State agencies, to centralize strategic policy powers within the Prime Ministry, coupled with a set of new appointments controlled by the Prime Minister himself. Among the most crucial of these various organizational changes, introduced step by step, has been the following:[8]

The creation of an Undersecretariat of Treasury and Foreign Trade in the Prime Ministers' office. This meant that the powers of both the Ministry of Finance and the Ministry of Commerce were dramatically reduced. Without control over the Treasury, the Ministry of Finance became, more or less, a general directorate of customs and taxation, akin to a department of internal revenue. Similarly, the detachment of foreign trade from the Ministry of Commerce dramatically curtailed its powers in the new era of export-oriented growth. The newly-established Undersecretariat of Treasury and Foreign Trade, on the other hand, attained the powers of a ministry, but remained a non-cabinet post headed by an appointed technocrat directly responsible to the Prime Minister.

Two new departments, a Department of Foreign Investment and a Department of Investment and Export Promotion and Implementation were also created in the Prime Ministers' office. The establishment of these departments centralized many activities previously scattered among various ministries, thus removing them from the jurisdiction of the traditional bureaucratic apparatus of the State and bringing them under the direct control of the Prime Minister.

The two other most critical State agencies, that is, the State Planning Organization and the Central Bank, were already attached to the Prime Minister's office

* For an elaboration on the developments deriving from these dilemmas, see Ziya Öniş in this volume (Editor's note).

8 The Annual Reports of the Turkish Businessmen's and Industrialists' Association provide a useful appendix on the calender of main economic policy measures including new legislation and administrative decisions on re-organization of centralized agencies, creation of new bodies, and the like. The OECD country surveys on Turkey include a similar monthly calendar of major policy decisions. Both sources contain detailed information on the dates and sequencing of the organizational changes outlined above. Also see Metin Heper, 'Motherland Party Governments and Bureaucracy in Turkey, 1983-1988', *Governance*, 2 (1989): 460-71.

prior to 1980. Also, during military rule (1980-1983), a High Coordination Council of Economic Affairs had been created, to be headed by the Prime Minister and including two vice Premiers, and the Ministers of Foreign Affairs, Finance, Trade, Agriculture, Industry and Energy. Thus, Mr Özal came to have direct control over appointments to all top executive positions of these organs as soon as the MP government was formed in 1983.

Last but not least was the creation of a [Board of] Mass Housing and Public Participation Fund (BMHPPF), again directly attached to the Prime Minister. Among the series of such 'Funds' created through the diversion of tax resources from the consolidated budget by the MP government, exempting them from the standard budgetary controls and placing them under executive jurisdiction, the BMHPPF has been the most important.[9]

The combination of these organizational changes has served to bring together, within the Office of the Prime Minister, a set of key agencies involved in strategic policy-making and implementation. The 'inner circle' has been composed of top executives of these agencies, directly appointed by the Prime Minister, comprising the Head of the Central Bank, the Undersecretary of Treasury and Foreign Trade, Undersecretary of the State Planning Organization, Head of the BMHPFF, Head of the Economic Affairs High Co-Ordination Council, and finally, the directors of two of the largest State banks, Ziraat Bank and Emlak Bank.

Equally important, if not more so, as these organizational changes, has been the Prime Minister's choice of the candidates for these positions. The concept of an 'inner circle' suggests a group of faithful followers appointed on the basis of personal trust and loyalty. It also implies that the powers of individual members in this inner circle depend upon the confidence and favour of the Prime Minister rather than the offices they occupy. The Prime Minister's choice of candidates suggests that this has indeed been the case.[10] The appointees to key 'inner circle' positions have shared a number of common characteristics. With few exceptions, they have been drawn from outside the career bureaucracy; none were politicians; all were relatively young, around 40 years of age and U.S.-educated for the most part. Some have been directly imported from the United States to head the agencies they were appointed to. All were 'unknown quantities' prior to 1983. In sum, the distinguishing characteristic of inner circle members has been their total loyalty to Prime Minister Özal, in the absence of allegiances

9 While the total number of such 'off-budget' funds financed through various earmarked revenues is estimated to be around one hundred, the bulk of the revenues tied up in them is accounted for by a mere half dozen. The BMHPPF is the single most important of these funds, accounting for nearly half of the total assets tied up in them, variously estimated to range between $3.5 and $5.7 billion in 1987/1988. Since May 1986, (under Act No. 3291) all publicly owned shares in the State economic enterprises designated for privatization have also been transferred to the BMHPPF, enhancing its importance as a public resource under direct control of the Prime Minister. See Oğuz Oyan, 'Fonlar, İstikrar Programı ve Özelleştirme', *Mülkiyeliler Birliği Dergisi*, no. 91 (1988), pp. 20-6 and also, *Financial Times*, 23 May 1988.

10 Hence dubbed as 'Özal's princes' by the press. See, for instance, *Cumhuriyet* (Istanbul daily), 14 January 1989.

within the bureaucratic establishment or party networks and factions.[11]

The Prime Minister's inner circle was initially greeted as a daring move to cut through Turkey's slow and deep-rooted bureaucracy; its members were viewed as 'Young Turks' ready to revolutionize a banking sector which had enjoyed decades of cheap money and freedom from external auditing, and hence had remained a morass of mismanagement, inefficiency, high operating costs, and doctored bad loans.[12]

The ramifications of ensuing policy insulation soon became apparent, however, as the Turkish financial markets failed to behave as anticipated in response to standard policy tools, and as frequent re-adjustments in the timing, sequencing and application of various policy measures had to be introduced. Chafing under the 'unpredictability' of such rapid shifts, the Turkish banking sector discovered that its institutionalized channels of access, contestation, and information, political as well as bureaucratic, were increasingly blocked. The inner circle remained insulated from the usual political (through Cabinet members and other MPs) or bureaucratic (through the ranks of the institutions they headed) pressures. Some of the views expressed in interviews these authors conducted with top executives in Istanbul's financial community in the summer of 1988 were to the effect that bureaucracy has been wiped out; the Cabinet has no agenda; the Ministers are like directors-general; and there is no one to talk to in Ankara.

These comments reflected the increasing marginalization of the bureaucratic apparatus of the state as well as the political bodies of the incumbent Motherland Party. They also expressed growing disenchantment with what has emerged as the new pattern of policy-making in the post-1983 era. Decisions are first formulated within the 'inner circle' and put into effect, then *afterwards*, either the Prime Minister himself or some members of his inner circle, explain the decisions taken and try to placate the vested

11 A Profile published in the *Financial Times* supplement on Turkey (14 May 1984) of Dr Namık Kemal Kılıç, Director of the Foreign Investment Department at the time, serves to provide a composite portrait. Described as a 'brisk 41-year-old', born in Çankırı and brought up in Ankara, he graduated from the University of Ankara in 1964 and worked for two years at the Ministry of Agriculture. He went to Michigan State University in 1967 and took a Master's degree in systems science (engineering). In 1972 he received a doctorate from the university's industrial engineering department. For the next four years, he taught there, and worked as consultant to the State of Michigan and the U.S. federal government. He gained experience in economic modelling and worked on the Agency for International Development's programme for South Korea, Mexico and Nigeria. Returning to Turkey to teach at Çukurova University's engineering and economics department in 1977, he began to press his ideas for eliminating subsidies on government. He was unsuccessful at first but caught the eye of the team which was beginning to gather around Turgut Özal..., etc. The profile above, directly taken from the *Financial Times*, is remarkably 'typical' of the Prime Minister's inner circle of technocrats, despite considerable turnover in actual membership. During the summer of 1988 when the present research was undertaken, the names most frequently cited as belonging to the 'inner circle' included Mr Yusuf Özal (Head of High Coordination Council of Economic Affairs and the Prime Minister's brother), Mr Ali Tigrel (Undersecretary of the State Planning Organization), Mr Rüşdü Saracoğlu (Head of the Central Bank), Mr Bülent Şemiler (Director of Emlak Bank), Mr Coşkun Ulusoy (Director of Ziraat Bank), Mr Bülent Gültekin (Head of the Board of Mass Housing and Public Participation Fund). Assessments as to the relative powers of these figures were invariably couched in terms of their 'closeness' to the Prime Minister, rather than the importance of the organizations they headed.

12 See for instance, *Financial Times*, 24 January 1984; 20 May 1985; and 9 April 1985.

interest groups, either by initiating special meetings, or by arriving in person, at the scheduled regular meetings of various associations such as the Association of Turkish Banks, Chambers of Commerce, Turkish Industrialists' and Businessmen's Association, and the like.

The political quiescence of the Turkish banking sector in the face of such policy insulation presents an initial puzzle. Banks have been and continue to be the most powerful economic actors in Turkish society. Yet growing dissatisfaction with the ongoing pattern of policy-making and implemention has not translated itself into open challenge to the incumbent MP government. To reiterate, the argument presented below is that the Turkish banking sector has been both unable and unwilling to engage in overt confrontation; unable, because of the heavy presence of the state itself within the banking sector; and unwilling, because the 'shock treatment' of the oscillation between different degrees and types of regulation and de-regulation notwithstanding, banks have been riding on a wave of short-run profitability contingent upon extensive internal and external borrowing in the Turkish economy.

To elaborate further, closer scrutiny of the nature of financial markets in Turkey is necessary, for the 'outcome' of any economic restructuration programme is as much dependent upon the institutional configuration of existing financial markets as the professed aims of policy-makers and the choices they make.

Anatomy of the Turkish Banking Sector

The organization of financial markets in Turkey has been characterized by extremely tight networks linking the state to the banking sector and the banking sector to industry. The strong presence of the state in the banking sector and the high degree of interpenetration between finance and industry are a historical legacy of the early decades of the Republic (founded in 1923). Throughout the 1930s and 1940s, policies of industrialization through state initiative entailed the creation of a series of state-owned banks to provide credit and facilitate investments in specialized sectors of the economy - agriculture, housing, mining, textiles, maritime activities, and the like. In the pre-war decades, these banks mobilized resources for a wide array of 'public sector' infrastructural and industrial investments. Later, in the post-1950 period, when private enterprise prospered under protectionist state policies, which encouraged import substitution, the state banks played a key role in channelling foreign aid and credit as well as domestic public credit to private industry. Interlocking ownership of banks and corporations gained further momentum as the nascent private conglomerates began to move into financial markets towards the end of the 1950s. Thus, during the inflationary expansion of the economy in the 1960s and 1970s, bank ownership became the sine qua non of comparative advantage in financial markets, with a series of private commercial deposit banks controlled by the so-called 'Groups'.

The resultant oligopolistic structure of the banking sector has been described in terms of three interlinked features.[13] First, the Turkish financial sector is characterized by an overwhelming dominance of banks, and the correspondingly limited role of other financial institutions. Bank deposits constitute two thirds of total financial instruments in Turkey. Thus, for all practical purposes, to talk about the Turkish financal system is to talk about banks.

Secondly, the banking sector, in turn, is also highly concentrated. Four major banks account for a substantial component of the total assets, deposits and credits generated by the banking sector (Table 8.1). These four banks (Ziraat Bank, İş Bank, Akbank, and Yapı Kredi Bank) control around 60 per cent of total credits; they account for 65 per cent of total deposits in the system.[14]

The ten largest banks listed in Table 8.1 include both state-owned deposit banks and also private commercial banks owned by large conglomerates - 'The Groups'. A few words about these different categories of banks is necessary to convey the general picture.

There are 10 specialized state deposit banks in the Turkish financial system, four of which are listed in Table 8.1 above.[15] In 1987, these ten banks represented 51.5 per cent of total assets of deposit banks in Turkey. Most were established in the early decades of the Republic (between 1923-1946) by special decrees, to provide credit and facilitate investments in specialized sectors of the economy as well as operating as regular deposit banks.[16]

Products of an era earmarked by industrialization through state initiative, they have provided credit facilities for a wide array of industrial and commercial enterprises, subsequently becoming equity holders with a controlling interest in many instances. Today, some of these banks are owners of state economic enterprises, others are equity holders in a variety of private sector companies, as well as operating as regular commercial banks.

The ascendancy of private commercial deposit banks in the system is predominantly a post-1946 phenomenon, lent impetus by the industrialization through private initiative policies of the post-1945 multi-party era, roughly up to the late 1970s. This is also the period in which the nascent private conglomerates began to move into the banking sector. More specifically, a new banking law, passed in 1957 (Act No. 7129)

[13] On the institutional structure of the Turkish banking sector, see, *inter alia*, Özcan Ertuna, *Finansal Kurumlar*, Ankara: Teori Yayınları, 1986; Öztin Akgüç, Türkiye'de *Bankacılık*, İstanbul: Gerçek Yayınevi, 1987; and Selçuk Abaç, *Turkish Banks and the Banking System*, Istanbul: Eurocurrency Publications, 1986.

[14] The oligopolistic structure of the Turkish banking system has remained highly resilient in the restructuration policies of the 1980s' decade, as revealed by Öztin Akgüç's annual trend reports published in the monthly journal *Banka ve Ekonomik Yorumlar* (Istanbul).

[15] In addition to the four listed in Table 8.1, the State-owned deposit banks include Anadolu Bank, İller Bank, Etibank, Sümerbank, T. Öğretmenler Bank, and Denizcilik Bank. Two of these, T.Emlak Kredi Bank and Anadolu Bank, were merged in 1988. If the three state-owned investment banks and the Central Bank itself are included, the number of State banks in the system becomes 14.

[16] Thus, for instance, the T. Emlak Kredi Bank is the only bank legally empowered to grant housing credit and engage in real estate development activities, in addition to providing all regular commercial banking services.

Table 8.1: The Largest Ten Banks in Turkey (December 1988)

Banks	Total Assets (million TL.)	% Share in Total	Cumulative % Share
1. T.C. Ziraat Bank (State-owned)	8,882,010	22.7	22.7
2. T.C. İş Bank (Quasi-State)	6,064,685	15.5	38.2
3. Akbank (Group-owned)	3,151,065	8.0	46.2
4. Yapı ve Kredi Bank (Group-owned)	3,043,785	7.8	54.0
5. T.Emlak Kredi Bank (State-Owned)	2,776,651	7.1	61.1
6. T. Halk Bank (State-owned)	1,889,234	4.8	65.9
7. T. Vakıflar Bank (State-owned)	1,606,934	4.1	70.0
8. Pamukbank (Group-owned)	1,289,318	3.3	73.3
9. T. Ticaret Bank (Group-owned)	1,229,443	3.1	76.4
10. T. Garanti Bank (Group-owned)	1,130,489	2.9	79.3
Other Banks (51 Banks)	8,112,357	20.7	100.0
TOTAL	39,175,966		

Source: Türkiye İş Bankası, *Review of Economic Conditions*, (Supplement), no.1, (January-March, 1988).

removed credit ceilings on lending to enterprises in which banks were themselves equity holders.[17] In the subsequent two decades of inflationary growth (perhaps better described as periods of rampant inflation alternating with stabilization measures and contracting growth, symptomatic of 'import substitution' behind protective barriers), interlocking ownership of banks and corporations gained momentum. Of the five private commercial banks listed in Table 8.1 above, all are controlled by large conglomerates.

A final very important structural feature of the current financial system is that the banks (both State and private) have equity holdings in affiliated companies, often with

[17] Ceilings were re-imposed in 1979 through a special decree-law (No. 28, 31 August 1979) modifying the relevant articles of Act No. 7129. The Bank Act of 1983 also includes credit ceilings to limit interlocking ownership.

controlling interest.[18] The resultant interlocking ownership of financial institutions and corporations has meant that the distinction between 'public' and 'private' banks is often not so clear cut as it initially appears. Hence it may be more appropriate to talk about 'oligopolistic public-private conglomerates' in the Turkish banking system, as suggested by one student of comparative Middle Eastern financial systems.[19]

The extremely tight networks linking state to financial interests and then to industrial capital, may provide one possible explanation of why the Turkish banking oligopoly has refrained from political opposition despite extreme policy insulation. The government has substantial powers and control over the financial system, given the dominance of state banks and the interpenetration of finance and industry. Mr Özal's political strategy has been to include the top executives of the two largest State banks in his inner circle, in addition to the Head of the Central Bank. But in all three cases, the appointments to these key positions have been from outside the traditional banking system. Thus, the old guard of the Turkish banking oligopoly (public and private) has not only been deprived of a voice in the immediate policy formulation and implementation process, but also found it impossible to mobilize group action to challenge the increasing autonomy of the Prime Minister's inner circle. The Association of Turkish Banks, a body with compulsory membership, having both state-owned and private banks under its umbrella, has proved 'meaningless' as an organizational vehicle, although dominated by the old guard of banking circles.[20]

However, ascribing the political quiescence of Turkey's banking oligopoly solely to the institutional structure of the sector itself would be misleading. Individual banks have found the new era of restructuration highly profitable, despite much private criticism of the Prime Minister's inner circle as 'young boys playing games', to quote from an interview these authors conducted. Thus it could well be argued that so long as individual banks have continued to profit, the Turkish banking oligopoly has been unwilling to openly challenge the prevailing policy exclusiveness, preferring to ride on a short-run wave of expansion based on extensive internal and external borrowing from which the sector as a whole appears to have reaped the lion's share. To elaborate

---

18 According to a special Commission report of the State Planning Organization in 1982, 18 of the 26 private commercial banks were 'Group' owned. See, 'Banking and Credit Policies and Measures', in *Fifth Five-Year Plan, Special Commission Report on Banking and Credit*, Ankara: The State Planning Organization, 1982, p.9. For a journalistic attempt to map out the interlocks, see Mustafa Sönmez, *Kırk Haramiler. Türkiye'de Holdingler* (İstanbul: Özlem Yayıncılık, 1987).

19 See Clement Henry Moore, 'Islamic Banks and Competitive Politics in the Arab World and Turkey', *The Middle East Journal*, 44 (1990): 234-55.

20 The Association of Turkish Banks was created in 1958 through special provisions of the Banking Act (No. 7129) on a corporatist model (in institutional terms) of singular, monopolistic representation. The general assembly of the Association includes all banks, but voting rights are defined according to the assets of individual banks. The largest State bank, Ziraat Bank, is a permanent member of the Executive Board as stipulated in the statute of the Assocation; the Board itself is dominated by large banks, notably large State banks. The association's ineffectiveness in organizing group action was demonstrated when it attempted to implement a 'gentleman's agreement' which set interest rates (for current accounts) at 33 per cent, shortly after the government decision to free them in June 1980. Among the earliest violators of the gentleman's agreement were the large state banks, and by February 1981 interest rates had shot up to 80 per cent.

this point further, it will be necessary to have a closer look at the specific policies of de-regulation implemented in the post-1980 period, and the micro-politics of banks in the context of those policies.

Macro-Politics of 'Tight Regulation' Prior to 1980

Observes of the Turkish financial scene have been almost unanimous in describing the pre-1980 period in terms of 'tightly-administered system' characterized by 'extensive state intervention'.[21] The political logic behind the indisputably extensive bureaucratic regulations centred on state control over the allocation of two critical resources in the economy, namely, foreign currency and credits. Both the 'price of foreign currency' and the 'price of credits' were administratively defined at below market rates, and bureaucratically allocated according to 'policy and/or political priorities'.

An overvalued exchange rate policy (that is, the price of foreign currency officially fixed at below real market value) was accompanied by the exclusive monopoly of the Central Bank over foreign currency transactions. The commercial banks (state or private) were prohibited from holding foreign currency in deposit accounts or reserves. This meant that the Central Bank purchased the foreign currency earnings of exporters below real market value (that is, at the fixed official exchange rate) and allocated it (cheaply) among importers. Thus, import requests from import licence holders (who deposited the equivalent amount in TL at the offical exchange rate with a commercial bank) were processed by the Central Bank. Depending upon the foreign currency reserves of the Central Bank and priorities established by the State Planning Organization, the available foreign currency was selectively distributed. A chronic balance of payments deficit coupled with the over-valued official exchange rate meant that the demand for foreign currency was almost invariably in excess of supply, resulting in long waiting lists. The existence of a flourishing 'unregulated' parallel market in foreign currency is self-explanatory.

The second most important set of controls in the pre-1980 period entailed administered interest rates for deposits and credits in the banking system, again below market prices. Hence, numerous sectors of the economy were subsidized through low cost credit - public enterprises, agriculture, artisans and small traders, and the like. Specific quantity directives, interest surcharges and rebates, preferential tax treatments, and the like further served to manipulate the cost of credit. The extensiveness of these administrative controls meant that only an estimated one quarter of total credit was free from government controls.[22] It also meant that in practice, all investments benefited from encouragement schemes of one type or another, that is, the policy of low cost credit. [23]

The dynamics of the banking sector in the 1950-1980 period were shaped by the combination of these two sets of political- cum-bureaucratic controls over the price and

[21] See for instance, A. H. Hanson and C. R. Neal, *Interest Rate Policies in Selected Developing Countries, 1970-1982* (Washington D.C.: World Bank Industry and Finance Series, 14, 1986,) pp. 121-8.

[22] Ibid., p. 121.

[23] See The State Planning Organization, 'Banka Kredi Politikaları ve Tedbirleri', p.3.

allocation of foreign currency and credits, resulting in what is frequently described as 'riskless banking' by the bank executives themselves.

Prohibited from foreign currency transactions, banks were effectively cushioned from short-term fluctuations in world currency markets. They 'bought and sold Turkish money'. To capture deposits at administratively-defined low interest rates, an elaborate network of 'branch offices' developed, with an estimated average number of 250 new branch offices opened annually between 1970 and 1981.[24] 'Cheap' loans, or State subsidized credit at preferential interest rates, were in turn channelled into 'The Group' investments; the interlocking ownership of financial institutions and corporations was accompanied by less than arm's length lending and underwriting practices.

What this brief characterization serves to underline is that the often repeated depiction of Turkish financial system in the pre-1980 period as 'tightly regulated' refers to the existence of an elaborate edifice of bureaucratic regulations built up to control the price and allocation of foreign currency and credits.

Macro-Politics of De-Regulation and Micro-Politics of Banks in the Post-1980 Period

The dramatic shift towards a strategy of 'liberalization' in the post-1980 period has thus entailed successive attempts to de-regulate interest as well as foreign exchange rates. In actual implementation, this has meant 'high' interest rates (with two brief attempts to actually 'liberate' them) and floating rates of foreign exchange. The ramifications for the banking sector as a whole have been momentous, although the outcome remains far short of the monetarist ideal of 'full liberalization'.

The micro-politics of banks in the new era of 'de-regulation' have been based on simultaneous changes in both markets. The adoption of a crawling-peg exchange rate from May 1981 onwards, with the Central Bank empowered to establish the parity of the Turkish lira on a daily basis, meant, in effect, the removal of price controls over foreign currency.

Equally, if not more, important were the concomitant changes introduced in the foreign exchange regime, allowing commercial banks to engage in foreign currency operations, thus ending the historical monopoly of the Central Bank. A series of discrete measures were progressively introduced through special decrees, permitting commercial banks to hold foreign currency in their legal reserves, granting them autonomy to use proceeds from export sales, transfer the income and sales proceeds of foreign direct investments, generate short-term foreign credits for themselves directly and to extend foreign currency loans and determine the exchange rate for large transactions, as well as allowing individual depositors to open domestic foreign currency accounts. The cumulative outcome of these changes has been to decentralize the majority of commercial transactions in foreign currency, hitherto the exclusive domain of the state (through the Central Bank), to the banking sector. Thus the role of the Central Bank in foreign currency markets became essentially a regulatory and supervisory one.

---

[24] In 1986, the total number of branch offices of deposit banks in the system reached 6,244 (Akgüç, *Türkiye'de Bankacılık*, p. 82).

The most immediate consequence of the decentralization of foreign currency operations, when coupled with the softening of restrictions on capital inflows from abroad and the introduction of an export encouragement scheme, was the arrival of international banks which had so far eschewed Turkish financial markets. The number of foreign banks in Turkey went up from 4 in 1977, to 22 by the end of 1988 (Table 8.2).

Table 8.2: Foreign Banks in Turkish Financial Markets

Banks	Date	Specialization	Ownership
Osmanlı Bank	1863	General-Commercial	French
Banco Di Roma	1911	General-Commercial	Italian
Hollantse Bank	1921	General-Commercial	Dutch
Arap-Türk Bank	1977	General-Commercial	Libyan
Citibank	1981	Trade-Finance-Funding	American
Bank Mellat	1982	Trade-Finance-Funding	Iranian
BCCI (*)	1982	" "	Luxemburg
Türk Bank Ltd.	1983	" "	Cypriot
Habib Bank Ltd.	1983	" "	Pakistan
Hanover Trust	1984	" "	American
Chase Manhattan	1984	" "	American
F.N.Bank of Boston	1984	" "	American
Saudi-American	1985	" "	Saudi-American
Chemical Mitsui	1985	" "	American-Japanese-Turkish
Irving Trust/Tütün (**)	1985	General-Commercial	American-Turkish
BNP-AK (***)	1985	Trade-Finance-Funding	French-Turkish
Koç-Amerikan (***)	1986	" "	American-Turkish
Bahrain/Kuwait	1986	" "	Bahrain-Kuwait
Banque Indosuez	1986	" "	French
Standard Chartered	1986	" "	British
Credit Lyonnais	1988	" "	French
Körfez Bank	1988	" "	Qatar

* BCCI: Bank of Credit and Commerce International

** Irving Trust subsequently withrew from the Turkish financial markets over policy conflicts with Yaşar Group, owners of Tütünbank.

*** BNP-Ak is a Bank Nationale de Paris and Akbank joint venture. Akbank is the largest private bank in Turkey, part of the Sabancı conglomerate. Koç-American Bank is again a joint venture between American Express and the KOÇ group. The Koç Group ranks as the third largest conglomerate in Turkey, after İş Bank (partly-state owned) and OYAK (Army Mutual Assistance Organization owned by the Military). Chemical Mitsui's Turkish partner is again a large 'Group', ENKA.

The large Turkish banks, long protected from fluctuations in world money markets and burdened with the operating costs of vast branch networks and agonizing bureaucracy, lacked the flexibility to immediately shift their activities from passive deposit taking and credit-issuing to aggressive international trade financing in the new era of export expansion. To quote from an interview held by the authors with a top bank executive, 'We used to wait for customers to walk in through the door; now we have to try to anticipate their needs'. Hence, international banks, with their vastly superior networks around the world, experienced in management and electronic fund transfer technologies, initially met little competition in Turkey in carving a lucrative niche for themselves in trade finance and funding operations. But by 1985, many of the prominent private 'Groups' had given birth to a new generation of 'trade-finance banks', either in joint ventures with foreign banks (as seen in Table 8.2) or independently.[25]

The slowness of the over-branched, over-staffed traditional deposit banks in shifting into foreign currency markets also provided scope for the emergence of a number of new and small independent trade-finance banks of domestic origin. These enterprising new mavericks, employing aggressive Madison Avenue techniques, were able to take advantage of the expanding foreign trade and funding markets, and established themselves in a banking sector long dominated by the 'Groups'. Such names as Esbank, Netbank, Finansbank, İktisat Bank, Ekonomi Bank, İthalat/İhracat Bank, Adabank, and the like have come to represent what one of the old guard described during our interview with him as 'the sporty end of the banking market', different in image and style as well as mode of operation from the traditional banks.

The high returns on short term 'trade-finance' and 'funding' operations in foreign currency has in part been linked to the export boom of the 1980s, encouraged by lavish subsidies particularly on manufactured goods as well as fortuitous external circumstances in the Middle East markets. In dollar terms, exports nearly quadrupled, going up from $ 2.3 billion in 1979 to $ 8.0 billion in 1985.[26] Equally important however, were generous capital inflows from abroad. Turkey's Debt-GNP ratio increased from 27.8 per cent in 1980 to 53.1 per cent in 1986, stimulated both by growing confidence in Turkey's credit worthiness in international financial circles, and also generous official support in view of Turkey's geo-political position.[27] The increased ability of the economy to borrow from foreign sources in the post-1980 period has thus enabled trade banks to generate funds from abroad, as well as attracting business from prominent

---

25 Among the most visible indicators of the shift towards foreign currency operations in the banking system as a whole have been changes introduced at the top executive level. A recent study comparing recruitment and succession patterns of top management in the banking sector in pre- and post-1980, emphasizes that the older, traditional banks began to recruit U.S.-educated, relatively young, aggressively mobile top executives in the 1980s in preference to promotions from within the old guard. See Behlül Üsdiken, 'The Impact of Environmental Change on Characteristics of Top Management Teams', paper presented at the Ninth EGOS Colloquium, Berlin, 11-14 July 1989.

26 See Halis Akder, 'Turkey's Export Expansion in the Middle East, 1980-1985', *The Middle East Journal*, 41 (1987), pp. 553-67, and Merih Celasun and Danny Roderik, *Debt, Adjustment and Growth. Turkey* (Chicago: University of Chicago Press, 1989).

27 Celasun and Roderick, *Debt, Adjustment and Growth. Turkey*, p.313, Table 10.1. For alternative estimates, see TÜSİAD, *Dış Borçlar. Tahmin ve Analiz* (İstanbul: TÜSİAD, 1987).

exporters. As described to these authors by some bank executives in the summer of 1988, in recent years the real function of banks is acting as brokers in foreign currency transactions; people are going out of the banking business into the funding business; deposit taking and credit-issuing are no longer profitable.

These comments by top banking executives suggest that 'traditional banking' of the pre-1980 variety is no longer deemed an attractive source of profits. To be able to explain why, it is necessary to look at interest rate policies of the post-1983 period.

The Turkish experiment with 'de-regulation' of interest rates has been confined to a strategy of fixed but 'high' rates, with two brief but important attempts to actually 'free' them. The first attempt to lift ceilings on interest rates dates back to June 1980. Initially heralded as the emancipation of banking in Turkey and later dubbed as 'June Banking', it led to a cut-throat competition for deposits with catastrophic results for all participants concerned. Banks and financial houses (money brokers) raced to capture deposits by offering higher and higher rates. In a very short period, lending rates shot up, threatening an avalanche of bad debts arising from the business community's growing inability to settle its loan obligations. The so-called financial houses, that is, money brokers or 'bankers', which had collected deposits at unusually high interest rates (giving promissory notes, post-dated checks as well as certificates of deposits of banks as guarantee for the vast funds they collected on the basis of very limited assets), were soon faced with a tide of bad loans, unable to cover their promised interest rates and re-purchase guarantees. When the largest of these brokers crashed in 1982, followed by a run on some of the smaller banks (five of which subsequently crashed), the Central Bank was forced to step in by pumping huge sums of money into the sector. Following the crisis, a series of urgent measures were taken in money and capital markets to liquidate the brokers; interest rates were brought down and once more became fixed; and a new law was passed (in 1983) to bring banking practices under tougher regulation and closer discipline.[28]

After this well-publicised episode, a more cautious strategy of fixed rates with frequent re-adjustments within a wide margin has become the norm. The basic strategy has been one of steering clear of two pitfalls. On the one hand, nominal interest rates on deposits have been frequently revised to keep them on a par with inflation and hence avoid a flight of savings from the banking system. On the other hand, to ward off the possibility of massive defaults by credit users and a threatened collapse of banks, similar to the 1980-1982 incident, ceilings have been imposed to keep rates under control. Thus, variable interest rates have been determined according to the general trends of the economy, notably the rate of inflation.

This strategy of frequent re-adjustments in fixed rates has dramatically narrowed the profit margins of traditional commercial banks in credit operations. Higher deposit rates have increased the cost of loanable funds. So banks have found that unless they sacrificed their profit margins, or took on the risk of non-performing loans, they had to remain confined to a very narrow base of sound credit customers. Inevitably, commercial banks have been squeezed at both ends, and they have had to reduce their profit

[28] For journalistic accounts of the events of this period, see Emin Çölaşan, *12 Eylül. Özal Ekonomisinin Perde Arkası* (İstanbul: Milliyet 1984); and idem, *Banker Skandalının Perde Arkası* (İstanbul: Milliyet Yayınları, 1984).

margins. Nonetheless, their potential pool of sound interest customers, that is, enterprises able to bear the high credit costs without the risk of non-performing loans, has been steadily decreasing in numbers. The grip of high interest rates upon banks was further tightened when the Central Bank announced (on 14 October 1988) a decision to 'free' interest rates, for the second time since 1980. But within a week, ceilings were re-established since the interest rates had risen 'high enough'. By various estimates, the number of sound credit customers, who could borrow at the prevailing high rates of interest towards the end of 1988, did not exceed 300 enterprises at best.[29]

This progressive decline of profit margins in conventional banking operations has meant that large commercial banks, which have traditionally relied upon their vast deposit bases, have found liquidity in Turkish currency a liability. Not only has deposit-taking at high interest rates become expensive, but also credit seekers have grown fewer in numbers. Thus to quote from one of our interviews, 'buying and selling Turkish money is not profitable so long as interest rates remain high'.

What has compensated for the progressive decline of profits in conventional banking operations has been the concomitant increase in central government borrowing. From 1984 onwards, the central government has increasingly resorted to issuing short-term Treasury bills and longer-term government bonds in financing public sector cash deficits. These default-free, tax-exempt and high-interest bonds have become the most popular avenue of investment for large commercial banks, held against their liquidity requirements.[30] Again, a direct quotation from an interview with the top executive of one of the largest commercial banks will serve to summarize this point: 'Interest rates have lost their importance. We buy and sell foreign currency now. And, of course, we invest in State bonds.' Thus, given higher interest rates on government bonds than on deposits (Table 8.3), large commercial banks have been a major beneficiary of increased public sector borrowing in the domestic economy.

The broader implications of increases in domestic borrowing, which grew as a proportion of GNP from about 35 per cent in 1981-1982 to nearly 45 per cent in 1983-1984 and to 49 per cent in 1985-1986, is beyond the scope of discussion in this chapter.[31] The short term implications for the banking sector have clearly been very favourable. Riding on the wave of domestic borrowing, coupled with the concomitant inflow of international funds, Turkish banks have found the new era of 'de-regulation' highly profitable.

---

29 The difficulties of banks in finding credit worthy customers at the ongoing lending rates made the headlines in the daily newspapers when two banks from among the top ten decided to issue press releases. See *Cumhuriyet*, 4 December 1988, and *Hürriyet* (Istanbul daily), 20 December 1988.

30 For proceedings of two round-table discussions concerning the implications of the so-called 'super-interest' government bonds, see *Banka ve Ekonomik Yorumlar*, 21 (1984), pp. 13-33, and 22 (1985), pp. 7-26.

31 For a discussion on increased domestic borrowing in the post-1980 period, see Celasun and Roderik, *Debt, Adjustment and Growth. Turkey*, pp. 149-52. The figures quoted are from p. 150.

Table 8.3: A Comparison of Interest Rates on Government Bonds and Bank Deposits, 1986

	Maturity	Interest Rate (%)		Maturity	Interest Rate (%)
GOVERNMENT BONDS	1 year	53.11	CURRENT ACCOUNTS	1 month	30.0
	2 year	52.09		3 months	40.0
	3 year	Variable		6 months	45.0
				1 year	52.0

Source: Figures released by Ministry of Finance, as quoted in Ziya Öniş and Süleyman Özmucur, 'The Role of the Financial System in the Creation and Resolution of Macroeconomic Crises in Turkey', 1988, typescript.

Conclusion

Our initial point of departure in the present study was the broader concern of changing State-society relations in Turkey in the 1980s' decade. We began with a series of questions gleaned from a theoretical literature, that is fraught with manifest problems of alternative paradigms. Our attempt to approach these questions through a de-limited study couched at the sectoral level was in part a reaction to the excessive reification of 'the State' in this theoretical literature. We hoped to pin down the concrete referents of 'the State' which appears to gain or lose autonomy, retreat or expand, engage or disengage itself from society and/or economy, depending upon which approach one adopts from among the proliferating theses on changing State-society relations.

Our analysis in the foregoing pages has emphasized changes in the logic and mode of state intervention, rather than its degree or scale. We underlined that after nearly a decade of implementation of an official policy of economic re-structuration, the anatomy of the Turkish financial system remains essentially unchanged. State banks continue to figure prominently among the oligopolistic giants of the Turkish financial system; their interpenetration with private conglomerates remains as tight as ever. The state has neither been been trimmed down (in budgetary or personnel terms), nor 'privatized'.

But while the centrality of the state remains intact, the form and type of state action appears to have changed. Policy formulation and implementation have become increasingly encapsulated within a narrow inner circle of technocrat-planners, insulated from institutionalized channels of intermediation and bargaining (bureaucratic and political) in the domestic arena. Thus, the new logic of intervention, based upon the monetarist imperatives of international financial institutions, has been accompanied by policy insulation of a type often associated with authoritarian regimes. Such policy insulation, we argued, has been contingent upon waves of increased foreign and domestic borrowing and hence its longevity depends upon continued economic expansion.

The financial sector, more so than any other sector of the economy, has been both a mirror and also an instrument of 'development policies' in Turkey. To study the financial sector is to focus upon the most powerful actors - banks - in Turkish society. Even so, to venture from a concrete investigation of change within an historically specific period towards a theoretical discussion of the transformation in State-society relations is at best a perilous task. With due apologies for the methodological leap, we would like to conclude by adding a footnote to the increasing literature on 'the State tradition' in Turkey.

The centrality of the State in Turkish society and its pivotal role in the organization of the economy has frequently been ascribed to an abiding State tradition. Political life has been viewed through the optics of State primacy, a powerful centralized State which retains the prerogative of allowing, denying or transforming the dynamics arising outside itself. Without debating their theoretical validity, such State-centric analyses presume a certain continuity in the role of the Turkish state, past and present. Empirical study here suggests that such a role, paramount as it may be, has not always been the same. In fact, it has undergone changes which can only be understood with reference to the projects and activities of groups and classes in the domestic and international arena. To the extent that the character, mission and capacities (nature and strength) of the Turkish state have been, and continue to be, subject to re-definition and re-constitution in interaction with society, the apparent continuities in State tradition may indeed be illusory.

9

Manufacturing Industries: Giants with Hesitant Voices

Yılmaz Esmer

Introduction

In this chapter we explore the nature of the interface between the state and the industrial sector in Turkey. Our aim is to analyze the organizational structure and behaviour of the Turkish industrial sector from an 'interest group politics' perspective. More specifically, we attempt to investigate the methods the representatives (both in a personal and organizational sense) of the manufacturing industries employ in furthering their interests.

Metin Heper in this volume argues that interest group politics in Turkey fits neither pluralism nor varieties of corporatism. The key variable in Heper's analysis is the degree of 'stateness'. He asserts that the Ottoman-Turkish tradition differs significantly from the various modalities of European feudalism with respect to this crucial variable. Hence the inapplicability of the two models to the Turkish case, which represents a particular combination of the two major factors that shape 'politics in general and interest group politics in particular'- its position on the Gemeinschaft-Gesellschaft continuum and the degree of 'stateness'. Not all students of Turkish interest group politics agree with Heper. Robert Bianchi, for example, is of the opinion that 'the existing institutional structure of Turkish associational life provides a much finer base for the further expansion of corporatism than for the gradual development of pluralist democracy'.[1] He notes:

> In modern Turkey the ongoing competition between pluralist and corporatist modes of representation has been a recurrent source of conflict in the relations of differentially organized interests with the state and with one another. But the intensity and broader implications of these conflicts have varied substantially in three different historical periods depending on the degree and nature of linkages between associations and political parties. First, during the Kemalist period all types of associations were clearly subordinated to a one-party apparatus and authoritarian state, which effectively suppressed the expression of interest conflict through either pluralist or corporatist channels. Second, under the Democratic and Justice Party governments corporatist and pluralist structures gradually became alternative networks for mobilizing supports and neutralizing opponents and for ensuring that different constituencies would receive vastly different treatment from the political authorities. This dualistic system of associational repre-

---

[1] Robert Bianchi, *Interest Groups and Political Development in Turkey* (Princeton: Princeton University Press, 1984).

> sentation promoted new pressures for abrupt and radical action, both from above and from below, to purge the system of its most glaring inconsistencies and inequities. Even though relatively privileged segments of associational leadership shared a narrow consensus supporting such arrangements, widespread discontent with their performance bred still stronger support for groups confronting the state and one another with conflicting proposals for the fundamental redesign of associational life and of the regime itself. Third, the success of the [Republican] People's Party in fashioning a social democratic coalition significantly strengthened the pluralist network during the 1970's and enhanced the possibility that discriminatory features of the corporatist bargaining process might have been ameliorated or overridden by the countervailing force of popular sovereignty if a democratic framework had been retained.[2]

Thus, Bianchi thinks that pluralist and corporatist forms have co-existed in modern Turkey, albeit with a heavy tilt towards the latter. Indeed,

> The network of corporatist associations is not yet universal in its coverage of occupational categories. In many sectors organizational structure remains quite undifferentiated, membership continues to be a form, and participation is generally sporadic. Nevertheless, in terms of organizational strength, financial soundness, control over rewards and sanctions against members, and effective access to authoritative decision-makers, the corporatist network enjoys a clear superiority over the still sprawling and fragmented pluralist network. In contrast to the fitful, uneven, and highly visible development of voluntary associability, the network of modern Turkish corporatism has expanded slowly, steadily and quietly. Its Ottoman foundations in business and agriculture were strengthened by the Kemalists, extended by the Democrats to include most of the free professions, and widened further by the Justice Party to encompass *esnaf* [artisans] as well.[3]

Thus, unlike Heper, Bianchi believes that the Turkish case bears a strong resemblance to corporatism and that, furthermore, the roots of this corporatist structure can be traced back to the Ottoman Empire.

In the present essay, we seek some clues from the manufacturing industries sector as to the nature of interest group politics in Turkey, limiting ourselves to the post-1983 era. Although this author would be extremely hesitant to call the developments of this period a 'liberal revolution' as Dankwart A Rustow has,[4] it is clear that certain major transformations took place after the Motherland Party came to power in 1983. Among these, the following are especially worthy of mention for our purposes:

A radical liberalization of the foreign exchange regime;

A sharp departure - at least in rhetoric - from the discourse of 'mixed-economy', which had almost been a State ideology for decades in favour of complete reliance on market forces with as little government involvement, subsidies and controls as possible;

A shift from import substitution to export-oriented policies and lifting of most controls over imports;

[2] Ibid., pp. 356-7.

[3] Ibid., p. 350.

[4] Dankwart A. Rustow, 'Turkey's Liberal Revolution', *Middle East Review*, 17 (1985), pp. 5-11.

Enabling local governments to gain control over significant financial resources thus reducing their dependence on the central government;
Applying for full membership in the European Community, and, in full reversal of past policies, strongly encouraging contacts, partnerships, exchanges, etc. between private companies, associations, and foundations in Turkey and abroad;
Pursuing, whether of will or necessity, a policy of heavy foreign borrowing which more than doubled the country's foreign debts in a matter of less than five years.

Although it is clear that historical and cultural variables play a very significant role in determining the nature of interest groups and interest articulation in a polity, it would not be unexpected for such radical changes to have an impact, too. It is for these reasons that, as Heper notes in this volume, the post-1983 period is especially interesting for studying interest group politics in Turkey.

In our attempt to study this topic from the perspective developed by Heper we shall make use of the results of a survey of the managers or owners of industrial firms (all members of the Istanbul Chamber of Industry) and a survey of the Turkish press during that period. Data collected from the first survey are based on a duly selected sample and a standard interview schedule while the survey of the press is much more informal and impressionistic. Thus, perhaps, any conclusions drawn from the latter should be regarded as hypotheses rather than confirmed findings.

It has already been stated that our discussion of interest groups is limited to the manufacturing industries sector and we would like to begin with an evaluation of the significance of this sector within the whole economy. Needless to say, the size and importance of the industrial sector relative to the country's economy is an important control variable for our study.

Manufacturing Industries Sector

In Table 9.1, we present the relative shares in Gross Domestic Product of the major sectors from the beginning of the Republican era up to 1987. It is observed that up until 1960, the share of industry in total Gross Domestic Product (GDP) shows minor fluctuations and certainly does not display an upward trend. However, between 1960 and 1987, we observe a steady increase with the share being nearly doubled during this period. As late as 1970, the share of agriculture is noticeably higher than the share of industry. Yet in 1987 the industrial sector accounted for almost a third of Turkey's total GDP while the share of agriculture was only 17 per cent. It is also interesting to note that the shares of services and construction show very little change between 1923 and 1987. Thus, industry is the only sector that has steadily increased its share, and reached a level that compares favourably with many industrialized countries. For example, the share of industry (including construction) in total GDP in 1985 was 31 per cent in U.S.A., 41 per cent in Japan, 40 per cent in Federal Germany, 34 per cent in France, 36 per cent in U.K., 39 per cent in Italy, 34 per cent in the Netherlands, 24 per cent in Denmark, 33 per cent in Belgium, 29 per cent in Greece, 40 per cent in Portugal, 36 per cent in Spain. The difference between the structure of GDP in Turkey and in these countries is the relative sizes of the agricultural and service sectors.

Table 9.1: Sectoral Shares in Turkey's GDP (%)*

	Agriculture	Industry	Construction	Services
1923	39.8	13.2	2.6	41.7
1930	45.8	11.4	4.5	35.6
1940	38.7	18.9	3.4	38.4
1950	41.6	14.6	3.8	37.9
1960	37.6	17.1	4.8	37.7
1970	27.3	21.4	6.7	41.8
1980	21.1	25.3	4.9	45.6
1985	17.5	31.6	3.8	44.9
1987	17.1	32.5	4.0	44.8

* Row totals do not add up to 100 since 'import duties' and 'imported bank service charges' are not included.

Source: Süleyman Özmucur and Yılmaz Esmer, 'Total Factor Productivity in Turkey', research report prepared for the World Bank, Istanbul, 1988.

Another question of significance with respect to the importance of the industrial sector in the economy is the distribution of the labour force. The sectoral distribution of the economically active population in 1950 and 1980 is given in Table 9.2. Within that 30-year period, the proportion of those employed in manufacturing industries doubled. In 1980, the total industrial sector employed 17 per cent of the economically active population over the age of 15, as opposed to 58 per cent for the agricultural and 25 per cent for the service sectors. In the same year, comparable figures for the industrial sector were 29 per cent for Greece, 37 per cent for Spain, 37 per cent for Portugal, 32 per cent for Denmark and 32 per cent for the Netherlands.

Table 9.2: Sectoral Distribution of the Economically Active Population (Age 15 and above)

	1950	%	1980	%
Agriculture	8,085,178	78.9	9,972,361	57.9
Mining	53,235	0.5	131,522	0,8
Manufacturing	578,700	5.7	1,888,743	11.0
Electricity, gas and water	9,199	0.1	32,988	0.2
Construction	113,610	1.1	753,257	4.4
Trade	259,721	2.5	1,356,135	7.9
Transportation	125,240	1.2	529,111	3.1
Services	540,179	5.3	2,384,757	13.9
Unknown	485,179	4.7	170,696	1.0
Total	10,250,241	100.0	17,219,571	100.0

Source: Özmucur and Esmer, 'Total Factor Productivity in Turkey'.

It is also instructive to trace the changes in the sectoral breakdown of Turkish manufacturing industries. An examination of the figures in Table 9.3 reveals that chemicals and petroleum products, food and beverages, machinery and transport equipment, and finally textiles and leather are the four major sectors of Turkish manufacturing industries. In 1984, these four sectors accounted for 78 per cent of the total value added in Turkish manufacturing industries. On the other hand, a quick glance at the time series data shows that both the food and beverages and textiles sectors have been decreasing steadily in relative importance. However, during the 35-year period between 1950 and 1984 the share of chemicals and petroleum products increased four-fold. The increase is 300 per cent in metal industries and - although not so spectacular - certainly very significant in machinery and transport equipment. Taken together, Tables 9.1 and 9.3 point to two important developments in the Turkish economy that the share of agriculture in GDP has been decreasing in favour of industry and within the industrial sector, the shift is away from the more traditional and agriculture-based industries (such as food, beverages, tobacco, textiles and leather) and towards metal and chemical industries.

Table 9.3: Sectoral Shares in Value Added in Manufacturing Industries (%)

Sector	1950	1960	1970	1980	1984
Food, beverages and tobacco	40	35	28	18	21
Textiles and leather	30	25	19	17	15
Forest products, furniture	3	4	4	3	3
Paper and printing	3	4	3	3	4
Chemicals and petroleum products	6	9	17	22	23
Non-metalic mineral products	4	4	5	7	5
Metal industries	3	6	6	8	9
Machinery, transport equipment	11	12	17	20	19

Source: Özmucur and Esmer, 'Total Factor Productivity in Turkey'.

It may also be noteworthy that the composition of the total value added in manufacturing industries in Turkey is very similar to a number of market economies in Europe (Table 9.4).

The relative sizes of various sub-sectors within the manufacturing industries sector with respect to the size of the labour force are given in Table 9.5. We have already noted that the share of food, beverages, tobacco and textiles in total GDP has been decreasing. An examination of the figures in Table 9.5 reveals that this statement is only 'half true' with respect to the distribution of the economically active population. Indeed, the proportion of the economically active population in the food industries went up from 14.8 to 17.6 per cent between 1950 and 1980, not a significant increase, perhaps, but certainly a reversal of the trend observed for the sectoral distribution of GDP. On the other hand, the share of textiles has been decreasing considerably. It should also be noted that the proportion of workers in chemicals-petroleum and metal industries rose significantly during this period.

Table 9.4 : Sectoral Distribution of Value Added in Manufacturing Industries in Selected Countries in 1984 (%) (1980 Constant Prices)

	Food and Beverages	Textiles	Machinery and Transportation Vehicles	Chemicals	Other
West Germany	10	5	41	9	34
France	17	7	35	9	32
U.K.	13	7	33	11	36
Italy	11	18	25	8	38
Netherlands	19	4	28	13	37
Denmark	22	6	23	8	40
Belgium	19	9	24	12	35
Greece	20	21	11	8	39
Portugal	16	28	11	7	37
Spain	13	15	20	8	44
Ireland	32	10	18	15	25
Turkey	21	16	16	11	37

Source: Özmucur and Esmer, 'Total Factor Productivity in Turkey'.

Another important measure that must be considered for a comprehensive review of the industrial sector from an interest group politics perspective is the size distribution of firms in this sector. Needless to say, a sector that consists of thousands of very small firms cannot be expected to exhibit similar patterns of interaction with the state as a sector which is made up of few but very large establishments.

Unfortunately, such size measures as capital, gross earnings, and the like are not available for all firms. However, data on the number of employees are available. Table 9.6 gives the size breakdown of the Turkish manufacturing industries (up to 1984) according to this criterion. It is interesting that, between 1970 and 1984, there were almost no changes in the structure of the manufacturing industries with regard to size. One certainly cannot speak of a trend towards larger firms if one's measure of size is the number of persons employed. However, it is observed that the relative contributions of the size groups to the total value added in manufacturing industries has shifted considerably. Firms with more than 1,000 employees, for example, constituted less than 1 per cent of the sector in terms of numbers in 1984, but accounted for over 23 per cent of the value added. Similarly, firms with over 200 employees made up a mere 7.0 per cent of the total number of establishments in manufacturing industries, but produced nearly two-thirds of the valued added.

Table 9.5: Distribution of the Economically Active Population in Manufacturing Industries (Age 15 and above)

	1950		1975		1980	
	n	%	n	%	n	%
Food, beverages and tobacco	85,772	14.8	199,628	13.7	332,988	17.6
Textiles and leather	269,487	46.6	433,950	29.8	537,094	28.4
Forest products and furniture	62,130	10.7	178,510	12.3	200.412	10.9
Paper and printing	9,950	1.7	44,341	3.0	51,468	2.7
Chemicals and petroleum	11,551	2.0	57,572	3.9	110,842	5,9
Non-metalic mineral products	21,655	3.7	54,746	3.8	106,054	5.6
Metal industries	6,739	1.2	71,996	4.9	103.129	5.5
Machinery,transportation equipment	103,754	17.9	287,246	19.7	367,983	19.5
Other manufacturing industries	7,662	1.3	129,294	8.9	72,773	3.9
Total	578,700	100.0	1,457,283	100.0	1,888,743	100.0

Source: Özmucur and Esmer, 'Total Factor Productivity in Turkey'.

Up to this point, we have tried to give a description of the Turkish industrial sector as a whole without making a distinction between public and private. However, this distinction is of utmost importance for our purposes. We have established that the industrial sector, as a whole, is a major force in the economy of Turkey and its relative share has been and is expected to continue increasing. But what is the share of the public sector within manufacturing industries? Table 9.7 provides a clue to this question.

Table 9.6: Size Breakdown of Manufacturing Industries (Private Sector)

	Size of Firm	No. of Firms (rel.freq)	No. of Firms (cumulative)	Value Added (rel.freq)	Value Added (cumulative)
1970	10-19	40.5	100.0	5.8	100.0
	20-49	33.2	59.6	12.2	94.2
	50-99	12.8	26.4	11.7	81.9
	100-199	6.8	13.6	11.7	70.2
	200-499	4.8	7.0	25.4	58.5
	500-999	1.5	2.3	15.5	33.1
	1000+	0.8	0.8	17.6	17.6
	n=4566				
1980	10-19	46.4	100.0	5.1	100.0
	20-49	32.0	53.6	10.4	94.9
	50-99	10.7	21.6	11.1	84.5
	100-199	5.6	10.9	14.6	73.4
	200-499	3.6	5.3	22.5	58.8
	500-999	1.1	1.7	16.7	36.3
	1000+	0.6	0.6	19.7	19.7
1984	10-49	73.8	100.0	12.8	100.0
	50-99	12.8	26.1	9.2	87.2
	100-199	6.4	13.3	12.7	78.0
	200-499	4.6	7.0	22.8	65.3
	500-999	1.5	2.4	19.4	42.5
	1000+	0.9	0.9	23.1	23.1
	n=8396				

Source: Özmucur and Esmer, 'Total Factor Productivity in Turkey'.

In Table 9.7, the data for 1983 and 1984 include only firms with 25 or more employees, while establishments with 10 or more employees are included in the rest of the series. (This is due to a change of definition by the State Institute of Statistics). However, even then, in 1984 the private sector produced close to two-thirds of the total value added in manufacturing industries. If data were available for the whole sector rather than only for firms with 25 or more employees, the share of the private sector would be significantly greater since almost all public firms are large enterprises with considerably more employees than 25. Nevertheless, two points are clear: the relative share of the private sector within manufacturing industries is high; this relative share exhibits a clear upward trend.

How does this sector interact with the state? How are they organized? How do they make their demands known? Can they openly speak of their group interests, or do they cast these in terms of broader 'public and national' interests? It is these questions that we now turn our attention to.

Table 9.7: Value Added in Large Manufacturing Industries

	Public		Private	
	Billion TL	%	Billion TL	%
1970	15.5	54.2	13.1	45.8
1971	21.1	56.0	16.6	44.0
1972	24.5	51.8	22.8	48.2
1973	25.3	46.5	29.1	53.5
1974	37.2	49.9	37.3	50.1
1975	42.2	48.1	45.6	51.9
1976	47.9	42.6	64.6	57.4
1977	59.4	39.8	89.9	60.2
1978	82.8	34.8	155.1	65.2
1979	129.3	33.1	261.0	66.9
1980	332.9	40.4	491.0	59.6
1981	717.2	49.3	738.7	50.7
1982	949.3	46.8	1077.4	53.2
1983	1043.7	42.4	1420.3	57.6
1984	1329.6	37.4	2229.4	62.6

Source: Özmucur and Esmer, 'Total Factor Productivity in Turkey'.

Manufacturing Industries Sector: Corporatist, Pluralist or Something Else?

In outlining the theoretical framework of the present study, one of the questions implied by Heper (Chapter 1) is whether the groups are organized into an unspecified number of multiple, voluntary, competitive, non-hierarchically ordered and self- determined (as to type or scope) categories, or into a limited number of singular, compulsory, non-competitive, hierarchically ordered and functionally differentiated categories.

The case of the Turkish industrial sector is certainly much closer to the latter categorization than the former. The chambers of industry in various provinces are founded by law. They are semi-public organizations with compulsory membership and are the 'official' representatives of their members' interests. They are linked to a higher body - Union of Chambers - in the capital. Both individual chambers and the union must conform to procedures specified by law for electing their officers. As such, these organizations are certainly 'compulsory, non-competitive, hierarchically ordered'. Their organizational structure fits the ideal-type corporatist model perfectly.

However, the Turkish industrial sector has a number of 'voluntary, competitive and non-hierarchically organized' associations as well, which certainly act - and are recognized by the general public - as interest groups. Among them, one is especially worth mentioning: Turkish Industrialists' and Businessmen's Association (shortly referred to as TÜSİAD). In the words of one of its former chairmen, Mr Şahap Kocatopçu, TÜSİAD was founded by those large firms which constituted only a minority in the

Union of Chambers, and which longed for an attitude outside of political influences, without a connection to a political party, defending long-term national interests and a free market economy.[5] As one of the leading spokesmen for the industrial sector, Kocatopçu said:

> The TÜSİAD, in carrying out its activities, will be close to the governments according to the degree of their loyalty to a free market economy and mixed economy. But this does not entail being close to a [political] party.... Our TÜSİAD, with its 220 members, has remained like a club; it does not represent the private sector as a whole, yet.... If we wish the dialogue with the government to continue, TÜSİAD should take up problems with the government instead of discussing them in the open. In other words, it should know to keep its mouth shut. That is, instead of letting the press know of its views, TÜSİAD will take them to the government, will fight for them if necessary, and when agreement on a certain view is reached, that will be announced as the government's view.... Many persons who are in fierce competition with each other in many fields of business have agreed on a common denominator in TÜSİAD. The points that are agreed upon are: (1) Defending democracy; (2) staying outside the orbit of a political party; (3) giving priority to the country's interests.[6]

These remarks provide many interesting and clear clues to the nature of interest group politics in the Turkish industrial sector. In fact, many of the points discussed in chapter 1 find direct resonance in the words of Mr Kocatopçu. But before turning to a more qualitative analysis, it is in order to summarize the quantitative results of the survey that has already been mentioned.

In 1987, a survey was carried out by the present author and three colleagues to investigate the problems, priorities and expections of the business world.[7] Supported and published by TÜSİAD, some results of this survey are directly relevant to our topic.

The survey covered 1,004 firms selected from among the 6,347 members of the Istanbul Chamber of Industry. There is no question that the sample provided a more than adequate representation of Istanbul's industrial sector. Furthermore, Istanbul in 1987 accounted for 54.5 per cent of the number of private manufacturing firms with 10 or more employees in Turkey. 65.5 per cent of all persons employed by this sector (again, private firms with ten or more employees) are in Istanbul - a city that produces 45.8 per cent of the country's total value added in industry (private sector), including village industries and establishments of all sizes.[8] A sample of this size from Istanbul, therefore, undoubtedly represents a very major portion of the private industrial sector in Turkey. We should also mention that the sample was stratified according to size and sub-sector to assure adequate representation for all groups.

It will be particularly useful to review the results of the survey with regard to opinions on the role of the government in solving problems; problems with the state per se (public service, government offices, municipalities); and problems and preferences

---

5 *Tercüman* (Istanbul daily), 24 August 1985.

6 *Tercüman*, 24 August 1985. Our translation.

7 Yılmaz Esmer, Hamit Fişek, Ersin Kalaycıoğlu, Süleyman Özmucur, *İş Dünyasının Sorunları. Öncelikler, Beklentiler ve Çözümler* (İstanbul: TÜSİAD, 1987).

8 Ibid., p. 2.

concerning associational groups that 'represent' the sector. Table 9.8 gives the percentages of firms mentioning certain problems as the 'most important' and 'one of the four important' that they are faced with. The last column gives the proportion of those owners/managers who expect some kind of direct governmental action for the solution of a particular problem.

Table 9.8: Most Important Problems Faced by Industrial Firms

Problem	Most Important	One of Four Most Important	Governmental Action Mentioned (Among 3 solutions)
Short term finance	31.0	42.1	78.4
Long term finance	6.3	20.4	77.2
Personnel	19.2	37.3	15.3
Marketing	5.1	17.0	20.4
Exporting	5.2	20.3	135.1
Importing	2.5	15.3	182.8
Other firms	1.6	10.8	71.9
Production	9.5	26.2	52.9
Investments	2.6	27.0	92.6
Public services	2.5	15.8	
Government office	3.5	4.9	
Municipalities	3.5	16.1	
Associations	0.4	4.9	

Source: Yılmaz Esmer, Hamit Fişek, Ersin Kalaycıoğlu and Süleyman Özmucur, *İş Dünyasının Sorunları. Öncelikler, Beklentiler, Sorunlar* (İstanbul: TÜSİAD, 1984).

The data presented in Table 9.8 lead us to the following conclusions. First, the percentage of industrial firms that see the state or its agents as the source of their most important problems, is not very significant. Even when we consider column 2, we observe that only 5 per cent of the total sample regard problems with government offices as one of their four major woes. Municipalities, a constant source of complaint, are mentioned only by 16 per cent as one of the four problems. We shall deal with the nature of these problems below. Secondly, some sort of governmental action is deemed to be necessary for the solution of almost every problem.[9] With the notable exception of personnel and marketing, the Turkish industrial sector expects the state to alleviate or solve its problems in all areas. This attitude is not very different from

[9] The percentages in the last column of Table 9.8 can exceed 100.0 since many firms mention more than one kind of governmental action for the solution of a problem.

that of the ordinary citizen who expects much more than his Western counterpart from the 'paternal State'. Thirdly, The proportion of firms that mention the associations which represent them - compulsorily or voluntarily - as a source of problem is very low. Is this because there are no problems in interest articulation and representation by these associations or because not much is expected from this mode of interest group activity? One wonders.

Table 9.9 : Problems Related to Public Services (%)

Inadequacy of energy	22.2
Price of energy	19.2
Clean water	4.0
Industrial wastes	6.1
Inadequacy of postal and telephone service	11.1
Inadequacy of transportation service	23.2
Other problems	14.1

Source: Esmer, et.al., *İş Dünyasının Sorunları.*

Table 9.10 : Problems Related to Government Offices (%)

Regulations and by-laws	22.6
Attitude and behaviour of higher level bureaucrats	9.7
Knowledge and adequacy of higher level bureaucrats	3.2
Attitude and behaviour of lower level bureaucrats	12.4
Knowledge and adequacy of lower level bureaucrats	5.9
Slow operation of the system	19.4
Redtape	21.5
Other problems	5.4

Source: Esmer, et.al., *İş Dünyasının Sorunları.*

Tables 9.9, 9.10 and 9.11, reproduced from the TÜSİAD study, summarize the nature of the problems directly related to the state. It is also interesting that even the representatives of the private industrial sector hardly mention privatization, for example, as a solution to energy or other infra-structural problems and inadequacies. The solutions for problems related to public services are sought not in radical reforms, such as the privatization of the enterprises that provide these services, but rather in the minor adjustments to be effected by the public enterprises themselves.[10]

10 Esmer et al., *İş Dünyasının Sorunları*, p. 55.

Table 9.11: Problems Related to Municipalities (%)

Decisions and actions of local administrations	32.2
Regulations and by-laws	18.8
Attitude and behaviour of higher level bureaucrats	5.4
Knowledge and adequacy of higher level officers	1.3
Attitude and behaviour of lower level bureaucrats	12.8
Knowledge and adequacy of lower level bureaucrats	3.4
Slow operation of the system	8.1
Redtape	8.1
Other problems	10.1

Source: Esmer, et.al., *İş Dünyasının Sorunları.*

Table 9.12 is especially instructive within this context. Only 2 per cent of the sample believe that the involvement of private enterprises is a solution to the problems related to public services.

Table 9.12: Solutions Mentioned to Problems Related to Public Services (%)

Reducing redtape	38.0
More public investments in these services	31.0
More concern by local administrations	20.0
Involvement of private sector	2.0
Privatization of enterprises providing public services	2.0
Other	7.0

Source: Esmer, et. al., *İş Dünyasının Sorunları.*

We know that in terms of GDP, value added and the number of persons employed, the private industrial sector in Turkey is a major economic force. We have also shown that this sector expects a great deal from the state, and believes that the solution to many of their problems lies with the state. What kinds of structures, then, exist to formulate the interests of the Turkish private industrial sector? In what terms are these interests formulated? Through what channels are they made known?

We have already noted that, in the Turkish case, both 'voluntary, competitive, non-hierarchically ordered, self- determined' and 'compulsory, non-competitive, hierarchically ordered' organizations exist and play a role. Indeed, not infrequently, these associations disagree on which is the 'legitimate' representative of the sector. The present situation, undoubtedly, is neither corporatist nor pluralist. Are current developments likely to favour one of these models in the near future? The TÜSİAD study, from which we have quoted extensively, asked respondents whether they favoured voluntary or compulsory membership associations to represent the private sector. 31 per cent replied that membership should be compulsory, 59 per cent favoured voluntary membership, and 9.9 per cent said both types should exist.[11] Judging by these data and also by the fact that some voluntary organizations have already been recognized by all parties concerned as legitimate interest groups, perhaps a transition to the pluralist model can be forseen. However, there is no question that it is yet too early to reach a final verdict.

Is Papa Alive and Well?

It is clear that interest group politics in Turkey cannot be fully understood without a careful consideration of the long tradition of a strong and dominant State that, according to some authors, could define public interest independently of social elites and interest groups. The image of a 'paternal State' is still very strong in the minds of Turks. They still expect the state to intervene directly and solve a wide variety of problems - from dealing with the housing shortage or protecting the family to controlling prices. We have already seen that even the representatives of the private industrial sector are a part of this strong tradition. To many, the term 'interest group' still has a pejorative meaning. It is not right, many feel, to speak about group interests, and the only legitimate interest is 'public interest' that can best be defined by the State.

This tradition poses a radically different conception of interest group politics in Turkey, and severely limits the applicability of both pluralist and corporatist models. However, it is also true that Turkish society has been undergoing important changes within the last decade. The major question, then, is the degree to which these recent developments have altered the old perceptions.

Up to this point we have mentioned only two major organizations that 'represent' the interests of the Turkish industrial sector: the chambers of industry and TÜSİAD. Although others - such as the Turkish Confederation of Employers' Unions, Council of Free Enterprise - could be mentioned within this context, a survey of the press since 1983 reveals that almost all statements made in the name of the industrial sector bear the signature of one of these two associations and their leaders. The interesting development of the last decade is the recognition of TÜSİAD - a voluntary organization that is not founded by law - as a legitimate representative of the interests of large industrialists. The following comments by the columnist Metin Toker are extremely interesting:

> Today, at a period when democracy is developing and the economy is being debated, there is great need for the TÜSİAD-like voices....TÜSİAD is an association whose duty is to be the spokesman for the interests of not only one particular section [of the private sector] but of the much conflicting interests of all sections of the private sector....A TÜSİAD, a Türk-İş [Confederation of Turkish Trade Unions], an association of artisans and craftsmen, and perhaps a consumers' protection association like the ones found in the West, are crucially valuable in the debates on the economy.[12]

Another columnist, Mehmet Barlas, writes that 'TÜSİAD is an organization based

11 Ibid., p. 64.

12 Metin Toker, *Milliyet* (Istanbul daily), 27 January 1986.

on the pressure group model and founded to protect the interests of Turkish [private] capital'.[13] But the press can still be hesitant about openly calling an organization an interest group:

> A *concealed* [our underlining] pressure group or the club of bosses, however it is called, every publication, every statement of TÜSİAD is first-page news in the daily papers. Their chairmen are at least as well-known as the most popular actors. Being a member of TÜSİAD - the cream of the business world - is a status symbol....[14]

We are devoting so much attention to TÜSİAD because it is the first example of an explicit interest group that is voluntary and that has gained so much prominence. The above quotation is very interesting in this respect. It recognizes the importance of TÜSİAD, but questions whether it is legitimate for an interest group to have so much say in public affairs. Is it acceptable for such an organization to be directly involved in politics? The following comment by the former chairman of the Istanbul Chamber of Industry clearly shows that - despite the recent developments - Turkey is still a long way from understanding and accepting the pluralist model: 'TÜSİAD... has become harmful for the Turkish economy. This association should be closed without wasting any time.'[15]

In conclusion, although it is impossible to say that there are unlimited numbers of voluntary, competitive organizations representing or intermediating the interests of the industrial sector, there are attempts in this direction and at least one voluntary association is changing the scene.

How are group interests expressed? At least in public statements, group interests are almost always justified by general societal interests. These words of Mr Ersin Faralyalı, former president of the Turkish Union of Chambers and Stock Exchanges, uttered at a meeting of the Union, are typical: 'On this rostrum, we must first express the interests of our country and then the interests of the private sector and the difficulties we are faced with.'[16] In a similar statement, the Chairman of TÜSİAD said: 'If the government policies and our beliefs are... conflicting and if we see that they [government policies] are developing in the opposite direction to this country's interests, then we must let public opinion know about this situation through the press.'[17] It is very seldom one comes across to a statement which is explicit about defending the interests of one social group only, regardless of the implications for the general public.

What are the channels and means of access for the interest groups? There is no doubt that personal connections are still a very important and effective channel, and are resorted to very often. Elite representation is also not uncommon. However, it seems that increased importance is being attached to reasoned arguments based on research findings. Both the chambers of industry - especially the Istanbul Chamber of Industry - and TÜSİAD support and publish the results of research by independent academicians. The latter, for example, supports resarch projects in such diverse fields

---

13 Mehmet Barlas, *Güneş* (Istanbul daily), 28 January 1986.
14 *Güneş*, 24 April 1988. Our translation.
15 *Güneş*, 20 January 1988.
16 *Güneş*, 2 April 1988.
17 *Nokta* (Istanbul weekly), 22 February 1987.

as traffic, foreign debts, or the economic potential of Turkish businessmen in Germany. The findings of these research projects are published, and very often presented in press conferences as well. Some of these reports become the source of heated debates. It is not unusual for a cabinet minister to issue a statement to support or criticize the results. It is too early to say that reasoned arguments based on solid research have become the most important channel of interest articulation. We cannot, however, ignore the fact that there is a tendency in this direction. At least, certain groups feel the need to support their demands by research.

Finally, what are the styles of interest articulation and how specific are the demands made? Our survey of the press shows that there is a tendency in the direction of more specific demands. Many of the statements made by industrial leaders and associations contain very specific demands about interest rates, subsidies, public borrowing, foreign trade regulations, and the like. But emotional ('affective') rather than to the point ('instrumental') statements are not infrequent. The following comments by the former chairman of the Istanbul Chamber of Industry provide an example:

> Who is the boss of export incentives? There is a committee at the State Planning Organization and then there is the Undersecretary of Treasury and Foreign Trade. It is being said that an office at the Undersecretarial level will be formed. There is an indeterminancy. Ankara is trying to divide. That cannot be. That was late [İsmet] İnönü's policy. Divide and rule. We must be careful against this, and stick together.[18]

Conclusion

We have tried to answer a number of important questions to determine the nature of interest group politics in Turkey, limiting ourselves to the industrial sector and the post-1983 period. Our conclusion is ambivalent, if not ambiguous: interest group activities in the industrial sector bear *resemblances* to both the corporatist and the pluralist models. However, one can easily observe the deep effects of Turkey's long tradition of a strong State. This crucial variable forces us to consider the Turkish situation as distinct from either one of these forms. Nevertheless, some rudimentary signs of pluralist development in recent years cannot be ignored.

---

[18] *Cumhuriyet* (Istanbul daily), 20 February 1987. Our translation. İsmet İnönü was second President of Turkey.

10

Politics and Big Business: Janus-Faced Link to the State

Yeşim Arat

Introduction

On 2 April 1971, twelve leading industrialists of the country issued a memorandum announcing the foundation of the first voluntary business association in Turkey: the Turkish Industrialists' and Businessmen's Association (TÜSİAD). Until then, business was organized into chambers such that membership was compulsory and goverment control tighter.[1] Yet, the impact of the memorandum was negligible. It did not even have the news value to be reported in Turkish dailies.[2]

By the 1980s, the situation had changed. TÜSİAD, by then called the 'Club of the Rich', was perceived by some as 'the Association that toppled the goverment'.[3] Although many doubted its legitimacy, TÜSİAD was a most visible, if not formal, representative of the private sector. Newspapers posed the question: 'Does TÜSİAD with its 200 or so members, or the Turkish Union of Chambers and Stock Exchange (TOBB) with its half a million members, represent the Turkish private sector?'[4] Businessmen who were not TÜSİAD members argued that the Association could speak only in the interest of big capital and that it should not claim to represent the interests of the Turkish private sector as a whole.[5]

Others charged that TÜSİAD was violating the law because the 1982 Constitution prohibited associations from engaging in politics - something that TÜSİAD clearly did. It was also claimed that the government followed TÜSİAD's advice instead of the formal representatives of business and commerce, such as the Istanbul Chamber of Commerce or the Turkish Union of Chambers.[6]

Did TÜSİAD have the power or influence it was alleged to have ? To throw some light on this question, I shall try to delineate the opportunities TÜSİAD had, and the constraints it faced, in its efforts to promote the interests of its members.

---

1 On the nature and evolution of organized interests in Turkey, see Robert Bianchi, *Interest Groups and Political Development in Turkey*, (Princeton: Princeton University Press, 1984); İlkay Sunar, 'Redemocratization and Organized Interests in Turkey', paper presented at workshop on 'Organised Interests and Democratic Consolidation in Southern Europe', Florence, Italy, 18-20 June 1987.

2 Istanbul dailies, *Cumhuriyet, Hürriyet and Milliyet* were surveyed. There was no coverage of TÜSİAD's founding.

3 *Hürriyet*, 21 January 1988.

4 *Cumhuriyet*, 20 May 1986 and interview with Mr Ali Coşkun, the then President of the Turkish Union of Chambers, in *Cumhuriyet*, 8 June 1986.

5 *Cumhuriyet*, 20 May 1986.

6 *Cumhuriyet* 13 February 1987.

The goals, if not the functions, of the Association changed over time. In the late 1970s, TÜSİAD sought a new government that could stabilize the economy and provide the crucial foreign exchange needed at the time. By the mid-1980s, the issue at stake was low cost credits. TÜSİAD, which was founded to strengthen big business against small business, now had to defend the interests of the big industrialists against the exporters.

Economic and political contingencies essentially helped to shape the Association's goals and at the same time limited its influence. In the late 1970s, TÜSİAD had to lobby for a new government because of the economic crises of import substitution industrialization (ISI) and the political crises of unstable governments. In the event, a military government was installed. By the mid-1980s, when a civilian government effectively put its stamp on politics, TÜSİAD had to bargain with that government, which allegedly supported private enterprise, yet, at least in the short run, opted for policies adverse to the interests of big industrialists. Ironically, TÜSİAD's links to the government set limits on how far the Association could influence the government. Members of the TÜSİAD community assumed important positions in the government, including the premiership (Turgut Özal). Government, however, came to have significant autonomy from the wishes of its constituents.

Establishment of TÜSİAD

TÜSİAD was founded because within the TOBB the big industrialists did not have the weight they thought they deserved. Before TÜSİAD was set up, big industrialists were members of the Chambers of Industry where the State enforced membership. Within the Chambers, there were conflicts of interest between the small number of big industrialists, mostly from Istanbul, and the large number of small industrialists from the periphery.[7] The big industrialists could afford more liberal economic measures and a less protected economy. They sought a higher share of scarce foreign exchange and credits to finance their large-scale operations. Unlike the small industrialists, they could afford higher wages. Because they were engaged in the production of durable consumer goods, they preferred levels of income that could support increasing internal demand. Lower wages would threaten the domestic market on which they were dependent to sell their goods. As members of the Chambers of Industry, they belonged to TOBB, the umbrella organization of Chambers of Industry, Commerce, and Stock Exchanges. The TOBB could not provide a platform to express the demands of the big industrialists against those of the commercial interests that dominated the Union.[8] Perhaps more importantly, the particular structure of the Chambers had lost its allure as a means of access to further economic and political gains; the Justice Party, which

---

7 Bianchi, *Interest Groups and Political Development in Turkey*, pp. 268-9.

8 Ibid. On the cleavages between Chambers of Industry and Chambers of Commerce, see Ayşe Öncü, 'Chambers of Industry in Turkey: An Inquiry into State-Industry Relations as a Distributive Domain', in *The Political Economy of Income Distribution in Turkey*, Ergun Özbudun and Aydın Ulusan, eds. (New York: Holmes and Meier, 1980). On the differences between big industrialists and other employer groups, also see Ziya Öniş and Ersin Kalaycıoğlu, both in this volume (Editor's note).

had been in power since 1965, had undermined the importing privileges of the Chambers before it was ousted by the military in 1971. After the military intervened, the Chambers lost their rights to allocate foreign exchange.[9]

Under those circumstances one of the two leading industrialists in the country, Mr Vehbi Koç, took the initiative to found TÜSİAD. Eleven others followed him in signing 'The TÜSİAD Founders Memorandum'.[10] Accordingly, it was hoped, the Association would contribute to Turkey's achieving the standards of living and industrialization already attained by the Western developed world.[11] Industrialists would be the 'leading power' in this development process.[12]

Beyond these resolutions, as mentioned above, the Association aimed to promote the interests of big business against the small entrepreneurs.[13] Big business could afford to pay higher wages than more labour-intensive smaller businesses. The strategy of the Association, entailed collaboration with labour. Prominent spokesmen of the Association, such as Mr Vehbi Koç and Mr Ertuğrul Soysal, were making conciliatory statements towards demands from labour. Unlike the Turkish Confederation of Employers Unions, TÜSİAD did not have a militant stance against trade unions and high wages the latter asked for.[14]

Organizational Characteristics

TÜSİAD is a small association with select membership. On 2 August 1971, eighty-six big industrialists signed the letter propagating the 'Aims and Views' of the newly established Association. By 1987, there were two hundred and forty-three members. According to the by-laws, the board of directors decides on who can become a member. Even though the criteria of admission have never been explicity stated, big industrialists rather than traders, even when the latter are rich, are preferred.

In 1985, the share of TÜSİAD members in production and employment within the top hundred industrial organizations in Turkey reached 80 per cent.[15] TÜSİAD members now represent about one thousand associate companies. As such, the Association accounts for about half the production and employment of (private) manufacturing industry. Because leading industrialists also own banks, a large proportion of the private

---

9 Atilla Eralp, 'The Politics of Turkish Development Strategies', in *Turkish State, Turkish Society*, Andrew Finkel and Nükhet Sirman, eds. (London: Routledge, 1990).

10 The twelve industrialists who signed the 'The TÜSİAD Founders Memorandum' were: Mr Vehbi Koç of Koç Holding Company (HC), Dr Nejat Eczacıbaşı of Eczacıbaşı HC, Mr Sakıp Sabancı of Hacı Ömer HC, Mr Selçuk Yaşar of Yaşar HC, Mr Raşit Özsaruhan of Metaş Joint Stock Company (JSC), Mr Ahmet Sapmaz of Güney Industries JSC, Mr Feyyaz Berker of Tekfen JSC, Mr Melih Özakat of Automotive JSC, Mr İbrahim Bodur of Çanakkale Ceramics, Mr Hikmet Erenyol of Electro-Metallurgy JSC, Mr Osman Boyner of Altınyıldız Textiles JSC, Mr Muzaffer Gazioğlu of Cement Industries JSC.

11 'The TÜSİAD Founders Memorandum', 2 April 1971.

12 The TÜSİAD by-laws, as reprinted in *TÜSİAD 1979 Yılı Çalışmaları* (İstanbul: TÜSİAD, 1980), p.3.

13 Bianchi, *Interest Groups and Political Development in Turkey*, pp. 261, 269-71.

14 Ibid, pp. 270-71.

15 Mustafa Sönmez, *Kırk Haramiler. Türkiye'de Holdingler* (İstanbul: Gözlem, 1987), p. 162.

sector banking community as well as insurance companies, construction companies and other service sectors are represented.[16]

A small selective membership has its advantages. Because only big industrialists or their representatives are admitted to TÜSİAD, it has a strong financial base. Not every member pays the same. The board of directors decides on the fee when a new member is admitted. In 1988, the lowest membership fee was 4 million Turkish Liras, or then approximately 2,700 U.S. dollars. Mr Koç and Mr Sakıp Sabancı, the two biggest industrialists of the country, were each paying 60 million Turkish Liras, or approximately 40,000 U.S. dollars.[17] The substantial revenue base of the Association is apparent from its costly public activities.

The small selective membership also ensures homogeneity. As already noted, the Association comprises big entrepreneurs - mostly industrialists. Relative homogeneity of membership means relative homogeneity of interests regarding which macro-economic policies to support. The members personally know each other, and have voluntarily come together in TÜSİAD. Yet, cleavages exist. At times, exporters and domestic market-oriented industrialists have been in conflict with one another regarding the policies TÜSİAD would support. In a 1984 TÜSİAD general assembly meeting, Mr Halit Narin, a leading textile industrialist, was highly critical of government policies which favoured exporters over the investing industrialists. For the exporters, Mr Atilla Yurtçu of İzdaş Holding Company and Mr Şarık Tara of Enka Holding Company opposed Mr Narin in support of export promotions. The dispute was duly covered in the Turkish press.[18]

Even amongst the big industrialists,size differences were not irrelevant. The bigger industrialists could at least for some time afford to live with policies that were not particularly favourable to them, whereas the smaller ones could not. For example, in the 1987 TÜSİAD general assembly, Mr Sabancı argued that the industrialists had to learn to live with inflation, whereas Mr Ömer Dinçkök was adamantly opposed to the suggestion.[19]

Yet these differences of interest were not significant enough to undermine the basic homogeneity of the Association. It is true that selection of members and payment of dues were clearly not based on democratic processes. Yet one could talk of a consensual democracy in the way decisions were reached and policies made. Informal briefings and social contacts among members allowed for decisions that were supported by virtually all members. The Association was voluntary; there were no resignations.

TÜSİAD was led by eminent businessmen who had clout in the business world. There was a continuity of leadership because those whose term of office ended were re-elected to the high level decision-making bodies. Mr Feyyaz Berker of Tekfen Group of Companies presided over the Association during its first decade, between 1971 and 1980. Mr Ali Koçman of Koçtuğ Shipping Group (1980-1984), Mr Şahap Kocatopçu, a professional manager of Koç Group of Companies (1984-1985), and Mr Sabancı of Sabancı Group of Companies (1985-1987), and Mr Ömer Dinçkök of Akkök Group

16 TÜSİAD, *The Turkish Economy* (Istanbul: TÜSİAD, 1987).

17 *Cumhuriyet* 21 May 1988.

18 *Inter alia, Rapor* (Istanbul monthly), 21 January 1984.

19 *Cumhuriyet*, 13 November 1987; 15 November 1987.

of Companies (1987-1989), followed. Members of the High Advisory Council and the Council of Presidency were also eminent industrialists who were mostly re-elected to their positions.[20] Candidates for leadership positions were decided informally amongst a small circle without any open competition.

With a small and cohesive membership, a strong financial base and powerful leadership, TÜSİAD was well equipped to pursue its goals. The Association primarily disseminated information to shape public opinion. Its publications included reports on the State of the economy and government policies (including development plans and state budgets), sector studies, and a monthly review, *Görüş*. Its publications were widely distributed; they were sent to the members of the Cabinet and Parliament, higher civil servants, private sector executives, academics and journalists. Conferences, seminars and dinners were arranged to discuss economic issues. In a country where resources to disseminate information on public policies or economic and political questions are scarce, the impact of TÜSİAD's activities reverberated. TÜSİAD cultivated links with foreign business associations and chambers of commerce and industry, and thus further enhanced its relative status in domestic politics.[21]

Because of its economic power, it came to have a wide audience. TÜSİAD publications and activities were duly reported. Daily newspapers and other publications of differing persuasions gave wide coverage to the Club of the Rich.

Economic and Political Crises and TÜSİAD

TÜSİAD's prominence and activities increased over the years. The economic and political crises of the late 1970s constituted a turning point. The political stance the Association assumed against the government was unprecedented in Turkish political life. Thus, it gave rise to the perception that 'the Association toppled governments'.

Economic and political crises characterized the late 1970s. The ISI that defined post-World War II Turkish economic development had reached an impasse. Foreign exchange that was a necessary if not a sufficient condition of ISI was not available.[22]

Without foreign exchange, oil and other necessary inputs could not be imported. Industrial production came to a halt. Yet the industrialists had to continue to pay wages and their fixed costs.[23] In 1979, gross domestic product (GDP) fell by 0.4 per cent

---

20 For example, since 1982 only 7 members of the High Advisory Council (elected annually by the General Assembly and composed of eighty members until 1984 and sixty members since then) changed. Among the members of the Board of Directors, in 1985 six out of eleven members and in 1986 seven out of eleven members changed. All the newcomers were prominent businessmen or industrialists who had been involved in the founding of the Association. Data from *TÜSİAD Çalışmaları* for the years 1982- 1986.

21 On the constitutional standing of voluntary associations, see Ergun Özbudun in this volume. Also see Taha Parla and Ayşe Öncü, 'Militarism and Corporatism in Turkish Politics', unpublished manuscript, 1987.

22 Şevket Pamuk, 'İthal İkamesi, Döviz Darboğazları ve Türkiye, 1947-1979', in *Kriz, Gelir Dağılımı ve Türkiye'nin Alternatif Sorunu*, Şevket Pamuk, Korkut Boratav, Çağlar Keyder, eds. (İstanbul: Kaynak, 1987).

23 Çağlar Keyder, *State and Class in Turkey. A Study in Capitalist Development* (London: Verso 1987), pp. 188-96.

and industrial production went down by 5.4 per cent.[24] The rate of private investment continued to decline from 11.8 in 1977 to 11.1 in 1978 and to 9.7 in 1979.[25]

During 1978-1979, when the Social Democrats under Mr Bülent Ecevit were in goverment, shortages of essential goods prevailed. There were frequent power cuts and long lines in front of petrol stations and grocery stores. Scarcity of the basic items of consumption led to hoarding, smuggling and a large black market.

The economic crisis was accompanied by a political crisis. Political parties were polarized, and this polarization at the top fuelled the politization of the polity as a whole. Confrontations between the radical Right and the radical Left resulted in mounting violence. The death toll increased from about 200 in 1977 to 800-1,000 in 1978 to 1,500 in 1979.[26] The security forces of the state were ineffective against the militant Right and Left that clashed in the streets.[27] Finally, Parliament was paralyzed, unable even to elect a president.

In response to economic and political deterioration, TÜSİAD made its most visible public move to demand a change in the political-economic system. An unprecedented campaign to mobilize public support began. During a period of four weeks in May and June of 1979, four full page advertisements were published in seven newspapers and a weekly journal. 'Realistic Exit', 'The Nation is Waiting', 'Sharing Scarcity or Providing Plenty?', 'The Enemy of Welfare and Liberties', were the four captions under which the prevailing socio-economic and political problems were discussed.[28] All the socio-economic ills, namely the inability to export, scarcity of foreign exchange, necessity to import, insufficient energy, population growth, unemployment and inflation, were recounted, and policies that should be adopted were advocated: free enterprise encouraged, government controls abolished, the economy liberalized, state economic enterprises rendered more efficient, tax reform undertaken, less money printed and freedom of economic initiative respected.

In each of the four messages, there was a section in a box at the corner which stated TÜSİAD's primary mission:

> We, as members of the Turkish private sector, declare that the main force that will improve our welfare in a system of liberal democracy is free enterprise - free enterprise that has always prompted the individual to work harder and more productively. The developed nations of our age reached prosperity under conditions of freedom.... There is no alternative path.[29]

Even though their role in the consequent unfolding of events may have been limited, TÜSİAD's messages made a vibrant impact. In Turkey's State-centred polity neither big business nor any other group had earlier been engaged in such all-out confrontation

---

24 Korkut Boratav and Oktar Türel, 'Notes on the Current Development Problems and Growth Prospects of the Turkish Economy', *New Perspectives on Turkey*, 9 (1988), p. 38.

25 Ibid.

26 C.H.Dodd, *The Crisis of Turkish Democracy* (Walkington, England: The Eothen Press, 1983), p.7.

27 Kemal H. Karpat, 'Turkish Democracy at Impasse: Ideology, Party Politics and the Third Military Intervention', *International Journal of Turkish Studies*, 2 (1981), pp.1-43 and Lucille W. Pevsner, *Turkey's Political Crisis* (New York: Praeger, 1984), pp. 68-73.

28 TÜSİAD, *1979 Yılı Çalışmaları*, passim.

29 Ibid.

with the government. There was no tradition of organized interests pressuring government by public appeals. Big business had now deemed it necessary to invest in this singular political campaign. Both the nature of the campaign and the contents of the messages were subjected to intense scrutiny by the press. They were also reported on the radio and television.

Political Efficacy of TÜSİAD

In November 1979, the Ecevit government resigned, and the centre-right Justice Party under Mr Süleyman Demirel came to power. On 24 January 1980, about six months after TÜSİAD's public denouncement of the Social Democratic government, the new government introduced a new and radical package to stabilize and liberalize the economy in the general direction advocated by TÜSİAD.

Mr Turgut Özal, at the time Under-Secretary of the Prime Ministry, played a key role in the preparation of this stabilization programme. As a former member of TÜSİAD, one time President of the Metal Industry Industrialists Union, and a top-level executive in Sabancı Holding Company, Mr Özal was well attuned to the interests of the private sector and was a firm proponent of liberal economic policies.

The primary intention of the stabilization programme was to allow the price mechanism to regulate supply and demand. Markets would set the prices for goods and services which, under the prevailing conditions, meant an attempt to control demand and rampant inflation. Equally important, there was a move to adopt an export-oriented growth model to replace the ISI. Without the necessary political and social infrastructure, the prospects for the success of the economic package were dim, but the step was nevertheless taken.

On 12 September 1980, the military stepped in. Now, political violence and terrorism could be controlled. Politically unattractive measures, necessitated by the stabilization and liberalization policies, could be adopted. In fact, the activities of trade unions, the press, universities and voluntary associations were soon duly restricted. Reminiscent at least on the surface of the 'bureaucratic authoritarian model'[30] the military that came to power, though it had not stepped in to facilitate the 'deepening' of the economic structure, nevertheless provided the political framework in which the technocratic elite could make the export-oriented growth model work.

The military endorsed the economic policies favoured by the private sector, in general, and big business, in particular. Big business was thankful yet cautious. In this context, the letter that Mr Vehbi Koç sent to the new Head of State and ex-Chief of the General Staff, General Kenan Evren, on 3 October 1980, less than a month after the military intervened, is revealing.[31] In a section entitled 'What Should be Paid Attention To', the first point he made was that the military should be careful not to get bogged down in politics. He emphasized that it was therefore 'necessary for the army to return to the barracks after the major legislative adjustments were made'. Unless

30 Guillermo O'Donnell, *Modernization and Bureaucratic Authoritarianism. Studies in South American Politics* (Berkeley: University of California Press, 1973).
31 Sönmez, *Kırk Haramiler. Türkiye'de Holdingler*, pp. 346- 52.

there was a return to democracy, Mr Koç continued, links with the West would be jeopardized: 'Western countries and their institutions will be suspicious, and will not deliver their promises.'[32] Big business had been interested in opening up the economy to the West and felt threatened by the prospect of long-term military rule.

A year later, on 5 September 1981, Mr Ali Koçman, the then Chairman of TÜSİAD, expressed his 'gratitude to the 12 September operation' in the name of the Association, but listed a host of lingering economic problems including inflation, inefficiency of state economic enterprises and the problems of the industrial and banking sectors.[33] The Association was content to have the military step in, but economic ills were not necessarily relieved.[34] A technocratic civilian government could be more efficient in attacking economic problems. Big business, presumably, could have more leverage under a civilian government. Power that was vested in the military implied uncertainties regarding public policy choices. After all, in 1982 Mr Özal, the architect of the economic stabilization policies, had to resign because the military was in favour of less market-oriented policies following the crash in the money market.

When in 1983 Mr Özal and his Motherland Party came to power as a result of circumscribed elections,[35] they attempted to rationalize the economic system essentially along the lines TÜSİAD had proposed. To promote an export-oriented model of growth, radical measures were taken. Foreign exchange operations were greatly liberalized; the Turkish lira was further devalued; and price controls on state economic enterprises were relaxed, if not entirely abolished. A tight monetary policy to control internal demand and curb inflation was adopted. New tax laws and controls on wages (made possible by restricting the activities of the trade unions) and salaries changed the distribution of income against the middle and lower classes.[36] This helped to control internal demand, and encourage exports. The government provided more direct support to the exporters through tax exemptions and low-cost credit. Big industrialists that could find markets abroad would benefit from those policies. For industrialists who sought foreign exchange, the Özal government had the right credentials - a centre-right ideology, successful implementation of stabilization policies, a pro-market stance - to obtain the crucial funding from abroad. So, early in Mr Özal's term of office, big business was content and willing to wait for a favourable business climate.[37] The economic and political crises of the late 1970s were over. The economy had started growing again; inflation, though not as low as they had hoped, appeared to be under control; perhaps more crucially, once again foreign exchange became available. Had TÜSİAD attained

---

32 Ibid.

33 *Görüş*, 9 (1981), pp.5-11.

34 *Görüş*, 11 (1983), pp.9-18.

35 The military was keen to supervise the nature of the transition to civilian rule. The National Security Council had the right to veto party members and candidates. Restrictions were imposed for parties interested in partaking in the 1983 elections. Each party had to organize in at least half the provinces and in one third of the districts within those provinces. Some candidates were vetoed. See John H. McFadden, 'Civil-Military Relations in the Third Turkish Republic', *The Middle East Journal*, 39 (1985), pp.73-5.

36 Korkut Boratav, *Stabilization and Adjustment Programmes and Policies. Country Study-Turkey* (Helsinki: WIDER, 1987), pp. 14-24. Also see Oğuz Oyan, *24 Ocak Ekonomisinde Dışa Açılma ve Mali Politikalar* (Ankara : V Yayınları, 1987), pp. 56-65.

37 *Görüş*, 12 (1984), passim.

its goal ? Had it outlived its mission ?

Unique economic and political conditions accounted for the structural changes TÜSİAD sought to bring about. Economically, by the late 1970s, the ISI, if not exhausted, had come to the end of road. This economic model could not earn the foreign exchange which was necessary to keep it going. The oil crisis of the mid-1970s had precipitated a worldwide recession; the ISI efforts of other industrializing countries were already set back. Remittances from migrant workers in Europe, and later short-term borrowing with high interest rates from international banks, had deferred the crisis until the late 1970s.[38] There was now a need for a strategy of economic growth which could ensure a steady supply of foreign exchange. Either an export-oriented growth model was going to be adopted, or else foreign exchange had to be borrowed from abroad with the proper policies, that is, a stabilization package and a liberal and market-oriented ideology.

In addition to and quite independent from economic factors, political factors also necessitated change. The decade of the 1970s was characterized by a fragmented and eventually polarized political system. Despite the proliferation of smaller parties on the Right and the Left, the Justice Party (JP) of the centre-right and the Republican People's Party (RPP) of the centre-left were the two predominant political parties.[39] Yet, neither in the 1973 general elections (where RPP received 33.3 and JP 29.8 per cent of the votes) nor in the 1977 general elections (where RPP received 41.4 and JP 36.9 percent of the votes) could a single party emerge to form a majority government and lead the country out of economic and political crises.

During the 1970-1980 period, twelve unstable governments were formed in the context of an increasingly polarized and politicized polity. In Samuel P. Huntington's terminology,[40] political institutions were unable to channel political participation and discontent and there was no political will to impose political stability. In 1980, the JP government under Mr Demirel initiated the economic stabilization policies that would lead to structural change in the economy; however, it is questionable whether the exclusionary regime these policies implied could be brought about without a reconstruction of political space.

Hence the military intervention was crucial in restructuring the polity where political will could be exercised, if at the cost of political participation. In the process, the arena in which politics could take place was circumscribed. The (new) 1982 Constitution enhanced the power of the executive.[41] The president was now endowed with powers that would make him more effective against parliament and the political parties. The power of the government to pass decree-laws was increased. Perhaps more importantly, the

---

[38] Pamuk, 'İthal İkamesi, Döviz Darboğazları ve Türkiye, 1947- 1979', passim.

[39] Ergun Özbudun, 'Political Parties and Elections', in *Türkei Sudosteurope-Handbuch, Band IV*, Klaus-Detlev Grothusen, ed. (Gottingen: Vandenhoeck und Ruprecht, 1985), pp. 269-72.

[40] Samuel P. Huntington, *Political Order in Changing Societies* (New Haven: Yale University Press, 1968).

[41] Özbudun, 'Political Parties and Elections', pp.273-75 and Ersin Kalaycıoğlu, 'Turkish Political System in Transition: Multi-Party Politics in the 1980s', *Current Turkish Thought*, 56 (1985), pp. 16-22, For an overview, see Taha Parla, *Demokrasi, Anayasalar, Partiler ve Türkiye'nin Siyasal Rejimi*, (İstanbul: Onur, 1986) and Parla and Öncü, 'Militarism and Corporatism in Turkish Politics'.

new electoral laws made it easier for governments to have a parliamentary majority. The proportional representation formula was modified to provide additional seats to the party with most votes. A minimum of 10 per cent of the nation-wide vote was required for political parties to return members to parliament. A similar barrier was instituted in each electoral district.

The new Constitution allowed the State to extend its control over civil society. As Ergun Özbudun in this volume elaborates, the organization and activities of interest groups (trade unions, chambers, voluntary associations) were restricted. Strikes and collective bargaining practices of trade unions were circumscribed. The establishment and membership of associations became subject to close supervision and bureaucratic controls by the state. There was a ban on so-called 'political activities'. Political parties and interest groups were officially divorced.

These measures, especially the way they were implemented - being applied more stringently to trade unions than to business associations - could in effect curtail demands coming from the masses. Under these circumstances, a centre-right coalition of middle and upper middle classes could bring to power a government ready to implement the new growth strategy.

When the Motherland Party under Mr Özal came to power in 1983, TÜSİAD was particularly receptive. The Prime Minister, himself earlier a TÜSİAD member, had twenty ministers in his Cabinet, of which sixteen had worked in the private sector. The Ministers of Justice, Finance and Customs and a Minister of State had close ties with Enka Holding Company, and another Minister of State with Sabancı Group; both the Company and the Group have been leading TÜSİAD members. TÜSİAD had 'organic' links to the government in power.

However, TÜSİAD's links to the government had two-sided implications. It is true that the Association, despite its voluntary status, could have easy access to the government. Yet there was little tangible outcome. Within the export-oriented economic model, competition between industrialists and exporters gradually emerged. Furthermore, the government had to make critical choices to ensure growth and, later, keep a centre-right coalition intact through politically expedient policies. These choices were in conflict with the interests of big industrialists. The special links, that TÜSİAD had with the government, became an asset *for the government*, to contain demands coming from big business. TÜSİAD had to endorse the government's, policies despite its increasing dissatisfaction with them, because the Motherland Party at the time was the best bet for big business. At least in the short run, ideological affinity and personal contacts between the government and big business enhanced the relative autonomy of government from the demands of a powerful constituent in civil society.

The government aimed at growth through exports. Following the crisis of 1978-1979, GDP growth rates increased steadily.[42] Yet, despite the prevailing private enterprise ideology, much of this growth was due to public investment. Investment by the public sector remained higher than investment by the private sector.[43] The relative share of the private sector in total fixed capital investment decreased from 45.0 per cent in 1984

---

42 *OECD Economic Surveys, 1986/1987 Turkey* (Paris: OECD, 1987), p. 74.

43 Boratav and Türel, 'Notes on the Current Development Problems and Growth Prospects of the Turkish Economy', p. 38.

to 42.9 per cent in 1985, and remained at 42.9 per cent in 1986.[44]

Public investment was politically expedient.[45] The MP government invested in infrastructure and communications. Special extra-budgetary funds with net revenues of half the consolidated budget helped the MP government to increase its discretionary spending of public funds for politically advantageous purposes in order to maintain its centre-right coalition.[46]

Furthermore, these high rates of GDP growth and public spending could be maintained only with external financing. Between 1980 and 1986, the size of the outstanding external debt increased from 28 per cent to 53 per cent of the gross national product (GNP). The annual payments on the external debt jumped from 2 per cent to 8 per cent of GNP.[47] To maintain the growth rate, the Özal government became dependent on external borrowing. As the debt payments rose, it in turn became dependent on exports.

Exports increased after the Özal government came to power. The rate of increase was 25 per cent in 1984 and 12 per cent in 1985.[48] These high rates of export growth could be attained not only because internal demand was curbed or the rate of capacity utilization increased, but also because exporters were subsidized by the government.

When export credits were reduced in 1986 to fight inflation, a 6 per cent decline in exports occurred. Meanwhile, the foreign debt was increasing. Preferential export subsidies had to be used once again to increase exports and service the debt. The policy measures adopted in February 1988, which promoted a new subsidy schedule to encourage exporters to bring back their earnings, further underlined the government's alliance with the exporting groups.

All this time, the industrialists were kept at bay. They wanted cheaper credits and lower interest rates. Although Central Bank credits extended to the private sector increased in 1984, after the Özal government came to power, they had sharply declined by the end of that year. The credits extended to the public sector then surpassed those extended to the private sector, and this trend continued until 1987.[49]

TÜSİAD's criticisms of the government escalated over time as the government's policies became more detrimental to their interests. At a press conference in April 1985, Mr Şahap Kocatopçu, the then President of TÜSİAD, presented a list of criticisms: inflation, budget deficits, inefficiency of the state economic enterprises, unequal opportunities provided to the private sector as compared with the public sector, unfavourable credit policies, and high interest rates.[50] TÜSİAD reports began to be increasingly critical of the government. The report on 'Foreign Debt, Forecast and Analysis', which predicted an inevitable foreign exchange crisis unless necessary measures were immediately taken, attracted particular public attention: both Prime Minister Özal and

---

44 TÜSİAD, *The Turkish Economy*, p. 12. Also see Ziya Öniş in this volume (Editor's Note).

45 John Waterbury, 'Coalition-Building, Export-Led Growth and the Public Sector in Turkey', paper presented to the Middle East Studies Association Annual Meetings, Los Angeles, U.S.A., 2-6 November 1988.

46 Oğuz Oyan, 'ANAP'ın Fon Ekonomisi', *Görüş*, 15 September 1987, p.28.

47 *OECD Economic Surveys. 1986/1987 Turkey*, p. 25.

48 Ibid, p. 20.

49 Ibid, p. 40.

50 *Görüş*, 13 April 1985, pp. 4-14.

Minister of State Yusuf Özal harshly chided TÜSİAD to mind its own business.[51] After all, big business was their younger brother whom they could patronize!

By the end of 1987 and during 1988, Mr Ömer Dinçkök, the then President of TÜSİAD, was frequently quoted in the newspapers criticizing government policies: 'Inflation is high: the public sector is using up Central Bank credits ...[they] are being denied to the private sector.'[52] In 1988, in response to a questionnaire distributed amongst TÜSİAD members, 91 per cent thought that government policies were inadequate in improving credit facilities; 80 per cent pointed out that they were inadequate in solving unemployment; 82 per cent claimed that the policies pursued by the government had a negative impact on the sales of goods produced by the companies in the sector.[53] Conversely, for the industrialists who wanted low-cost credits for investment, Mr Özal's suggestion was that they should sell their villas![54]

Conclusion

TÜSİAD pursued its changing goals within a system of constraints and opportunities which also varied over time. Systemic factors independent of the Association made the latter's endeavours at times only partly effective. 1978 to 1980 was a period of crisis in Turkey during which TÜSİAD sought to change the parameters of the polity and the rules of the economy. Under the circumstances, a new system favourable to the private sector and capable of bringing in much needed foreign exchange could be initiated.

Within the new system, opportunities and constraints changed. Because of its ideological affinity and 'organic' ties, TÜSİAD could ensure a close dialogue with the government. Yet the tangible outcome of this dialogue was limited. Exporters were indispensable to the systemic needs of an export-oriented growth strategy, and, particularly towards the end of the decade, public spending became essential to the political interests of the government for maintaining its electoral coalition. Consequently, the government's support and subsidies went to the exporters and not to the industrialists, and the government did not reduce its spending to give private enterprise more scope. Precisely because of its ideological affinity and close ties, TÜSİAD could not seek an alternative government. Its demands had to be contained within the parameters set by high government spending and generous subsidies to exporters. Even though the Association was founded to articulate the interests of big business against small entrepreneurs, after 1980 TÜSİAD had to give voice to the demands of big industrialists, who needed to invest, against the exporters. The cleavage between the big and the small was superceded by the cleavage between investors and exporters.

---

51 Özal was quoted as saying, 'No one, especially businessmen, has the right to depict Turkey's situation as worse than it really is. Some have taken the axe in their hands and are cutting the branch they are sitting on'. Yusuf Özal in turn was quoted as saying, 'The TÜSİAD should occupy itself with the problems of the private sector rather than repeat the studies of the State Planning Organization; it should mind its own business', *Hürriyet*, 21 January 1988. My translation.

52 *Cumhuriyet*, 22 May 1987; 7 October 1987; 3 March 1988; 2 May 1988; 20 August 1988.

53 *Hürriyet*, 23 November 1988.

54 *Hürriyet*, 13 April 1988.

In retrospect, TÜSİAD as an association representing the organized interests of big business, could successfully communicate its needs. Its efforts as a voluntary association were unprecedented in the context of a State-oriented Turkish polity. Yet its effectiveness was ultimately defined by macro-level economic and political dictates independent of TÜSİAD.

The post-1980 Turkish polity was characterized by increased State control over civil society. Ironically, a government, allegedly committed to private enterprise and the market, assumed power only to exercise state controls over society in order to promote its own strategy of growth and satisfy, at least for a while, its own clientele. Even though individual entrepreneurs benefited from the system through personal ties, conditions favourable to private entrepreneurs in general and big industrialists in particular could not be created. Despite the affinity between big business and the government, the autonomy of the State from civil society has increased.

Part Four
CONCLUSION

11

Political Sources of Uncertainty in Business Life

Ayşe Buğra

This chapter is based on some of the findings of a research project on the political context of business activity in Turkey. * Our research is limited to big business, more specifically to holding companies with highly diversified activities in industry, trade and finance. Our observations on the attitudes of businessmen in Turkey are based primarily on biographical and auto-biographical material, personal interviews, publications of voluntary interest group associations, newspapers, magazines and periodicals.

The essay is organized in three parts. First, we present the basic elements of the theoretical framework of the study. Second, a number of observations are made concerning some aspects of the values and attitudes of businessmen in Turkey. Third, we try to explain the values and attitudes in question by discussing different types of state intervention in the business environment - those adopted in Turkey during the 1930s and 1980s.

Theoretical Backdrop

A study of business attitudes in a political context is, more than anything else, a challenge to the dichotomy established between the state and the market in the mainstream economic literature. There the market is viewed as a spontaneous order resulting from the free play of private interests. The emergence of the market and the market economy is thus analyzed as a 'natural' phenomenon which excludes any deliberate intervention from outside. In this view, intervention by the state replaces the logic of the market with a different logic. What one looks at are the ways in which state intervention restricts market activity. What is virtually excluded is the possibility that the intervention itself may actually play a role in helping the establishment of the market and/or in enlarging the scope of the market activity.

Although marginal to mainstream economic analyses, there nevertheless also exists a body of literature addressing itself to limitations of the standard economic approach concerning the role of the state in economic life. Particularly significant here is Karl Polanyi's seminal work, where the market economy appears not as a spontaneous, natural order, but as an 'instituted process' brought into being by deliberate state intervention. The market economy is thus not defined as a system where the totality of economic activity is conducted through self-regulating markets, that is, as one the functioning of which is free from outside control. Polanyi thinks that the establishment of a self-regulating market economy requires prior state activity in institution-building;

* The Project in question was supported by the Middle East Research Committee of the Ford Foundation, Cairo.

intervention is also required to protect the social fabric against the disruptive influence of the expansion of markets in all spheres of social life. The state thus plays a crucial role both in building and enlarging the domain of the market, and taking the necessary measures to protect society against the market. In Polanyi's words, '[t]here was nothing natural about *laissez-faire*; free markets could never come into being merely by allowing things to take their course'.[1]

Polanyi's statement acquires a new significance in the context of developing economies where the market system is underdeveloped and the business community is weak. In fact, post-Second World War development economics furnishes several interesting analyses of the role of the State in shaping the economy. Alexander Gerschenkron's *Economic Backwardness in Historical Perspective* may be considered a pioneering study in this area. Gerschenkron has shown that the institutions and ideologies which accompany economic development in late industrializing countries are considerably different from those found in countries which industrialized earlier. According to him, these differences can be explained with reference to the overwhelming presence of the state in economic life in late industrializing countries.[2]

We also find, in the now fashionable field of State-centred approaches to the study of political economy, an attempt to explore the forms as well as the extent of intervention. This literature emphasizes 'the society forming role' of the State and the need to study that role with reference to the dynamics of interaction between the state and society.[3] One interesting area of application for studies along these lines has proven to be the development experience of some East Asian countries such as Taiwan and South Korea. While in the past they had been presented as ideal types, illustrating the validity of neo-classical approaches to economic policy formation,[4] they now appear in a new light. We find, in these analyses, a contrast between the 'market augmenting' and 'market repressing' role of the State.[5] They imply, even if they do not fully explore, the necessity of studying the ways in which state action modifies rather than replaces the logic of the market.[6]

---

1 Karl Polanyi, *The Great Transformation* (Boston: Beacon Press, 1957), p. 139. Also see, Karl Polanyi, Conrad M. Arensberg, Harry W. Pearson, eds., *Trade and Market in the Early Empires* (Chicago: Gateway, 1957).

2 Alexander Gerschenkron, *Economic Backwardness in Historical Perspective* (Cambridge, Mass.: Harvard University Press, 1966).

3 See, in particular, Peter Katzenstein, 'Domestic and International Structures and Strategies of Foreign Economic Policy', *International Organization*, 31(1977), pp. 587-606 and pp. 879-919; Peter Evans, Dietrich Rueschmeyer and Theda Skocpol, eds., *Bringing the State Back In* (Cambridge: Cambridge University Press, 1985); and Stephen D. Krasner, 'Approaches to the State: Alternative Conceptions and Historical Dynamics', *Comparative Politics*, 16 (1984), pp. 222-44.

4 As a typical example of such approaches see Bella Balassa, 'The Leasons of East Asian Development', *Economic Development and Cultural Change*, 16 (1988), pp. 273-90.

5 Chalmers Johnson, 'Political Institutions and Economic Performance: The Government-Business Relationship in Japan, S. Korea and Taiwan', in *The Political Economy of South East Asian Industrialism*, Frederic C. Deyo, ed. (Ithaca and London: Cornell University Press, 1987).

6 This issue is extensively explored by Leroy P. Jones and El Sakong, *Government, Business and Entrepreneurship in Economic Development. The Korean Case* (Cambridge, Mass.: Council on East Asian Studies, Harvard University, 1980).

In standard neo-classical analyses, the market appears as the realm of private interests. Businessmen are considered to be directed solely by the motive of gain. As a broad generalization, the postulate of neo-classical rationality, according to which the maximization of self-interest is the sole objective of economic activity, can hardly be contested. People do pursue their self-interest. But how useful is this proposition in understanding the ways in which businessmen will respond to government policy? How useful is it, in other words, to understanding the market mechanism and the way state intervention will affect it? Any meaningful inquiry into these areas seems to require a closer examination of the rationality postulate.

A survey of economic theory yields valuable analyses of business activity developed around a criticism of the rationality postulate. One branch of such critical analyses can be associated with the names of several eminent economists such as Malthus, Menger, Knight and Keynes. Central to the contributions of these economists is the concept of uncertainty. According to them, uncertainty is the key element of managerial and entrepreneurial activity. The formulation of objectives, the perception of constraints and the choice of strategies, which together comprise what is called business behaviour, are shaped by the element of uncertainty about the ends and means of business activity. Business behaviour in a particular business environment can only be understood with reference to the nature and sources of uncertainty characterizing that environment. By combining the insights derived from these disparate lines of critical analysis, it is possible to make certain observations about business behaviour in Turkey.

The State Intervention and Business Attitudes

It would be appropriate to start an analysis of business attitudes in Turkey with a few notes on the self-image of Turkish businessmen. Self-image is defined here as a complex variable comprising diverse aspects of businessmen's evaluation of their position in society. Their perception of their rights and responsibilities as well as the sense of social power that they have, all appear as elements of the self-image of Turkish businessmen. It is obvious that in no society would these elements manifest a static character, remaining unchanged over time. Our emphasis here, however, is on continuity rather than change. It is our contention that the business outlook revealed in our recent interviews reflects a significant continuity throughout the post-Republican period (1923 to the present), and remains marked by the historical legacy of government-business relations in Turkey.

One of the most striking dimensions of the Turkish businessmen's self-image seems to be a lack of confidence about the legitimacy of activities carried out in pursuit of pecuniary gain. We find in the auto-biographies and public statements of businessmen an almost desperate attempt to justify business as a walk of life with reference to its social value. Turkish businessmen rarely express their pride about successful ventures, but try, instead, to apologize for their success, and never fail to mention its positive implications for the national economy as a whole. Similarly, the inviolability of private property rights does not at all seem obvious to them. They do not, in fact, appear to be sure about their legal rights and their ability to do whatever they please with their private property. Hence, they feel the need to indicate that wealth is not something to be ashamed of, and they justify it by accounting the ways in which they use their wealth for the benefit of their country.[7]

The same lack of confidence can be observed in their evaluation of the power that they have in political life and society. Whether it is justified or not, both the statements and the actual behaviour of Turkish businessmen reflect a certain sense of impotence to influence the direction of economic, social and political change. Closely related to this sense of powerlessness is a lack of efforts to develop any institutionalized form of consultation with bureaucrats and politicians, and seek individually the support of influential bureaucrats and/or politicians. As higlighted in a number of studies on the relationship between the market and the state in Turkey, businessmen often choose to circumvent rules and regulations rather than try to change them.[8] This leads to the emergence of certain doubts as to the very legality of business activity; businessmen are frequently seen to operate in a grey area between the realms of outlaws and honest citizens.[9]

On the basis of these observations, it would not be too difficult to conclude that business activity in Turkey is likely to exhibit certain characteristics which would not necessarily be conducive to a healthy development of the national economy. Businessmen would be likely to avoid long-term investment projects, and instead seek easy and quick ways of making high profits. Risk-taking and imaginative entrepreneurship would be in short supply and speculative activity quite rampant. The internal organization of the business firm, too, would reflect businessmen's evaluation of their powerlessness. In the legally shady area in which they function the element of trust between business partners is likely to acquire a crucial significance. Family ties and coming from the same home town would therefore play an important role in business affairs and hamper the professionalization of management. These seem to constitute, in fact, the most obvious behavioural and institutional characteristics of business activity in Turkey. What we wish to highlight here is the link between these characteristics and the self-image of Turkish businessmen, since we believe that as long as there is no fundamental change

---

7 We have provided a more detailed analysis of these issues in a review article on the auto-biographies of three leading Turkish businessmen. See Ayşe Buğra, 'The Late Coming Tycoons of Turkey', *Journal of Economics and Administrative Studies* (Istanbul), 1 (1987), pp. 143-55. In addition to the auto-biographies of Messrs Vehbi Koç, Sakıp Sabancı and Nejat Eczacıbaşı reviewed in this article, see also Alber Bilen, *Türk Sanayiinde Kırk Zorlu Yıl* (İstanbul: Milliyet Yayınları, 1988) and Bernar Nahum, *Koç'ta 44 Yılım* (İstanbul: Milliyet Yayınları, 1988).

8 Metin Heper presents a survey of these in his *The State Tradition in Turkey* (Walkington, England: The Eothen Press, 1985). An interesting event which took place in 1988 neatly illustrates the ideas explored in these studies: The Turkish Industrialists' and Businessmen's Association (TÜSİAD) conducted a survey which higlighted the dissatisfaction of its members with the current policy formation and implementation process. During the meeting organized to discuss the survey results with some members of the govrenment, however, businessmen refused to voice any strong opinions likely to offend the latter. They chose to avoid overt criticism of the government because they were afraid of the consequences of such a confrontation. Mr Ömer Dinçkök, the then President of the Association, was thus left alone by his constituency. Businessmen and industrialists refused to give a priority to their group interests over and above their short run, individual interests. This was probably one of the reasons leading to Dinçkök's resignation from his post shortly after the event.

9 'The grey' area is the expression used by one of the businessmen we interviewed.

in this self-image no amount of policy incentives can modify the business environment so as to minimize the divergence between social and private interests. It would also make institutionalized linkages between the state and interest groups impossible.

Two major categories of arguments have been developed to explain the emergence of the business outlook outlined above. According to the first argument, social attitudes towards business activity embedded in the cultural fabric of society have been critical. It is the traditional lack of respect towards, and an absence of recognition of the worth of their activities which explains the observed characteristics of Turkish businessmen, including their lack of confidence.[10] This argument is closely related to the generally accepted idea that the Muslim population in the Ottoman empire was not involved, or only marginally involved, in commercial activities which were largely controlled by non-Muslim minorities. As pointed out by one historian, the idea is so deeply-rooted in Ottoman studies that one can hardly find efforts to substantiate it.[11] The reason why Muslims were said to be excluded from the realm of commerce is in fact difficult to understand. One can hardly explain it with reference to Islam which condemns usury but does not pass any moral judgement against money-making activity. The fact that Mohammad himself was involved in commerce seems to be sufficient to render a religion-based explanation difficult to sustain. While it would be possible to conjecture that Ottoman rulers might have had unfavourable attitudes towards commercial dealings between Muslims and non-Muslims, that, too, was not the case. A recent study, in fact, argues: 'There is no evidence that any action on the part of the Ottoman government or the religious authorities was aimed at stopping Ottoman merchants from trading with foreigners within and outside the empire.'[12] The same study also documents the extensive involvement of Muslim merchants in extra-territorial trade from the fifteenth to seventeenth centuries.

The culturally-explained exclusion of Muslims from commercial activity, therefore, remains to be substantiated. The idea appears, however, as a significant element in nationalist discourse both during the 1908-1918 Young Turk experiment and the early years of the Turkish Republic. In the latter period, we find certain authors who referred to this phenomenon as a product of *Tanzimat* (Reform Period, 1839-1876). According to them, it was during the *Tanzimat* era that commerce and industry acquired their current status of second class occupations. They argue that it was in this period that the Muslim population of the Empire has begun to leave the realm of business. It is emphasized, however, that it would be wrong to see the exclusion of Muslims from business activities as a deep-rooted cultural phenomenon.[13]

Regardless of the type of explanation offered for the ethnic and religious make-up of the business community, during the twentieth century the significance of the private sector in the economic development of the country was always emphasized, and

[10] See, for example, Güvenç G. Alpender, 'Entrepreneurs and Private Enterprises in Turkey', in *The Turkish Administrator. A Cultural Survey*, Güvenç G. Alpender and Jerry R. Hopper, eds. (Ankara: USAID, 1967).

[11] Cemal Kafadar, 'A Death in Venice (1575): Anatolian Muslim Merchants Trading in the Serenissima', *Journal of Turkish Studies*, 6 (1986), pp. 191-217.

[12] Ibid., p. 210.

[13] See, for example, Yusuf Kemal Tengirşenk, *Türk İnkılabı Dersleri. Ekonomik Değişmeler* (İstanbul: Resimli Ay, 1935), p. 47.

the reluctance of the Muslim population to participate in business activity lamented as a serious problem both by politicians and intellectuals. These considerations were accompanied by the attempts of both the Union and Progress Party (1908-1918) and the Republican governments to 'create' a group of indigenous businessmen.[14]

The fact that the modern Turkish business community has developed as part of a social project undertaken by the State is often mentioned in State-centred explanations of business behaviour. It is argued that in both the Ottoman Empire and Republican Turkey the source of power was always special privileges. This approach often rests on the assumptions about an uninterrupted continuity in the State tradition in Turkey.[15] There is much to commend in this view which, among other things, has shown the omnipresence of the State in the Ottoman- Turkish polity and its significant implications for the structuring of the polity and society. As Metin Heper has recently indicated, the locus of the State has gradually shifted from the bureaucrats and the military to politicians, but the attitudes of both categories have remained the same.[16] The particular policies adopted by both groups have had a significant impact on business behaviour.

Two Types of State Intervention: Pre- and Post-1980 Periods

Under certain circumstances, a heavily interventionist government might provide an environment more favourable to the development of a self-confident business community than a less interventionist government. In fact, economic policy in the 1930s, in the so-called *étatist* period, was more favourable to the development of such a business community than the policies pursued by the Motherland Party governments in the so-called liberal period following the general elections in 1983. A comparison of this sort might seem too provocative to an economic historian, especially since we will be extrapolating from the impact of the Great Depression in shaping the economic strategy of the 1930s, in order to refute the well-established dichotomy between the state and market, and highlight the 'instituted' character of the latter.

The point that we are trying to make here is not that the strengthening of a weak business community could only be possible by extensive state support. While the idea has a certain validity, it has little relevance to the comparison that we will be making. It would, in fact, be extremely difficult to characterize the 1980s as a period when the state support given to businessmen was withdrawn. There was certainly a change in the type of protection as well as in the groups receiving it, but it has surely remained significant.[17] When we state that the *étatist* era was probably more favourable to the development of a self-confident business community, we are arguing that businessmen were then less preoccupied by the changes in government policy, and thus the state

---

14 Zafer Toprak, *Türkiye'de 'Milli İktisat'* (Ankara: Yurt Yayınları, 1982).

15 See, for example, Heper, *The State Tradition in Turkey* and Ahmet İnsel, *La Turquie entre l'ordre et développement* (Paris: l'Harmattan, 1984).

16 Metin Heper, 'The State, Political Party and Society in post-1983 Turkey', *Government and Opposition*, 25 (1990), pp. 321- 33.

17 See, on this subject, Ziya Öniş and Süleyman Özmucur, 'Supply-Side Origins of Macroeconomic Crises in Turkey', paper presented at the World Bank Conference, Madrid, May 1988.

was a somewhat less important concern in their day-to-day operations than has been the case during the 1980s.

The Motherland Party governments owe their liberal reputation largely to three objectives repeatedly emphasized in their discourse: elimination of price controls (including controls over the rate of interest and the foreign exchange rate), liberalization of the foreign trade regime (including more lenient policies towards foreign direct investment), and the privatization of state economic enterprises (SEEs). These objectives are still far from being fully realized.[18] We believe, however, that it would be more fruitful to seek elsewhere the factors behind the inability of the government to implement a 'market augmenting' strategy.

The most striking characteristic of Turkey's economic performance during the second part of the 1980s appeared to be an overwhelming instability reflected in the values of some basic economic indicators. There seems to exist little ambiguity as to the source of this instability: it stemmed from unpredictable economic policies. The uncertainty in question has to do, first and foremost, with the ways in which basic policy objectives have been defined. According to the formal policy statements, the mission of the Motherland Party governments is the implementation of a standard IMF stabilization programme. Prime Minister Özal was presented to the public as an economic wizard, and the proof of the pudding was going to be the success of the said programme. During the first few years of Özal's rule, his opponents directed their criticisms towards the appropriateness of the standard IMF recipe in general, and for the Turkish economy in particular. There were hardly any doubts about the conformity of the government's programme to this recipe. Later, it became clear that what was being implemented in the country was largely an expansionist programme with heavy state investment in infrastucture, which, it was hoped, would act as the engine of growth.

The ensuing budget deficits and an accelerating rate of inflation appeared as the end result of the economic strategy in question.[19] The basic uncertainty of an inflationary environment presented a major obstacle to the smooth functioning of the market. A government which had repeatedly declared its determination to fight the *étatist* tradition in Turkey in order to establish a real market economy was thus instrumental in bringing about a highly uncertain environment inimical to its alleged aims.

What is even more significant than the government's inability to assure price stability is the central place that the objective of controlling inflation continued to occupy in official discourse. Businessmen thus found themselves facing a doubly uncertain future. Price fluctuations resulting from government policy was only one element of uncertainty. A second, and perhaps a more significant factor, was the possibility of a major policy change at any moment. The business community simply did not know the basic parameters of the system, and, like farmers in a simple peasant community watching the clouds to predict the weather, they kept track of the signals to guess the

---

18 It is for this reason that one Turkish economist working in the United States expressed his doubts about the liberalism of the Motherland Party governments already in 1985. see Asım Erdilek, 'The Turkish Free Market in Jeopardy', *The Wall Street Journal*, 15 February 1985. Also see Ziya Öniş in this volume.

19 A recent study considers public deficits as the major cause of inflation in Turkey: Tansu Çiller and Mehmet Kaytaz, *Kamu Kesimi Açıkları ve Enflasyon* (İstanbul: İstanbul Ticaret Odası, 1989).

future course of events, that is, future moves by the government.

One implication of the growing budget deficit has been the significant rise in public debt and the pressures this has exercised on interest rates. Some economists in fact pointed to the 'crowding out effect' of government operations, whereby private sector firms have found themselves in a position to enter into competition with the government for loanable funds.[20] Since the government could set the rules of the game, the competition in question was a highly unequal one, leading members of the private sector to voice their complaints. It is interesting, however, that these complaints were directed more at the uncertainty about the rates of interest rather than their level. At a panel discussion on TV in 1989, for example, the Chairman of the Turkish Industrialists' and Businessmen's Association (TÜSİAD) pointed out that the interest rates were changed nineteen times in the course of the previous year, which made irrelevant all discussions about the rate of interest as a tool of economic policy.[21]

It is important to note here that what was being changed by the government was not only the level of interest rates but also the rules of the game in relation to determination of those rates. In February 1988, for example, interest rates were raised to 65 per cent. This decision led to many complaints on the part of businessmen who were adversely affected by high costs of credit. Then, in September 1988, the rates were reduced. A few months later, the government discontinued interest rate controls, and announced that they were going to be determined by the market. The banks immediately raised their borrowing rates, ferociously competing with each other to attract deposits. Next day, the government announced a new decision fixing the highest legal deposit rate at 85 per cent! This rather confusing development towards interest rate liberalization was generally interpreted as an act of punishment against certain private sector banks which were heavily involved in foreign exchange speculation. In any case, the whole episode left the business community with certain uneasy questions of a legal rather than economic nature. They found themselves in the position of trying to decide whether in Turkey foreign exchange speculation constituted a crime or not.[22]

The question of legal responsibilities and rights has in fact become very difficult to decide under the Motherland Party governments. Turkish businessmen were confused about legal issues particularly in two areas: the tax system and export promotion policies. In the first, the recurrent changes appeared as the source of two types of uncertainty. The unpredictability of future tax burdens was accompanied by the difficulty of figuring out the exact amount of taxes one had to pay. Businessmen thought, for example, that it was not very clear whether exporters' tax rebates were subject to value added tax. Many firms did not pay it, and those that did could not help feeling 'a bit stupid'.[23] The ambiguity in question presented a perfect incentive for tax evasion.

Businessmen were as unclear about their rights as about their responsibilities. The

---

20 For a discussion of this issue, see Demir Demirgil, 'Özel Sektörün Yatırım Eğilimindeki Durgunluk', *Türk Tarihi Dergisi*, no.2 (1985), pp. 68-71.

21 Panel discussion on TV, 'Industrialization and Alternative Policies', 5 May 1989.

22 This question was specifically raised in an article attempting to interpret the logic behind the policy move: See Deniz Gökçe, 'Terk', *Ekonomik Bülten* (Istanbul weekly), 7-13 November, 1988.

23 One of our interviewees told us that he was rather tired of feeling either like a crook or an incompetent manager.

exporters, who in theory should be the group most privileged by Motherland Party policies, operated on particularly slippery ground. The frequency of changes in the list of commodities benefitting from different types of export promotion measures made one feel dizzy. Equally confusing were the changes in the percentage of premiums and tax rebates as well as in the terms of repayment of export credits. It is not difficult to see that these changes, which constantly gave rise to and destroyed rents, created an ambiguity as to the content of acquired rights of businessmen. In fact, such an ambiguity was also present in the area of private property rights. For example, the delegation of powers to municipal governments, which in fact could be considered as a positive step in some ways, was instrumental in tampering with the nature of property rights. By using in a rather arbitrary fashion their recently acquired prerogative in issuing or withdrawing building permits, municipal governments radically altered both the value of the property and content of ownership rights.[24]

Business success in such an environment is contingent upon mastery in obtaining political favours in such a way as to influence the government's discretionary meddling in the economy, and the ability to make profits through quick responses to changes in the rules of the game. Consequently, the returns on carefully-planned investment strategies would be extremely small. What would also be quite low is the probability that a self-confident and self-reliant business community, that can play a positive role in economic development, would emerge out of this atmosphere.

We believe that in spite of the massive State intervention restricting the scope of the market, the economic atmosphere of the 1930s was in some ways more conducive to the emergence of such a business group. This statement should, however, be qualified: the economic model that the governments of the 1930s had in mind had very little to do with the institutional and behavioural characteristics of the standard model of capitalist development, where competition between small, independent firms has central place. What the authorities wanted was a modern, Western-looking economy which, nevertheless, had no resemblance to models of competitive capitalism. According to them, modern Western economies were characterized neither by the significance of competitive forces nor by a liberal outlook. A high industrial concentration and close ties between big, modern firms and the state appeared to the Turkish government as the crucial characteristics of these economies which they wanted the Turkish economy to resemble.

During the 1930s, politicians and intellectuals thought that liberalism was dead and buried everywhere, and protectionism was the order the day. In their analyses of the dynamics of underdevelopment of the Ottoman Empire, too, the absence of protectionist policies appeared as the key explanatory factor. According to them, the Ottoman Empire had remained underdeveloped because the policy makers were unable to capture the logic of economic development. This implied, in the 1930s, the inability to understand not the subtleties of the liberal economic model, but those of the mercantilist model. What was needed to reverse the historical trend, therefore, was to adopt a mercantilist policy. It was thought that not only mercantilism was the key notion

---

24 Some members of the Turkish Chamber of Architects have voiced their concern about these developments on many occasions. See, for example, the interview with Yücel Gürsel, the president of the Chamber, in *Sosyal Demokrat*, 8 (1988), pp. 26- 30.

to the analysis of the comparative dynamics of development and underdevelopment in the past, but it also provided a more relevant policy package than the liberal model to deal effectively with the contraints imposed by the international economy.[25]

During the 1930s, another point was emphasized, which had to do with the precarious nature of property rights in the Ottoman Empire. The insecurity of those rights was often underlined as a factor blocking the accumulation of capital and the development of a self-confident business community.[26] Corresponding to this particular emphasis, we find in the 1930s a widely shared idea concerning the significance of a secure and stable economic environment for the efforts to build a modern, Western-looking economy. Governments thus opted for an industrial strategy where big business firms would function in continuous dialogue and collaboration with government authorities, in an environment where both their rights and responsibilities were clearly defined by the requirements of economic development. In this setting, a high industrial concentration would be helpful to facilitate effective state control over the activities of private firms. The environment of the 1930s was appropriate for the emergence of private firms willing to play this state-assigned role.

The period was characterized by a protectionist international trade policy, extensive price controls, and an important role assigned to SEE's as the engine of industrial growth. Nevertheless, it was also characterized, first, by the stability of basic macroeconomic variables. Secondly, governments were quite sensitive about avoiding policy changes which would adversely affect the content of acquired rights. With regard to the first issue, governments had made a commitment to assure the stability of prices and maintain the value of the lira. These commitments were kept, and the businessmen faced very little uncertainty concerning the future values of these variables.

The stability of the system was largely assured through an ever increasing intervention in the economy. It is thus possible to view the situation in terms of an imaginary trade-off between non-interventionism and stability. There is some evidence suggesting that the businessmen of the era were more inclined towards stability. When we consider the type of complaints that businessmen had in the 1930s, we see that these complaints had less to do with policies that enhanced the role of the state than with policies introducing an element of instability in the system. The emergence of any type of uncertainty, either in relation to macro-economic variables or to business privileges and rights, appeared as a serious matter of concern. In their demands for the alleviation of such uncertainties, businessmen did not hesitate to call on the government to intervene.

The replacement of the *étatist* Minister of Economy, Mr Mustafa Şeref, by 'liberal' Mr Celal Bayar in 1932, can also be interpreted from this perspective. Economic historians of the era sometimes imply that Mr Şeref attracted the hostility of the private sector because of his radical *etatism.*[27] However, his views on the necessity of expand-

---

[25] See, for example, Tengirşenk, *Türk İnkılabı Dersleri* and Haldun Derin, *Türkiye'de Devletçilik* (İstanbul: Çituri Biraderler Basımevi, 1940).

[26] See, Derin, *Türkiye'de Devletçilik*; İsmail Hüsrev Tökin, *Türkiye'de Köy İktisadiyatı* (Ankara: Kadro Mecmuası, 1934), and Yorgaki Effimianidis, *Cihan İktisad Buhranı Önünde Türkiye* (İstanbul: Kağıtçılık ve Matbaacılık Anonim Şirketi, 1935).

[27] See, for example, Bilsay Kuruç, *Mustafa Kemal Döneminde Ekonomi* (Ankara: Bilgi Yayınevi, 1987).

ing the scope of the state sector played only a marginal role in the events that led to his forced resignation. The real conflict between Mr Şeref and the business community seems to have, at its origin, his attempts to reduce the rate of effective protection by imposing tariffs on imported raw materials. Ironically, the *étatist* Minister of Economy seems to have been trying to follow a trade policy based on the country's comparative advantage as a producer and exporter of agricultural raw materials. His attempts to implement a differential protection policy via the periodical preparation of protected items might also be interpreted as a reflection of a preference to distinguish the areas where Turkish industry could be competitive from those which could only be protected by totally overlooking all market indicators.[28]

Mr Şeref's successor, Mr Bayar, who was successful in obtaining the support of the private sector, was no more liberal in his policies than his predecessor. The real expansion of the state sector took place when Bayar was in office. A number of SEEs were established with the aid of Soviet experts and in some ways, the strategy reflected a much more *étatist* policy than Mr Şeref had in mind. Mr Şeref was trying to elaborate a strategy involving what was called 'key plants' (*santral fabrikalar*), that is, state-owned factories which would supply private firms with cheap inputs. The idea seems to have to encourage the small industry in the textile sector. In contrast, the public sector development policies during the Bayar era were directed at the establishment of 'integrated plants' (*koordine fabrikalar*), that is, self-sufficient state economic enterprises having few links with the private sector. Prominently absent from this second period were any policy efforts to encourage the development of small industry. On the contrary, the government seemed to be quite hostile to small competitive firms which, by virtue of both their smallness and competitiveness, were seen to be inimical to the development of a modern economy. In fact, explicit measures were adopted to limit increasing competition in industry, and these measures were supported by the Union of Industrialists.[29]

All through this period, following the resignation of Mr Şeref, the government in fact seemed careful not to make policy changes that would have adversely affected the business community. The privileges granted to the business community by the Act for the Encouragement of Industry (1927) were carefully maintained by avoiding any modification of the level of effective protection. The policy of differential protection through the preparation of periodically changing lists of protected items was abolished in 1934, in favour of an accross-the-board protectionism which left little room for discretion. In taxation, too, the government tried not to take away the exemptions granted to private sector firms with the 1927 Act, in spite of the difficulty of keeping its commitment to a balanced budget and monetary stability without increasing the tax burden. Each attempt of the government to impose additional taxes was met with a strong reaction

28 For a detailed discussion of the economic policies of the period, see, especially, İlhan Tekeli and Selim İlkin, *1929 Dünya Buhranında Türkiye'nin İktisadi Politika Arayışları* (Ankara: ODTÜ, 1977); İlhan Tekeli and Selim İlkin, *Uygulamaya Geçerken Türkiye'de Devletçiliğin Oluşumu* (Ankara: ODTÜ, 1982); Korkut Boratav, *Türkiye'de Devletçilik* (İstanbul: Gerçek Yayınevi, 1974).

29 Tekeli and İlkin, *Uygulamaya Geçerken Türkiye'de Devletçiliğin Oluşumu*, p. 219. The preparation of 'the Regulation on Overproduction' (*Sürprodüksiyon Kararnamesi*) in 1933 is an important illustration of the government's concern about this issue.

from the business community, whose opposition was not only directed at a possible increase of their own taxes, but also at similar increases in taxes paid by civil servants. A decline in the disposable income of civil servants was seen as a threat to business interests through its impact on domestic demand. The concern of business for the decline in domestic demand, in fact, led them to suggest to the government extremely non-market oriented policies. They proposed, in particular, that the government impose on civil servants the obligation to consume only domestically-produced items. The upward pressures that such a measure could exercise on prices could, according to business representatives, be checked by extensive price controls. We are thus faced with an extremely interesting situation where businessmen actually endorsed and supported price controls, which constituted one of the most *étatist* aspects of the strategy implemented in the 1930s.

The government's scrupulousness in not arbitrarily taking away the rights and privileges earlier granted to the private sector was partly instrumental in blocking an extensive reform in two crucial areas: the tax system and the agricultural sector. In the first area, the reluctance to infringe on business interests led the government to seek ways of increasing tax revenues through the imposition of non-progressive taxes often conflicting with the allocative function of the tax system. Agricultural reform projects, too, were largely blocked by the strong desire on the part of the government not to appear disrespectful towards private property. The legal changes brought about by the Republican governments in the period 1923-1940 were in the direction of the consolidation and expansion of private property rights.[30] The discussions about agricultural reform which became especially intense in the second half of the 1930s did not fail to provoke the expression of certain doubts concerning the government's attitude towards private property. However, it was important for the government to eliminate such doubts, which could generate anxiety not only in the agricultural sector, but in the business environment in general.

Conclusion

Had the government been successful during the 1930s in laying the foundations of a socially viable tax system and reforming agriculture, the development of a market economy could have proceeded on more solid grounds. These two areas appeared at the end of the 1930s among the weakest points of the Turkish economy. In turn, a most serious problem at the end of the 1980s' decade was the government-induced uncertainty about the parameters of the economy. In terms of the extent of arbitrary meddling in the rules of the game and the ensuing instability, the 1980s, in fact, compares quite unfavourably with the 1930s. Consequently, seizing and saving the day has been the basic norm of business behaviour. The development of a business community able to establish a healthy link between private and social interests has been seriously hampered. A satisfactory formal relationship between the business community and the State has yet to be realized.

---

[30] For instance, see Aydın Aybay, '1923-1939 Döneminde Mülkiyet Sorunu', in *Atatürk Döneminin Toplumsal ve Ekonomik Sorunları*, n.e. (İstanbul: İktisadi ve Ticari İlimler Fakültesi Mezunları Derneği, 1977).

12

Interest-Group Politics in post-1980 Turkey Lingering Monism

Metin Heper

Potential and Reality

At first sight, the decade of the 1980s in Turkey promised to usher in a new era in interest group politics. One came across developments during this decade that elsewhere contributed to the emergence of pluralism or different versions of corporatism. Developments favourable for the emergence of pluralism included attempts at rolling back the frontiers of the state - privatization of state economic enterprises, decentralization of government, and placing of emphasis on a market economy (Heper). * Mr Turgut Özal (Prime Minister from 1983 until 1989 and President since 1989) declared that the 1980s' decade in Turkey heralded unconstrained freedoms in economic entrepreneurship as well as freedoms of thought and conscience. Developments suitable for the advent of corporatism included, in the economy, a significant reconstruction (the strategy of import-substitution being replaced by that of export-orientation and the consequent increase in the internationalization of the economy), in the social sphere, the crystallization of a zero-sum game notion of class relations (largely a spin-off from the first process), and, in politics, a gradual weakening of the official ideology (Atatürkism) that earlier was used by the state elites to bring about social and political integration.[1]

Still, the 1980s in Turkey have hardly been conducive to the flourishing of pluralistic or corporatist interest group politics. The initial rationale behind privatization, that of spreading ownership to the public, was gradually replaced by a fiscal one of increasing government revenues. In any case, by the end of the decade, only a limited number of enterprises were privatized.[2] Decentralization of government turned out to be an effort not to promote political participation but to curb the influence of the traditional bureaucratic elites. Decentralization of government consisted of curtailing the tutelage powers of the Ministries of Interior and of Public Works and Resettlement over the metropolitan municipalities. In any event, decentralization stopped short at the level of the metropolitan municipality; it did not extend to the district municipalities.[3] Genuine political participation could, of course, take place only at the district level. The

---

* Here and below, references in parentheses refer to the chapters in this volume.

1 The processes of change initiated during the decade in question are elaborated by Ergüder, Öncü-Gökçe and Öniş, all in this volume.

2 Selim İlkin, 'Privatization of State Economic Enterprises', in *Consensus and Conflict in Turkish Politics. Dilemmas of Transition to Democracy*, Metin Heper and Ahmet Evin, eds., in preparation.

3 For an elaboration see Metin Heper, 'Motherland Party Governments and Bureaucracy in Turkey, 1983-1988', *Governance*, 2 (1989), pp. 463-5.

Motherland Party (MP) governments' (1983 to the present) unsympathetic approach to democracy as exemplified in this case, but also in other matters that are taken up below, was not helpful to the development of interest group politics.

Moreover, the MP governments rendered the civil bureaucracy less able to exercise autonomously whatever powers they still enjoyed. The first move here was to further politicize the bureaucracy.[4] Two factions within the MP (those leaning towards the now defunct religiously-oriented National Salvation Party and the ultra-nationalist Nationalist Action Party) managed to place their followers in a number of critical agencies. Secondly, several posts in the civil bureaucracy were made less secure; many functionaries were obliged to work on a contract basis. Thirdly, a number of what used to be relatively autonomous agencies were brought under close supervision by the government. For instance, a governmental decree made the Central Bank virtually no different from the regular ministries.[5] Thus, the traditional bureaucrats as potential participants in the corporatist policy-making process, were largely crippled.

It is true that the restructuring of the bureaucracy effected by the MP governments helped to centralize power within certain bureaucratic departments or agencies, and this could make it a more effective participant in corporatist policy-making. Indeed, in many agencies several committees, boards, and the like were eliminated, and authority was concentrated in the hands of a few individuals.[6] For instance, within the State Planning Organization a single department became responsible for matters pertaining to investments by foreigners in Turkey, thereby alleviating the problems generated by the fragmented nature of the bureaucracy (Öniş). Also, some newly created bureaucratic agencies such as the [Board of] Mass Housing and Public Participation Fund and the Undersecretariat of Treasury and Foreign Trade were furnished with wide responsibilities (Öniş). Yet, the bureaucrats who were recently appointed (often from outside the bureaucracy) and who amassed immense powers in their hands, acted independently of not only intra-bureaucratic pressures but also interest group associations (Öniş). Policy-formulation and implementation became increasingly encapsulated within a narrow circle of technocrat-planners, insulated both from institutionalized bureaucratic and political channels, and attached to a few decision makers in the executive (Öncü and Gökçe).

Furthermore, the parliamentary group of the MP and its party organization did not form an effective link between interest group associations and the top decision-makers. For reasons that cannot be elaborated here,[7] at the time the party was formed, few people thought that the MP could win the next general election. Consequently, many competent people did not join the party. Those who became party members had generally no previous political experience, and, therefore little political efficacy, and evinced

---

4 The politicization of the bureaucracy started in 1950 when the anti-Statist *Demokrat* Party came to power.

5 Metin Heper, 'The State and Debureaucratization: The Turkish Case', *International Social Science Journal*, no.126 (1990): 605-15.

6 Ibid.

7 For the political dynamics of Turkey before and after 1980, see Metin Heper and Ahmet Evin, eds., *State, Democracy and the Military. Turkey in the 1980s* (Berlin and New York: Walter de Gruyter, 1988) and Metin Heper and Jacob Landau, eds., *Political Parties and Democracy in Turkey* (London and New York: I.B. Tauris, Publishers, 1991).

a strong personal loyalty to Mr Özal. Also, the party was formed in great haste. In the process, many people with sympathies towards ultra-nationalism or radical Islam, too, joined the party. Quite a number of these people became members of Parliament, and later began controlling local party organizations. Consequently, a clash broke out between most members of the leadership group and others in the party.[8] Thus, it was not surprising that during the 1980s interest associations tended 'to contact the public bureaucracy or the members of the Cabinet directly, usually circumventing the TGNA [Turkish Grand National Assembly] deputies'.[9] In any case, the MP governments were 'not inclined to use the facilities of the TGNA in the law-making process'.[10]

One now observed in government 'the autonomization of an executive inner circle' in government, comprising the Prime Minister and a few technocrats around him.[11] For the leaders of interest group associations 'there...[was] no one to talk to in Ankara', since the inner circle allowed hardly anybody to lobby them. The inner circle formulated short-term policy decisions and immediately put them into effect. Then, the Prime Minister or another member of the inner circle appeared on the scene to *explain* the measures already taken and *placate* those who were adversely affected by those measures, either at special meetings or previously scheduled meetings of interest group associations (Öncü and Gökçe). The high-level contacts between the members of the inner circle and leaders of interest group associations that often attracted the attention of the mass media (Kalaycıoğlu) were, therefore, no more than monologues by the former. Besides, not all such encounters ended up by offering explanations; more often, such get-togethers were occasions for the members of the inner circle to communicate their instructions - for instance, 'sell your villas and augment your capital'-, if not their threats - for example, 'pay your taxes or else'.[12] As Kalaycıoğlu (in this volume) has noted, '[t]he tone and style of Mr Özal's talks, at the occasional meetings with the representatives of major commercial (as well as other interest) groups, and his public speeches indicate that he was more inclined to *instruct* the interest group members than *exchange views* with them'.

Mr Özal could get away with adopting such a posture towards the private sector because, during the 1980s, too, governments continued to have a significant leverage

---

8 Metin Heper, 'The State, Political Party and Society in post-1983 Turkey', *Government and Opposition*, 25 (1990), pp. 332-3.

9 Ersin Kalaycıoğlu, 'Cyclical Breakdown, Redesign and Nascent Institutionalization: the Turkish Grand National Assembly', in *Parliament and Democratic Consolidation in Southern Europe. Greece, Italy, Portugal, Spain and Turkey*, Ulrike Liebert and Maurizio Cotta, eds. (London and New York: Pinter, Publishers, 1990), p. 213.

10 Ibid., p. 202.

11 Thus, in her study of the executives of Turkish Industrialists' and Businessmen's Association (TÜSİAD), Şebnem Gülfidan has found that 52.2 per cent of first choices for *target* points of access to government was 'contacts with Prime Minister'. See Şebnem Gülfidan, 'Big Business and the State in Turkey: The Case of TÜSİAD', unpublished Ph.D. dissertation, Boğaziçi University, Istanbul, 1989, p. 118. As already noted, in 1989 Turgut Özal became President. Yet, despite the fact that Turkey essentially has a parliamentary system of government, Özal has continued to direct the economy from the Presidential Palace almost single-handedly. His 'representative' in government has been (until June 1991) Güneş Taner, Minister of State, whose clashes with leaders of interest group associations is chronicled below.

12 For one instance of such threats, see *Güneş* (Istanbul daily), 16 January 1988.

over the economy. Investments by public sector remained higher than those by the private sector (Arat). In a similar fashion, the State banks figured prominently in the financial system (Öncü and Gökçe). Governments determined key relative prices such as interest rates and exchange rates, and, furthermore, these rates were frequently changed, creating great uncertainty for and vulnerability on the part of the business community. The changes so effected were viewed as 'almost deliberately unpredictable policy moves' (Buğra). The situation was not any different concerning the favoured sector - foreign trade companies. The requirements to acquire the status of 'foreign trade company' were altered over time (İlkin). In any event, these companies remained directly dependent on a special set of government incentives (Öniş). Towards the end of the decade, they, too, received a cold shoulder from the government (İlkin).

The Motherland Party governments also have not amended in any significant manner the restrictive legal measures brought against interest group activity during the 1980-1983 period of military rule. These measures were the upshot of a deep distrust of spontaneous and pluralistic development of associational life, and derived from the overall aim of preventing the recurrence of what the military considered to be 'dysfunctional politicization' in the pre-1980 era (Kalaycıoğlu). Hence, extremely detailed and comprehensive legislation passed during the interregnum hedged basic associational freedoms with many qualifications. Among other things, a wide gap was created between the government and associational interest groups. Interest group associations were not allowed to pursue political aims, engage in political activities, get backing from or give support to political parties, or engage in joint action with trade unions. No association could be established with the aim of carrying out activities in violation of public interest or of taking action on the basis of social class. Associations could be dissolved by court decision in cases prescribed by law. They could also be suspended from activity by the competent administrative authority designated by law, pending a court decision in cases where delay would endanger public interest. As compared to the 1961 Constitution, the 1982 Constitution enlarged the scope of exceptional circumstances permitting the temporary suspension of an association by administrative authorities (Özbudun). To add insult to injury, Mr Özal from time to time threatened to close down some interest group associations when the latter criticized the economic policies pursued by his government, because the latter 'had been engaged in political activity'. Under the circumstances, throughout the decade of the 1980s, both the chambers ('professional organizations in the nature of public institutions') and voluntary associations have had a rough time in their relations with the government.

The State Versus Interest Group Associations

For a while during the post-1980 period, the chambers functioned as before, that is, as quasi-bureaucratic arms of governments. In the first place, they helped governments to set and enforce the standards for the exercise of certain professions. Ergüder's quotation (in this volume) from Robert Bianchi, that 'associations are confined to *regulate* their membership than to *represent* them' (my emphasis), well depicts the situation in the 1980s. It was for this reason that 'even the most major decisions concerning the structure and status of the Union of Chambers of Commerce and Stock Exchange (TOBB) were made without a prior dialogue between the TOBB representatives and the government'.[13] Mr Güngör Yener, the Chairman of the Ankara Chamber of Commerce retorted that it is time to halt the thinking of 'I do it, so will it be' (Kalaycıoğlu). Mr Yener implied that such a posture on the part of the government would force them to part company from the government.[14]

Secondly, chambers performed such functions as distribution of credits, purchase of government-subsidized products, and the like. Chambers of Commerce issued licences for the exporters and were instrumental in determining who obtained permission to export commodities (Kalaycıoğlu). In the process, 'they did not exhibit any systematic pattern of interest articulation; ....[They rather functioned] like state economic enterprises' (Ergüder). If they did not operate the way that governments wished they should; they were sometimes further 'bureaucratized'. For instance, in 1984, the Agricultural Credit Cooperatives were re-organized; their elected officials were replaced by government-appointed personnel (Ergüder).

Thirdly, through chambers, governments tried to direct the economic activities of the private sector so that those activities would not clash with overall economic policy. In 1987, an industrialist observed: 'Even today a businessman is under the command of the bureaucrats in Ankara' (Kalaycıoğlu). Some received better treatment. The favourites were taken along by the Prime Minister in his trips abroad so that they would find new outlets for their products (Kalaycıoğlu). As noted above, however, even the favourites were always left in a rather precarious position; from one day to another they did not know what to expect from the government.

It is with a view to this state of affairs that Kalaycıoğlu (in this volume) has come to the following conclusion: '...[the] basic features of the commercial interest groups of post-1983 Turkey seem to point to a trend for developing a *form* of state corporatism'.[15] As governments in Turkey had been distinctly differentiated from the 'interests' (Heper), what had developed was hardly state corporatism proper, a point Kalaycıoğlu has implied. It was regulation from above by governments which 'talked to others', but did not like 'to be talked to'.

For these governments thought that 'what...[was] good as espoused by the party government...[was] also good for Turkey, and there ...[was] "a public good" that...[was] disassociated from and elevated above the interests of economic (as well as social) groups' (Kalaycıoğlu). It was for this reason that governments were always interested in keeping a close eye over who were elected to the executive boards of chambers. They always tried to work with people who agreed with their economic policies (Kalaycıoğlu).

In 1986, the government went one step further and changed the organizational structure of the TOBB, despite stiff resistance from the business community. During the preparatory stages of this move the Union was not consulted.[16] Under the new system, five sectors, represented by the Union, were to set up thirty-member expert councils

---

13 Government's attempts in this direction is taken up below.

14 Towards the end of the 1980s, chambers indeed distanced themselves from the Motherland Party governments, a development we discuss below.

15 My emphasis.

16 *Milliyet* (Istanbul daily), 9 April 1986.

which would attend to the problems of the respective sectors. The fifteen-member executive board of the Union was to be elected by these councils. The apparent rationale was to further de-politicize the Union. Also, the chairman of the Union could no longer serve in that position for more than a total of ten years.[17] In reaction, Mr Ersin Faralyalı, the then Chairman of the Union said: 'I do not intend to be a civil servant.' [18] Mr Güngör Yener, Chairman of Ankara Chamber of Commerce in turn observed: '[These changes] reflect a philosophy of divide and rule.... If necessary, we would sever our ties with the government.' [19]

They indeed did this towards the end of the decade. As time went by, chambers remained less and less silent, or even moderate, in expressing their views concerning government economic policies. In particular, they severely criticized high interest rates and inflation.[20] Reaction from the government was typical: Prime Minister Özal accused the chambers of 'getting involved in politics'.[21]

Under the circumstances, the 1990 Union elections gained an added significance. The elections led to an intense competition between the governing party (MP) and one of the opposition parties - the True Path Party (TPP), led by Mr Süleyman Demirel, who had been on different occasions Prime Minister between 1965 and 1980. The then Chairman of the Union, Mr Ali Coşkun, (semi-clandestinely) supported in the past by the MP, this time sought the TPP's support. The TPP, however, came up with a candidate of their own, Mr Enis Yalım Erez. Upon this development, Mr Ali Coşkun witdrew his candidature, despite the efforts by senior MP politicians to dissuade him. In the event, Mr Erez was elected as the new chairman of the Union.[22] Upon his election, Mr Erez pointed out that he would strive to create a Union that 'everybody would respect'. During the next few months, the relations between the Union and the government continued to be a rather tense one. The Union kept on *challenging*, rather than *influencing* the government, even on matters in which it was hardly interested before. For instance, the Union criticized the government's indifference to the plight of the masses.[23] The worsening state-chambers relations resembled the state-voluntary associations relations of the same period; the latter, however, turned out to be more tumultous.

During the 1980s, a number of voluntary interest group associations in general, and TÜSİAD in particular, have been very much in the limelight. On the whole, these associations kept their distance from the governments (Esmer). Furthermore, as compared to their relations with the chambers, the governments had much less influence over the internal structure, and, therefore, the functioning of the voluntary associations. TÜSİAD itself had been a relatively small association with select membership. Its board of directors decided who whould become a member (Arat). The finding that 59 per cent of company owners/managers preferred voluntary associations to represent their sectoral interests as opposed to 31 per cent who favoured chambers for the same

---

17 *Cumhuriyet* (Istanbul daily), 30 March 1986 and 11 April 1986.
18 *Milliyet*, 9 April 1986.
19 Ibid.
20 See, for instance, *Milliyet*, 13 March 1988, and *Güneş*, 2 May 1988.
21 *Güneş*, 29 May 1988.
22 *Milliyet*, 14 May 1990; *Hürriyet* (Istanbul daily), 17 May 1990; 18 May 1990; and 27 May 1990.
23 *Milliyet*, 25 July 1990.

purpose (Kalaycıoğlu) reflected the relative autonomy of voluntary associations from the government.

Could this relative autonomy be translated into political efficacy? It is difficult to respond to this query in the affirmative. During the decade of the 1980s, the traditional suspicion on the part of governmental elites towards the intermediary structures[24] continued unabated. The term 'interest group' still had a pejorative connotation. It was not proper, businessmen felt, to speak about *group* interests; the only legitimate interest was *public* interest that could best be defined by the State (Esmer). The business community was seen as solely responsible for carrying out *economic* activities that did not clash with the overall objectives of government. Businessmen were expected not to meddle in other matters.

For instance, when in May 1990 Mr Sakıp Sabancı, head of Turkey's second largest conglomerate and the then Chairman of TÜSİAD, praised the Motherland Party government, even Mr Demirel, Chairman of the TPP, came up with a condescending, if not a sarcastic remark, about Mr Sabancı: 'Is the industrialist aspiring to the role of a politician?' Mr Demirel also implicitly threatened Mr Sabancı: 'As a businessman, what he did was not an intelligent thing to do. What else can I say?' An editorial in *Hürriyet*, Turkey's largest circulation newspaper, also expressed surprise that a businessman had poked his nose into politics: 'Not that we had belittled the whole affair, but because we had thought that everbody has a different responsibility we had not taken Mr Sabancı's comments seriously. But almost everybody reacted in some fashion to what... Mr Sabancı said.' [25] One of them was Mr Mehmet Gölhan, a high ranking member of the TPP, who pointed out that 'Mr Sabancı had talked on TV as a member of the Cabinet'.[26] When more recently TÜSİAD published a critical report about education in Turkey, again, as *Hürriyet* reported, the general atmosphere in the country was that of 'Everybody should mind his own business'.[27]

Consequently, during the 1980s, there was an almost total lack of confidence among the business community about the legitimacy of the activities carried out in pursuit of pecuniary gain only. This led to a desperate attempt to justify business as a walk of life with reference to its social value and to its positive implications for the economy as a whole (Buğra). Thus, 'it...[was] very difficult to come across a statement which...[was] very explicit about defending the interests of one social group only, regardless of the implications for the general public' (Esmer). It was still not considered appropriate to claim the Turkish version of 'what is good for General Motors is good for the United States'.

The upshot of this situation was the increased importance attributed by the voluntary interest groups to 'reasoned arguments based on research findings' (Esmer) in order to establish 'objectively' what was best for the country, and, only indirectly and

---

[24] For an elaboration of that tradition, see, *inter alia*, Metin Heper, 'Recalcitrance of the Turkish Public Bureaucracy to "Bourgeois Politics": A Multi-Factor Political Stratification Analysis', *The Middle East Journal*, 30 (1976): 485-500.

[25] *Hürriyet*, 30 May 1990.

[26] *Cumhuriyet*, 23 March 1990.

[27] *Hürriyet*, 20 September 1990 and 26 September 1990; *Cumhuriyet*, 20 September 1990.

implicitly, for themselves.[28] On those relatively rare occasions when a common point was reached between the government and voluntary interest groups, the latter presented it as the government's view (Esmer). Thus, it was not surprising that during the 1980s voluntary associations acted in a very hesitant and circumspect manner towards governments. An editorial in *Güneş* observed: 'Businessmen do not come up with new ideas either in economy or politics, and challenge the government. They are active only in the spheres of art and sports. Their most remarkable proposition to date is the need for birth control.' [29] A member described a typical TÜSİAD meeting as follows: 'The meeting starts with declarations that we agree with the government's economic policies. Then it turns out that the whole business community is against the government's policies on interest rates, imports, exports, banking sector, and the like. We do not, however, make these views of ours publicly known.' [30] When TÜSİAD does make its views publicly known it often does everything it can to soften, if not completely negate, them later. Once, the Association published a very critical report on Turkey's debt; when the government expressed its displeasure in rather strong terms the Association indicated that responsibility for the views advanced in the report belonged to the person (then a staff member at Boğaziçi University in Istanbul) who prepared the report, and not to the Association. Several businessmen explained this particular pattern of behaviour on the part of the Association - that Prime Minister Özal was a rather vindictive person and could ruin one overnight.[31] For most of the decade, all that the voluntary interest group associations did was to voice grievances and complaints in a feeble tone and after the implementation of policies (Kalaycıoğlu).

Even this they tended to do in exceptional situations and in an indirect fashion. In 1987, Mr Ömer Dinçkök, the then Chairman of TÜSİAD, indicated under which conditions and how TÜSİAD would act: 'If the government's policies are contrary to our beliefs and if they stray far away from the long-term interests of the country, then we would be obliged to inform public opinion of this situation, through the press.' [32] Later in the year, the TÜSİAD announced that it had set up a press bureau.[33] Rather than directly approaching governments, TÜSİAD makes its views known through the press, the reports it commissions to various people, seminars, symposia and conferences, and the like as well as through dinners with politicians, university staff members, journalists, and the like to discuss economic issues (Arat).[34] These activities are of course, substitutes for being consulted frequently by governments or having formal, regular meetings with governments. Concerning a rare get-together between Prime Minister Özal and some TÜSİAD members, one member observed: 'We received a warm welcome. We got the impression that he knows our problems.'[35] For the purpose of this

[28] Recently Mr. Cem Boyner, the then Chairman of TÜSİAD, said that regardless of the problems of the sector his Association represents, it was his Association's responsibility to concern itself with the state of the economy in general (*Hürriyet*, 24 June 1990).

[29] *Güneş*, 18 November 1987.

[30] *Milliyet*, 12 October 1986.

[31] Ibid., 26 August 1986 and 9 October 1987.

[32] *Nokta* (Istanbul weekly), 22 February 1987.

[33] *Güneş*, 1 August 1987.

[34] Also see Gülfidan, 'Big Business and the State', p. 140.

[35] *Milliyet*, 12 April 1988.

chapter, that the warm reception accorded them by the Prime Minister took them by surprise and that they were not expecting Mr Özal to be knowledgeable about their woes, are rather revealing.

Under the circumstances, TÜSİAD could not be politically effective. In the late 1980s, a plurality of TÜSİAD members interviewed (42 per cent) thought that it had been most successful in modifying unfavourable administrative decisions and that they were far less influential in stopping unfavourable legislation, getting favourable legislation enacted or having favourable administrative practices adopted.[36] In 1987, Mr Ömer Dinçkök, the then Chairman of TÜSİAD complained: 'The whole burden is on the private sector. Yet in the formulation of relevant decisions the private sector has no role to play.' [37]

During the 1980s not only governments have been rather harsh towards interest groups in general and voluntary associations in particular. Chambers, too, joined the bandwagon of those taking TÜSİAD to task concerning its 'rash acts'. Mr Ali Coşkun, while Chairman of the TOBB, stated: 'The TÜSİAD cannot criticize government policies....Such an act would be involvement in politics, and thus violate the Constitution and other laws' (Kalaycıoğlu). He also asserted that 'the TÜSİAD had become harmful for the Turkish economy' and that 'this association should be closed without delay' (Esmer).[38]

As with the chambers, towards the end of the decade, state-voluntary interest group relations also went through first a slow, then a rapid deterioration. Critical here was the emergence of a new breed of businessmen and industrialists - 'young, well-educated, and fast moving'.[39] An energetic team from among this new generation began to govern TÜSİAD. They were interested in broad social and political as well as economic matters. They were particularly troubled by the fact that the government did not set up some guidelines for the economy, and acted accordingly.[40]

Thus, they came up with harsh criticisms (rather than merely complaining feebly) about the government's slipshod running of the economy. They pointed out that it was no longer acceptable for the government to urge industrialists to invest, and not to consult them at all before adopting new measures and, in fact, formulate those measures at the spur of the moment.[41] In this new TÜSİAD-government confrontation, the then TÜSİAD Chairman Mr Cem Boyner gradually began not to mince his words. On one occasion, he pointed out that earlier the government's economic policy had been no more than a 'fairy tale' and that now it had become a 'tragic story'.[42] On another occasion, he said that the government should realize that people are citizens, and not

36 Gülfidan, 'Big Business and the State', p.140.

37 *Cumhuriyet*, 20 February 1987.

38 For a similar statement by the Chairman of Istanbul Chamber of Commerce, see *Güneş*, 20 January 1990.

39 Sinan Öz, 'New Business Culture in Turkey', *Turkish Daily News* (Ankara), 30 October 1989.

40 Osman Ulagay, 'TÜSİAD, Eğitim, SHP', *Cumhuriyet*, 21 September 1990. Also see the interview with the then chairman of TÜSİAD (Mr Cem Boyner) in the Supplement to *Milliyet*, 23 April 1990.

41 *Cumhuriyet*, 30 July 1990.

42 Ibid., 30 May 1990.

subjects or slaves who can be pushed around.[43] Mr Boyner urged the government not to conceive of the private sector as its rival, if not its enemy, but accept it as its partner; he added that in modern societies people are not in need of chaperoning.[44] In a rare act of solidarity, the TÜSİAD membership as a whole became united behind Mr Boyner.[45]

The government's reaction to Mr Boyner was equally harsh. Mr Güneş Taner, then Minister of State responsible for economic affairs, demanded: 'Why are members of TÜSİAD crying? Do they now earn less? Are they in the red? They should disclose to us their 1989 profits.'[46] Mr Güneş added that, 'Mr Boyner's holding company sells suits for exorbitant prices';[47] 'Mr Boyner should not hide behind others [the TÜSİAD]; he should enter into politics and compete out in the open.[48] Mr Boyner retorted back: 'I should like to think that those who aspire to public service would be mature enough to distinguish their political aspirations from the long-term interests of the community.'[49] When Mr Boyner also stated that there was a need for early elections, Mr Taner again came up with the usual accusation - that Mr Boyner was getting involved in politics. This was followed by the interrogation of Mr Boyner by the Public Prosecutor, a development that made Boyner even more bitter: 'The fault for my being here [at the Public Prosecutor's office] would belong to those who cannot put up with democracy.' [50] The statement by the Chairman of Istanbul Chamber of Industry in support of Boyner was more dramatic, and showed very clearly the business community's lingering apprehension of the State: 'We are with you...[Mr. Boyner] to the scaffold.' [51]

At the end of the decade, the relationship between voluntary organizations and the State in Turkey had turned into an open and bitter political and personal confrontation. One minister put his finger on what was happening: 'This time...[the businessmen] are doing something different. Instead of voicing their specific economic grievances, they are resorting to politicking.' [52] The business community had lost all hope concerning the present cadres of politicians. Mrs Suna Kıraç, Assistant Chairperson of the Executive Board of Koç Holding, Turkey's largest conglomerate, called in late 1989 for elite representation in parliament: 'For devising policies to maintain a healthy economy there is a need for the presence of people in the Parliament who would express the business community's views.' [53] Earlier, the more militant business community in

---

[43] Ibid., 24 January 1990 and 30 May 1990.

[44] Ibid.

[45] Ibid., 17 September 1990.

[46] Ibid., 6 June 1990.

[47] *Milliyet*, 6 June 1990.

[48] Ibid., 19 June 1990.

[49] Ibid.

[50] *Hürriyet*, 24 July 1990. The ministers were divided on Mr Boyner's interrogation, too. Some, like the then State Minister Işın Çelebi, said that in democracy the TÜSİAD should be able to express its views freely; others kept silent. *Hürriyet*, 27 July 1990. Mr. Taner himself rejected the innuendos that he had been instrumental in encouraging the prosecution against Mr Boyner, by saying that he had entered into a polemic with Mr Boyner only to defend the views he believed in. *Milliyet*, 24 July 1990.

[51] *Milliyet*, 27 July 1990.

[52] *Hürriyet*, 31 May 1990.

[53] *Milliyet*, 17 December 1989.

İzmir, Turkey's third largest city, had come up with the suggestion of a more radical 'solution': 'If Mr Özal does not listen to us, we should take to the streets!' [54]

The government's reaction to this rebellious attitude on the part of the business community was three-pronged: (1) cajole; (2) if that does not work, threaten; (3) in any case, never give in. A leading columnist in *Hürriyet* summed up the government's approach as follows: 'The State Minister Güneş Taner spends Tuesdays in Istanbul. Not unlike the Ottoman pashas sent to quell riots in the frontier regions, he holds talks with businessmen: at times, he tries to find out the latter's problems; at other times, he threatens them about the likely consequences of their actions.'[55] The government itself was of two minds. The leading columnist in *Hürriyet* explained:

> There are two possibilities. Either the riotous bosses will be given an object lesson or the government will initiate a dialogue with them. With regard to these two courses of action, the ministers have alredy been divided among themselves into hawks and doves. The fact that the Motherland Party recently lost the TOBB elections strengthens the hand of the hawks.[56]

Nevertheless, the government initially wavered between different strategies. Mr Taner first announced that a Business Council with 112 members would be established and economic decisions would be taken at the monthly meetings between this Council and the government.[57] A month later he said that 'the dialogue...[between the government and the business community] will be turned into a continuous one'.[58] But Mr Taner did not invite the Chairmen of TÜSİAD (Mr Boyner) and the TOBB (Mr Erez) to his next meeting with leading businessmen.[59] Two weeks later, the caption of a news item in *Hürriyet* was, 'Economic War Starts': Mr Taner had chosen to make public through the mass media the names of the firms who ('because of the adverse effects of the Gulf crisis') had unduly raised the prices of their products.[60] The government had once more chosen to treat the business community severely.

Lingering Monism

During the 1980s, State-interest group relations in Turkey continued to manifest unmistakable signs of monism in the absence of both pluralism and neo-corporatism. In fact, the State came to have more autonomy vis-à-vis interest groups. Prime Minister Turgut Özal, along with an inner circle of ministers and technocrat-planner administrators, mostly recruited from among Turks who had been working in the United States, made all the critical economic decisions virtually without consulting the traditional civil bureaucracy, the Parliament and the political parties as well as interest groups. These were short-term policy decisions which were put into effect immediately. They were constantly revised not in response to pressures coming from outside but when the

---

54 Ibid., 18 September 1989.
55 *Hürriyet*, 29 July 1990.
56 Ibid., 2 August 1990.
57 *Hürriyet*, 20 June 1990.
58 *Milliyet*, 18 July 1990.
59 Ibid., 1 August 1990.
60 *Hürriyet*, 14 August 1990.

inner group thought that new policies were necessary.

There was now an even greater gap between the state and interest groups not only because of further centralization of economic decision-making process and those decisions being made by tecnocrat-bureaucrats but also due to more restrictive legal restraints on interest group activity, which was effected during the interregnum of 1980-1983 and left largely intact during the years of the MP government.

This gap was not narrowed down even when for a while the government seemed to have a close affinity with one interest group - the foreign trade companies. While in France the State's encouraging the development of a societal group (the *notaires*) ended up in a clientelistic relationship and led 'to severe constraints on the power of the State to effect changes in the group's position in society',[61] in Turkey foreign trade companies remained dependent upon the state; they were always in a precarious position vis-à-vis the state; and they easily fell from favour (Öniş, İlkin).

Initially, the MP governments were aloof from all other interest groups and their associations, including the chambers. Only towards the end of the decade were they interested in the TOBB elections; when they were unsuccessful, they ignored the Union all together. In desperation, the Union changed its above-party posture, and tried to confront the MP governments on political platforms. The Union challenged the MP governments, but could not influence them. A similar development took place in the state-voluntary interest groups relations, too.

To the extent the chambers and voluntary interest group associations chose to confront governments head on, the latter by-passed them and preferred to deal with businessmen on an individual basis; businessmen as individuals, were, of course, more vulnerable. Governments treated businessmen as individuals even when the latter represented others; Mr Taner's remark that Mr Boyner should not hide behind others is a case in point. This course of action on the part of the members of government was an upshot of a very strong State - a State that did not accord legitimacy to intermediary structures. It was a State which itself decided what was best for society. Thus, in the eyes of the state elites all that the associations could do was 'to plead from the sublime state aid to the ailments of their members' (Kalaycıoğlu), as individuals, one must add. For instance, the MP governments have not expected TÜSİAD to convey to them its members' preferences and demands, let alone participate in the making of economic decisions.[62] Businessmen as individuals were to support the MP by their contributions and carry out their activities as dictated by the governments. If they strayed away from this pre-ordained role they could be ruined by selective measures adopted by the governments. For instance, during their polemic, Mr Taner threatened to lower the tariff for the goods Mr Boyner's holding company produced. This intimidation did not materialize, but there were cases earlier where such threats were carried through.[63]

Under the circumstances, it was only natural that the business community was pervaded with a lack of confidence about their political efficacy deriving, among other things, from the on-going apprehension felt towards the State. Mr Meriç Köyatası,

---

61 Ezra Suleiman, 'State Structures and Clientelism: The French State Versus the "Notaires"', *British Journal of Political Science*, 17 (1987), p. 277.

62 Gülfidan, 'Big Business and the State', p. 137.

63 For instance, Okumuş Holding was ruined in this fashion.

who directs the economics page of *Hürriyet*, recently claimed that in Turkey it took courage to establish an association, and, because they think they might get into trouble with the State, many businessmen as well as professionals did not actively support their associations.[64]

Instead, businessmen preferred to have direct contacts with government agencies (Kalaycıoğlu). Through this pattern of interface with government they could not easily participate in policy formulation. Until recently, however, this did not create much of a problem because businessmen did not try to impinge upon governments and influence policy. A survey in 1987 covering a major portion of the private industrial sector, found that for managers of the firms in this sector, as problems related to government offices, (1) 'regulations and by-laws' (22.6 per cent), (2) 'redtape' (21.5 per cent), (3) 'slow operation of the system' (19.4 per cent), and (4) 'attitudes and behaviour of lower level bureaucrats' (12.4 per cent) were far more important than both 'attitudes and behaviour of higher level bureaucrats' (9.7 per cent) and 'knowledge and adequacy of higher level officers' (3.2 per cent) (Esmer). Were businessmen interested in influencing or participating in the making of public policy then the managers would not have given short shrift to the attitudinal and cognitive characteristics of the higher level civil servants. Instead, managers were interested in such things as rules, and the lower level civil servants who carried out those rules and policies, and thus, in the way rules and policies were implemented. This significant finding points to the fact that regulation from above, in the absence of effective pluralist and neo-corporatist interest group politics, has still been a fact of life in Turkey during the 1980s.

Businessmen attempted individually to obtain concessions for themselves as individuals. Even such a prestigious interest group association as TÜSİAD was referred to as a 'club of bosses' (Esmer). Here the implication of 'personal touch' is unmistakable. Thus, in the 1987 survey of managers in the private industrial sector already noted, it was found that 'the contacts between *corporate interests* and *the government...* looked so satisfactory that more than 95 per cent of the firm owners and/or managers interviewed failed to register any current or potential demands from ...the government' (Kalaycıoğlu). But that was not the whole story, as Arat (in this volume) has indicated: 'even though individual entrepreneurs benefited from the system through personal ties, conditions favourable to private entrepreneurs [as a whole] could not be created.'

Since system-wide changes were what the new breed of businessmen were after, the question that remains to be addressed is whether towards the end of the decade interest group politics in Turkey took a turn towards pluralism or neo-corporatism. As already noted, governments wished to see neither pattern of interest group politics developing in Turkey. The new breed of businessmen for their part longed to see some *improvements*, essentially in the *present pattern*.

One set of suggestions made by businessmen *could* give the impression that they wanted the adoption of neo-corporatist arrangements. In 1986, Mr Sakıp Sabancı proposed to Özal the merger of the TOBB and TÜSİAD.[65] In 1987, Mr Ersin Faralyalı, the then Chairman of the TOBB, indicated that in Turkey negotiations take place only between labour and employers and that the government, too, should come into

---

64 Meriç Köyatası, 'Devlet Babanın Bayramı', *Hürriyet*, 2 May 1990.

65 *Milliyet*, 1 May 1986.

the picture.[66] More recently, Mr Boyner emphasized the need for consensus among all parties.[67] Other sets of suggestions again made by businessmen *could* lead one to think that they were after a pluralistic pattern of interest group politics. Significant here were constant complaints that governments were not consulting businessmen.[68] Yet, to date, businessmen in Turkey have not entertained the idea that they could effectively articulate their interests and views. It is true that they have always demanded that governments consult with them, but the impression one gets from their statements on this issue is that for them the most important thing is that the governments pay attention to their specific and often individual *problems*. Lately, they have particularly underlined the need for stable policies, that is, policies that are not frequently altered. Who devised them was of secondary importance. They did come up with proposals for economic strategies that they hoped governments could adopt. Their attitude was, as Mr Sabancı recently put it, that of 'Let us do our homework and try to persuade the government to adopt our proposal; in the last analysis, however, it is the government which would take a decision, which may be diametrically opposed to ours'.[69]

As a concluding remark it may be noted that Theda Skocpol's argument that 'the meaning of public life and the collective forms through which groups become aware of political goals and work to attain them arise not from societies alone but at the meeting point of [S]tates and societies'[70] seems to apply even to France with a strong State but not to Turkey with a stronger State. In France, the State has not smothered civil society; in Turkey it has virtually done so. Consequently, in Turkey interest group politics has evolved characteristics quite different from those in France. Also, over time, the configuration of interest group politics in Turkey has been more resistant to change than its counterpart in France.

---

66 Ibid., 10 December 1987.

67 Ibid., 21 January 1990.

68 See, *inter alia*, *Milliyet*, 10 October 1987; *Güneş*, 4 June 1988; *Hürriyet*, 27 January 1990.

69 *Nokta*, 14 October 1990.

70 Theda Skocpol, 'Bringing the State Back In: Strategies of Analysis in Current Research', in *Bringing the State Back In*, Peter B. Evans, Dietrich Rueschemeyer and Theda Skocpol, eds. (Cambridge, etc.: Cambridge University Press, 1985), p. 27.

Major References Cited

Abaç, Selçuk. *Turkish Banks and the Banking System*. Istanbul: Eurocurrency, 1986.

Akder, Halis. 'Turkey's Export Expansion in the Middle East, 1980-1985', *The Middle East Journal*, 41 (1987): 553-67.

Akgüç, Öztin. *Türkiye'de Bankacılık*. İstanbul: Gerçek Yayınevi, 1987.

Alderman, Geoffrey. *Pressure Groups and Government in Great Britain*. New York: Longman, 1984.

Alford, R. and R. Friedland, *Powers of Theory*. Cambridge: Cambridge University Press, 1985.

Almond, Gabriel A. 'Corporatism, Pluralism and Professional Memory', *World Politics*, 35 (1983): 245-60.

Almond, Gabriel A. and G. Bingham Powell, Jr. *Comparative Politics, Process and Policy*, 2nd edition. Boston: Little, Brown and Co., 1978.

Alpender, Güvenç G. 'Entrepreneurs and Private Enterprises in Turkey', in *Turkish Administrator. A Cultural Survey*, Güvenç G. Alpender and Jerry R. Hopper, eds. Ankara: USAID, 1967.

Ansay, Tuğrul. 'Law of Persons', in *Introduction to Turkish Law*, Tuğrul Ansay and Don Wallace, Jr., eds. Deventer: Kluwer Law and Taxation Publishers, 1987.

Aybay, Aydın. '1923-1939 Döneminde Mülkiyet Sorunu', in *Atatürk Döneminin Toplumsal ve Ekonomik Sorunları*, n.e. İstanbul: İktisadi ve Ticari Ilimler Fakültesi Mezunları Derneği, 1977.

Ayberk, Ural and Emre Boduroğlu. 'Turkish Interest Groups Facing the European Community', *Yapı Kredi [Bank] Economic Review*, (Istanbul), 3 (1989): 125-58.

Avcıoğlu, Doğan. *Türkiye'nin Düzeni. Dün, Bugün, Yarın*. Ankara: Bilgi Yayınevi, 1969.

Azarya, Victor and Naomi Chazan. 'Disengagement from the State in Africa: Reflections on the Experience of Ghana and Guinea', *Comparative Studies in Society and History*, 29 (1987): 106-31.

Badie, Bertrand and Pierre Birnbaum. *The Sociology of the State*, trans. by Arthur Goldhammer. Chicago: University of Chicago Press, 1983.

Baer, Gabriel. 'The Administrative, Economic, and Social Functions of Turkish Guilds', *International Journal of Middle East Studies*, 1 (1970), 28-50.

Balassa, Bela. 'The Lessons of East Asian Development', *Economic Development and Cultural Change*, 16 (1988): 273-90.

Bendix, Reinhard. *Kings or People. Power and the Mandate to Rule.* Berkeley: University of California Press, 1978.

Berger, Suzanne. 'Introduction', in *Organizing Interests in Western Europe. Pluralism, Corporatism and the Transformation of Politics*, Suzanne Berger, ed. Cambridge: Cambridge University Press, 1981.

Bianchi, Robert. *Interest Groups and Political Development in Turkey.* Princeton: Princeton University Press, 1984.

Bilen, Alber. *Türk Sanayinde Kırk Zorlu Yıl.* İstanbul: Milliyet, 1988.

Birnbaum, Pierre. *States and Collective Action. The European Experience.* Cambridge, etc.: Cambridge University Press, 1988.

Birnbaum, Pierre. 'The State versus Corporatism', *Politics and Society*, 11 (1981): 490-501.

Boratav, Korkut. *Türkiye İktisat Tarihi, 1908-1985.* Ankara: Gerçek Yayınevi, 1988.

Boratav, Korkut. *Stabilization and Adjustment Programmes and Policies. Country Study-Turkey.* Helsinki: Wider, 1987.

Boratav, Korkut. *Türkiye'de Devletçilik.* İstanbul: Gerçek Yayınevi, 1974.

Boratav, Korkut and Oktar Türel. 'Notes on the Current Development Problems and Growth Prospects of the Turkish Economy', *New Perspectives on Turkey*, 2 (1988): 37-50.

Birtek, Faruk. 'The State and the Transition to Capitalism in England and Turkey: A Socio-Cultural Model', unpublished Ph.D. dissertation, University of California, Berkeley, 1978.

Buğra, Ayşe. 'The Late Coming Tycoons of Turkey', *Journal of Economics and Administrative Studies* (Istanbul), 1 (1987): 143-55.

Cawson, Alan. *Corporatism and Political Theory.* Oxford: Basil Blackwell, 1986.

Cawson, Alan. 'Conclusion: Some Implications for State Theory', in *Organized Interests and the State. Studies in Meso-Corporatism*, Alan Cawson, ed. London, etc.: Sage, 1985.

Celasun, Merih and Danny Roderik. *Debt, Adjustment and Growth. Turkey.* Chicago: University of Chicago Press, 1989.

Chalmers, Douglas A. 'The Politicized State in Latin America', in *Authoritarianism and Corporatism in Latin America*, James M. Malloy, ed. Pittsburgh: University of Pittsburgh Press, 1977.

Coleman, William D. 'State Corporatism as a Sectoral Phenomenon: The Case of the Quebec Construction Industry', in *Organized Interests and the State. Studies in Meso-Corporatism*, Alan Cawson, ed. London, etc.: Sage, 1985.

Cox, Andrew. 'Neo-Corporatism versus the Corporate State', in *The Corporate State. Corporatism and the State Tradition in Western Europe*, Andrew Cox and Noel O'Sullivan, eds. Aldershot, England: Edward Elgar, 1988.

Cox, Andrew and Jack Hayward. 'The Inapplicability of the Corporatist Model in Britain and France: The Case of Labour', *International Political Science Review*, 4 (1983): 217-40.

Çelik, Nuri. *İş Hukuku Dersleri*. İstanbul: Marmara Üniversitesi Eğitim ve Yardım Vakfı, 1986.

Çölaşan, Emin. *12 Eylül. Özal Ekonomisinin Perde Arkası*. İstanbul: Milliyet, 1984.

Çölaşan, Emin. *Banker Skandalının Perde Arkası*. İstanbul: Milliyet, 1984.

Çiller, Tansu and Mehmet Kaytaz, *Kamu Kesimi Açıkları ve Enflasyon*. İstanbul: İstanbul Ticaret Odası, 1989.

Demirgil, Demir. 'Özel Sektörün Yatırım Eğilimindeki Durgunluk', *Türk Tarihi Dergisi*, 1 (1985): 54-6.

Derin, Haldun. *Türkiye'de Devletçilik*. İstanbul: Çituri Biraderler Basımevi, 1940.

Dodd, C.H. *The Crisis of Turkish Democracy*. Walkington, England: The Eothen Press, 1983.

Dyson, Kenneth H.F. *The State Tradition in Western Europe. A Study of an Institution and Idea*. Oxford: Martin Robertson, 1980.

Easton, David. *A Framework for Political Analysis*. Englewood Cliffs, New Jersey: Prentice-Hall, 1965.

Effimianidis, Yorgaki. *Cihan İktisad Buhranı Önünde Türkiye*. İstanbul: Kağıtçılık Matbaacılık A.Ş., 1935.

Ehrmann, Henry W. *Interest Groups on Four Continents*. Westport, Conn.: Greenwood Press, 1983. First printed in 1958.

Eldersveld, Samuel, Sonja Hubee-Boonzanjer and Jan Kooiman. 'Elite Perceptions of the Political Process in the Netherlands, Looked at in Comparative Perspective', in *The Mandarins of Western Europe. The Political Role of Top Civil Servants*, Mattei Dogan, ed. New York, etc.: John Wiley, 1975.

Eralp, Atilla. 'The Politics of Turkish Development Strategies', in *Turkish State, Turkish Society*, Andrew Finkel and Nükhet Sirman, eds. London: Routledge, 1990.

Erdilek, Asım. 'The Turkish Free Market in Jeopardy', *The Wall Street Journal*, 15 February 1985.

Ergüder, Üstün. 'The Motherland Party, 1983-1989', in *Political Parties and Democracy in Turkey*, Metin Heper and Jacob Landau, eds. London and New York: I.B. Tauris, 1991.

Ergüder, Üstün and Richard Hofferbert. 'Restoration of Democracy in Turkey? Political Reform and the Elections of 1983', in *Elections in the Middle East. Implications of Recent Trends*, Linda L. Layne, ed. Boulder, Colorado: Westview Press, 1987.

Ergüder, Üstün. 'Politics of Agricultural Price Policy in Turkey', in *The Political Economy of Income Distribution in Turkey*, Ergun Özbudun and Aydın Ulusan, eds. New York: Holmes and Meier, 1980.

Ergüder, Üstün. 'Politics of Agricultural Taxation in Turkey', unpublished Ph.D. dissertation, Syracuse University, U.S.A., 1969.

Ertuna, Özcan. *Finansal Kurumlar.* Ankara: Teori, 1986.

Esener, Turhan. *İş Hukuku.* Ankara: Ankara Üniversitesi Hukuk Fakültesi, 1978.

Eser, Kadir. *Dış Ticaret Sermaye Şirketleri.* Ankara: İş Bankası, 1989.

Esmer Yılmaz, Hamit Fişek, Ersin Kalaycıoğlu and Süleyman Özmucur. *İş Dünyasının Sorunları. Öncelikler, Beklentiler ve Çözümler.* İstanbul: TÜSİAD, 1988.

Evans, Peter, Dietrich Rueschmeyer and Theda Skocpol, eds. *Bringing the State Back In.* Cambridge: Cambridge University Press, 1985.

Finer, Samuel E. 'State-and Nation-Building in Europe: The Role of the Military', in *Formation of National States in Western Europe*, Charles Tilly, ed. Princeton: Princeton University Press, 1975.

Frieden Jeff. 'The Third World Indebted Industrialization: International Finance and State Capitalism in Mexico, Brazil, Algeria, and South Korea', *International Organization*, 35 (1981): 407-31.

Gerschenkron, Alexander. *Economic Backwardness in Historical Perspective.* Cambridge, Mass: Harvard University Press, 1966.

Goetsky, Janine. 'The Neo-Corporatist Issue in France', in *Political Stability and Neo-Corporatism. Corporatist Integration and Societal Cleavages in Western Europe*, Ilja Scholten, ed. London, etc.: Sage, 1987).

Gökalp, Şerafettin. *Açıklamalı Dernekler Kanunu ve İlgili Mevzuat.* İstanbul: Yetkin, 1986.

Gökçe, Deniz. 'Terk', *Ekonomik Bülten* (Istanbul weekly), 7-13 November 1988.

Gülfidan, Şebnem. 'Big Business and the State: The Case of TÜSİAD', unpublished Ph.D. dissertation, Boğaziçi University, Istanbul, 1989.

Güran, Sait. 'Administrative Law', in *Introduction to Turkish Law*, Tuğrul Ansay and Don Wallace, Jr., eds. Deventer: Kluwer Law and Taxation Publishers, 1987.

Gürcan, Ali Niyazi. *Dış Ticaret Sermaye Şirketleri.* Ankara: İş Bankası, 1986.

Haggard, Stephen. 'The Politics of Adjustment: Lessons from the IMF's Extended Fund Facility', *International Organization*, 39 (1985): 505-34.

Hale, William: *The Political and Economic Development of Modern Turkey.* London: Croom Helm, 1981.

Hanson, A. H. and C.R. Neal. *Interest Rate Policies in Selected Developing Countries.* Washington, D.C. : World Bank Industry and Finance Series, 14, 1986.

Harrison, Reginald J. *Pluralism and Corporatism. The Political Evolution of Modern Democracies.* London, etc.: George Allen and Unwin, 1980.

Hayward, Jack. 'Interest Groups and the Demand for State Action', in *State and Society in Contemporary Europe*, Jack Hayward and R.H. Berki, eds. Oxford: Martin Robertson, 1979.

Heper, Metin. 'Extremely "Strong State" and Democracy: The Turkish Case in Comparative Perspective', in *Modernity and Democracy*, Deborah Grenium, ed. for Israel Academy of Sciences and Humanities. Leiden: Brill, forthcoming.

Heper, Metin. 'Dynamics of Inter-Governmental Relations in post-1983 Turkey', in *Structure of Local Politics in the Middle East*, Takeji Ino, ed. Tokyo: Institute of Developing Economies, 1991.

Heper, Metin. 'The State and Debureaucratization: The Turkish Case', *International Social Science Journal*, no.126 (1990): 605-15.

Heper, Metin. 'The State, Political Party and Society in post-1983 Turkey', *Government and Opposition*, 25 (1990): 321-33.

Heper, Metin. 'The Executive in the Third Turkish Republic, 1982-1989', *Governance*, 3 (1990): 299-319.

Heper, Metin. 'The Motherland Party Governments and Bureaucracy in Turkey, 1983-1989', *Governance*, 2 (1989): 457-68.

Heper, Metin, ed. *Local Government in Turkey. Governing Greater Istanbul.* London: Routledge, 1989.

Heper, Metin. 'Introduction', in *Democracy and Local Government. Istanbul in the 1980s*, Metin Heper, ed. Walkington, England: The Eothen Press, 1987.

Heper, Metin. 'Introduction', in *The State and Public Bureaucracies. A Comparative Perspective*, Metin Heper, ed. New York, etc.: Greenwood Press, 1987.

Heper, Metin. *The State Tradition in Turkey.* Walkington, England: The Eothen Press, 1985.

Heper, Metin. 'The State and Public Bureaucracies: A Comparative and Historical Perspective', *Comparative Studies in Society and History*, 27 (1985): 86-110.

Heper, Metin. 'A *Weltanschuung*-turned-Partial Ideology and Normative Ethics: "Atatürkism" in Turkey', *Orient*, 1 (1984): 83-94.

Heper, Metin. 'A Methodological Note on Bureaucratic Modernization: Prevalent Attitudes of the Turkish Civil Servants', *International Review of Modern Sociology*, 12 (1982): 75-103.

Heper, Metin. 'Transformation of Charisma into a Political Paradigm: "Atatürkism" in Turkey', *Journal of the American Institute for the Study of Middle Eastern Civilization*, 1 (1980-81): 65-82.

Heper, Metin. 'Center and Periphery in the Ottoman Empire with Special Reference to the Nineteenth Century', *International Political Science Review*, 1 (1980): 81-105.

Heper, Metin. 'Recalcitrance of the Turkish Public Bureaucracy to "Bourgeois Politics": A Multi-Factor Political Stratification Analysis', *The Middle East Journal*, 30 (1976): 485-500.

Heper, Metin and Ahmet Evin, eds. *State, Democracy and the Military. Turkey in the 1980s.* Berlin and New York: Walter de Gruyter, 1988.

Heper, Metin and Jacob Landau, eds. *Political Parties and Democracy in Turkey.* London and New York: I.B. Tauris, 1991.

Huntington, Samuel P. *Political Order in Changing Societies.* New Haven: Yale University Press, 1968.

İlkin, Selim. 'Privatization of State Economic Enterprises', in *Consensus and Conflict in Turkish Politics. Dilemmas of Transition to Democracy*, Metin Heper and Ahmet Evin, eds., in preparation.

İnan, Nurkut and Cüneyt Ozansoy. 'Yasama Faaliyeti Açısından 12 Eylül', *Yapıt*, no. 14 (1986): 3-43.

İnsel, Ahmet. *La Turquie entre l'ordre et développement.* Paris: l'Harmattan, 1984.

İrem, Nazım. Interest Groups-Government Interface: The Case of Turkish Businessmen's and Industrialists' Association', unpublished M.A. thesis, Bilkent University, Ankara, 1990.

Jessop, Bob. *The Capitalist State.* Oxford: Martin Robertson, 1982.

Johnson, Chalmers. 'Political Institutions and Economic Performance: The Government-Business Relationship in Japan, S. Korea and Taiwan', in *Political Economy of the New Asian Industrialism*, Frederic C. Deyo, ed. Ithaca and London: Cornell University Press, 1987.

James, Leroy P. and El SaKong. *Government, Business and Entrepreneurship in Economic Development. The Korean Case.* Cambridge, Mass.: Council on East Asian Studies, Harvard University, 1980.

Jordan, A.C. and J.J. Richardson, *Government and Pressure Groups in Britain.* Oxford: Clarendon Press, 1987.

Kafadar, Cemal. 'A Death in Venice (1575): Anatolian Muslim Merchants Trading in the Serenissima', *Journal of Turkish Studies*, 10 (1986): 191-219.

Kalaycıoğlu, Ersin. 'Cyclical Breakdown, Redesign and Nascent Institutionalization: The Turkish Grand National Assembly', in *Parliament and Democratic Consolidation in Southern Europe. Greece, Italy, Portugal, Spain and Turkey*, Ulrike Liebert and Maurizio Cotta, eds. London and New York: Pinter, Publishers, 1990.

Kalaycıoğlu, Ersin. 'Türk Yasama Sistemi ve Siyasal Temsil', in *Türk Siyasal Hayatının Gelişimi*, Ersin Kalaycıoğlu and Ali Yaşar Sarıbay, eds. İstanbul: Beta, 1986.

Kalaycıoğlu, Ersin. 'Turkish Political System in Transition: Multi-Party Politics in the 1980s', *Current Turkish Thought*, no. 56 (1985): 2-38.

Kalaycıoğlu, Ersin. *Karşılaştırmalı Siyasal Katılma.* İstanbul: İstanbul Üniversitesi Siyasal Bilimler Fakültesi, 1983.

Karpat, Kemal H. 'The Ottoman Views and Policies toward the Orthodox Christian Church', *Greek Orthodox Theological Review*, 31 (1986): 131-55.

Karpat, Kemal H. 'Turkish Democracy at Impasse: Ideology, Party Politics and the Third Military Intervention', *International Journal of Turkish Studies*, 2 (1981): 1-43.

Karpat, Kemal H. 'Structural Change, Historical Stages of Modernization and the Role of Social Groups in Turkish Politics', in *Social Change and Politics in Turkey. A Structural-Historical Analysis*, Kemal H. Karpat, ed. Leiden: Brill, 1973.

Katzenstein, Peter, ed. *Between Power and Plenty.* Madison: University of Wisconsin Press, 1978.

Katzenstein, Peter. 'Domestic and International Structures and Strategies of Foreign Economic Policy', *International Organization*, 31 (1977): 587-606.

Keeler, John. *Politics of Neocorporatism in France.* Oxford and New York: Oxford University Press, 1987.

Keyder, Çağlar. *State and Class in Turkey. A Study in Capitalist Development.* London: Verso Press, 1987.

King, Roger. *The State and Modern Society. New Directions in Political Sociology.* London: Macmillan, 1986.

Kozanoğlu, Hayri. 'İhracatı Teşvik Sistemini Geliştirme', 1989, typescript.

Kozlu, Cem. *Uluslararası Pazarlama.* İstanbul: İş Bankası, 1982.

Krasner, Stephan D. 'Approaches to the State: Alternative Conceptions and Historical Dynamics', *Comparative Politics*, 16 (1984), 222-44.

Krueger, Anne O. *Foreign Trade Regimes and Economic Development. Turkey.* New York: Columbia University Press, 1974.

Krueger, Anne O. 'The Political Economy of Rent-Seeking Society', *American Economic Review*, 64 (1974): 291-303.

Kuruç, Bilsay. *Mustafa Kemal Döneminde Ekonomi.* Ankara: Bilgi Yayınevi, 1987.

Lawau, George. 'Political Pressures by Interest Groups in France', in *Interest Groups on Four Continents*, Henry W. Ehrmann, ed. Westport, Connecticut: Greenwood Press, 1958.

Lehmbruch, Gerhard. 'Concertation and the Structure of Networks', in *Order and Conflict in Contemporary Capitalism. Studies in the Political Economy of Western European Nations*, John H. Goldthorpe, ed. Oxford: Clarendon Press, 1988.

Linz, Juan J. 'A Century of Politics and Interests in Spain', in *Organizing Interests in Western Europe. Pluralism, Corporatism and the Transformation of Politics*, Suzanne Berger, ed. Cambridge: Cambridge University Press, 1981.

Ludington, Nicholas S. and James W. Spain. 'Dateline Turkey: The Case for Patience', *Foreign Policy*, 50 (1983): 150-68.

Maier, Charles. 'Preconditions for Corporatism', in *Order and Conflict in Contemporary Capitalism. Studies in the Political Economy of Western European Nations*, John H. Goldthorpe, ed. Oxford: Clarendon Press, 1988.

Mardin, Şerif. 'Center-Periphery Relations: A Key to Turkish Politics ?' *Daedalus*, 102 (1973): 169-90.

Mardin, Şerif. 'Power, Civil Society and Culture in the Ottoman Empire', *Comparative Studies in Society and History*, 11 (1969): 258-81.

McFadden, John H. 'Civil-Military Relations in the Third Turkish Republic', *The Middle East Journal*, 39 (1985): 69-85.

Miliband, Ralph. *The State in Capitalist Society.* London: Weidenfeld and Nicolson, 1969.

Millard, Frances. *Pressure Politics in Industrial Societies.* London: Macmillan, 1986.

Moore, Clement Henry. 'Islamic Banks and Competitive Politics in the Arab World and Turkey', *The Middle East Journal,* 44 (1990): 234-55.

Nahum, Bernar. *Koç'ta 44 Yılım.* İstanbul: Milliyet, 1988.

Nettl, J.P. 'The State as a Conceptual Variable', *World Politics,* 21 (1968): 554-92.

Neyzi, Nezih. 'The Middle Classes in Turkey', in *Social Change and Politics in Turkey. A Structural-Historical Analysis.* Kemal H. Karpat, ed. Leiden: Brill, 1973.

Nordlinger, Eric. *On the Autonomy of the Democratic State.* Cambridge: Harvard University Press, 1981.

O'Donnell, Guillermo. 'Corporatism and the Question of the State', in *Authoritarianism and Corporatism in Latin America,* James M. Malloy, ed. Pittsburgh: University of Pittsburgh Press, 1977.

O'Donnell, Guillermo, *Modernization and Bureaucratic Authoritarianism. Studies in South American Politics.* Berkeley:Institute of International Studies, University of California, 1973.

Okyar, Osman. 'Turkey and the IMF: A Review of Relations', in *IMF Conditionality,* John Willamson, ed. Washington, D.C.: Institute for International Economics, 1983.

Oyan, Oğuz. 'Fonlar, İstikrar Programı ve Özelleştirme', *Mülkiyeliler Birliği Dergisi,* no. 91 (1988), pp. 20-6.

Oyan, Oğuz. *24 Ocak Ekonomisinde Dışa Açılma ve Mali Politikalar.* Ankara: V Yayınları, 1987.

Oyan, Oğuz. 'ANAP'ın Fon Ekonomisi', *Görüş,* 15 September 1987.

Oyan, Oğuz and Ali Rıza Aydın. *İstikrar Programından Fon Ekonomisine.* Ankara: Verso, 1987.

Öncü, Ayşe. 'Cumhuriyet Döneminde Odalar', *Cumhuriyet Dönemi Türkiye Ansiklopedisi,* 50 (1984): 1566-76.

Öncü, Ayşe. 'Chambers of Industry in Turkey: An Inquiry into State-Industry Relations as a Distributive Domain', in *The Political Economy of Income Distribution in Turkey,* Ergun Özbudun and Aydın Ulusan, eds. New York: Holmes and Meier, 1980.

Öncü, Ayşe. 'Inter-Organizational Networks and Social Structures: Turkish Chambers of Industry', *International Social Science Journal,* 21 (1979): 646-60.

Öniş, Ziya. 'Organization of Export-Oriented Industrialization: The Turkish Foreign Trade Companies in Comparative Perspective', 1988, typescript.

Öniş, Ziya. 'Inflation and Import Substituting Industrialization: An Interpretation of the Turkish Case', *Journal of Economics and Administrative Studies* (Istanbul), 1 (1987): 56-72.

Öz, Sinan. 'New Business Culture in Turkey', *Turkish Daily News* (Ankara), 20 October 1989.

Özbudun, Ergun. *Türk Anayasa Hukuku.* Ankara: Yetkin, 1986.

Özbudun, Ergun. 'Political Parties and Elections', in *Türkei Sudosteuropa-Handbuch, Band IV*, Klaus Detlev Grothusen, ed. Göttingen: Vandanhoeck und Ruprecht, 1985.

Özbudun, Ergun. *Social Change and Political Participation in Turkey.* Princeton: Princeton University Press, 1976.

Özel, Mustafa. *Dış Ticarette Sermaye Şirketleri.* Ankara: Türk-Trade, 1988.

Özmucur, Süleyman. *Türkiye'nin Milli Geliri.* İstanbul: İstanbul Ticaret Odası, 1987.

Özsunay, Ergun. *Medeni Hukukumuzda Tüzel Kişiler.* İstanbul: İstanbul Üniversitesi Hukuk Fakültesi, 1982.

Pamuk, Şevket. 'İthal İkamesi, Döviz Darboğazları ve Türkiye, 1947-1979', in *Kriz, Gelir Dağılımı ve Türkiye'nin Alternatif Sorunu*, Korkut Boratav, Çağlar Keyder and Şevket Pamuk, eds. İstanbul: Kaynak, 1987.

Panitch, Leo. 'The Development of Corporatism in Liberal Democracies', in *Trends Toward Corporatist Intermediation*, Philippe C. Schmitter and Gerhard Lehmbruch, eds. London: Sage: 1979.

Parla, Taha. *Demokrasi, Anayasalar, Partiler ve Türkiye'nin Siyasal Rejimi.* İstanbul: Onur, 1986.

Pevsner, Lucille W. *Turkey's Political Crisis.* New York: Praeger, 1984.

Pizzorno, Alessandro. 'Interests and Parties in Pluralism', in *Organizing Interests in Western Europe. Pluralism, Corporatism and the Transformation of Politics*, Suzanne Berger, ed. Cambridge University Press, 1981.

Poggi, Gianfranco. *The Development of the Modern State. A Sociological Introduction.* London: Hutchinson, 1978.

Polanyi, Karl. *The Great Transformation.* Boston: Beacon Press, 1957.

Polanyi, Karl, Conrad M. Arensberg and Harry W. Pearson, eds. *Trade and Market in the Early Empire.* Chicago: Gateway, 1957.

Poulantzas, Nicos. *Political Power and Social Classes.* London: New Left Books, 1973.

Rustow, Dankwart A. 'Turkey's Liberal Revolution', *Middle East Review*, 17 (1985): 5-11.

Sağlam, Fazıl. 'Türk Hukuk Yapısı Nasıl Değiştirildi? 12 Eylül Yasaları', *Cumhuriyet* (Istanbul daily), 9-13 November 1987.

Salisbury, Robert. 'Interest Groups', in *Handbook of Political Science, Vol. IV., Non-governmental Politics*, Fred I. Greenstein and Nelson W. Polsby, eds. Reading, Massachusetts, etc: Addison-Wesley, 1975.

Saybaşılı, Kemali. 'Chambers of Commerce and Industry, Political Parties and Government. A Comparative Analysis of the British and the Turkish Case', *Studies in Development* (Ankara), 11 (1976): 117-36.

Saybaşılı, Kemali. 'Türkiye'de Özel Teşebbüs ve Ekonomi Politikası', *Gelişme Dergisi* (Ankara), 13 (1976): 83-98.

Scase, Richard. 'Introduction', in *The State in Western Europe*, Richard Scase, ed. London: Croom Helm, 1980.

Schmitter, Philippe C. 'Neo-Corporatism and the State', in *The Political Economy of Corporatism*, Wyn Grant, ed. London: Macmillan, 1986.

Schmitter, Philippe C. 'Models of Interest Intermediation and Models of Societal Change in Western Europe', in *Trends Toward Corporatist Intermediation*, Philippe C. Schmitter and Gerhard Lehmbruch, eds. London: Sage, 1979.

Schmitter, Philippe C. 'Still the Century of Corporatism?' *Review of Politics*, 36 (1974): 85-131.

Skocpol, Theda. 'Bringing the State Back In: Strategies of Analysis in Current Research', in *Bringing the State Back In*, Peter B. Evans, Dietrich Rueschemeyer and Theda Skocpol, eds. Cambridge, etc.: Cambridge University Press, 1985.

Sönmez, Mustafa. *Kırk Haramiler. Türkiye'de Holdingler.* İstanbul: Gözlem, 1987.

Stallings, Barbara. 'International Lending and the Relative Autonomy of the State: A Case Study of Twentieth Century Peru', *Politics and Society*, 14 (1985): 257-88.

Steinbach, Udo. 'Turkey's Third Republic', *Aussen Politik*, 3 (1988): 237-56.

Stepan, Alfred. *The State and Society. Peru in Comparative Perspective.* Princeton: Princeton University Press, 1978.

Strayer, Joseph R. *On the Medieval Origins of the Modern State.* Princeton: Princeton University Press, 1970.

Suleiman, Ezra. *Private Power and Centralization in France. The Notaries and the State.* Princeton: Princeton University Press, 1988.

Suleiman, Ezra. 'State Structure and Clientelism: The French State Versus the "Notaires"', *British Journal of Political Science*, 17 (1987): 257-79.

Suleiman, Ezra. *Politics, Power and Bureaucracy in France. The Administrative Elite.* Princeton: Princeton University Press, 1974.

Sunar, İlkay. *State and Society in the Politics of Turkey's Development.* Ankara: Ankara University Faculty of Political Science, 1974.

Tanör, Bülent. *İki Anayasa. 1961-1982.* İstanbul: Beta, 1986.

Tekeli, İlhan and Selim İlkin. *1929 Dünya Buhranında Türkiye'nin İktisadi Politika Arayışları.* Ankara: ODTÜ, 1977.

Tengirşenk, Yusuf Kemal. *Türk İnkılabı Dersleri. Ekonomik Değişmeler.* Ankara: Yurt, 1935.

Thompson, David. *Democracy in France. The Third and Fourth Republics.* London: Oxford University Press, 1958.

Tilly, Charles. *Coercion, Capital and European States, AD 990-1990.* Oxford: Basil Blackwell, 1990.

Togan, Sübidey, Hasan Olgun, and Halis Akder. *Recent Developments in External Economic Relations of Turkey.* Istanbul: Türk Trade, 1987.

Tökin, İsmail Hüsrev. *Türkiye Köy İktisadiyatı.* Ankara: Kadro Mecmuası, 1934.

Tönnies, Ferdinand. *Community and Society*, trans. and ed. by Charles Loomis. New York: Harper and Row, 1963.

Turan, İlter. 'Political Parties and the Party System in post-1983 Turkey', in *State, Democracy and the Military. Turkey in the 1980s*, Metin Heper and Ahmet Evin, eds. Berlin and New York: Walter de Gruyter, 1988.

TÜSİAD. *1980 Sonrası Ekonomide Kamu-Özel Sektör Dengesi.* İstanbul: TÜSİAD, 1988.

Uysal, Süleyman. 'Türkiye'de Teşvik Sistemi ve Etkinliği', 1989, typescript.

Varlık, Bülent. 'Dış Ticaret Sermaye Şirketleri', 1989, typescript.

Wiarda, Howard J. 'Corporatism and Development in the Iberic-Latin World: Persistent Strains and New Variations', in *The New Corporatism. Social-Political Structures in the Iberian World*, Fredrick B. Bike and Thomas Stritch, eds. Notre Dame and London: University of Notre Dame Press, 1974.

Williamson, Peter J. *Corporatism in Perspective. An Introductory Guide to Corporatist Theory.* London, etc.: Sage, 1989.

Williamson, Peter J. *Varieties of Corporatism. A Conceptual Discussion.* Cambridge: Cambridge University Press, 1985.

Wilson, Frank L. *Interest-Group Politics in France* Cambridge, etc.: Cambridge University Press, 1987.

Wilson, Graham K. *Interest Groups.* Oxford: Basil Blackwell, 1990.

Wilson, Graham K. *Business and Politics. A Comparative Introduction.* London: Macmillan, 1985.

Wolff, Peter. *Stabilization Policy and Structural Adjustment in Turkey, 1980-1985.* Berlin: German Development Institute, 1987.

Yavuz, Fehmi. 'Özel Teşebbüs ve Plânlı Kalkınmamız', in *Doç.Dr. Cem Sar'a Armağan,* n.e. Ankara: Ankara University Faculty of Political Science, 1972.

Yeşilada, Birol. 'New Political Parties and the Problems of Development in Turkey', *New Perspectives on Turkey,* 1 (1987): 35-62.

Contributors

Yeşim Arat is Associate Professor of Political Science at Boğaziçi University, Istanbul. Professor Arat has contributed to such journals as *Muslim World* and *International Political Science Review*, and such collected volumes as *The Yearbook for Comparative Social Research*, and is author of *Patriarchal Paradox. Women Politicians in Turkey.*

Ayşe Buğra is Associate Professor of Economics at Boğaziçi University. Author of a book in Turkish, she has contributed to such journals as *Current Anthropology, Technological Forecasting and Social Change, Review of Radical Political Economics, Labor Capital and Society, Studies in Development* (Ankara), *Journal of Economics and Administrative Studies* (Istanbul), *MAUSS*, and *Interventions Economiques.*

Üstün Ergüder is Professor of Political Science at Boğaziçi University. Author of two books in Turkish, he has contributed to such journals as *Journal of Public Policy* and such collected volumes as *Democracy and Local Government. Istanbul in the 1980s, Local Government in Turkey. Governing Greater Istanbul, State, Democracy and the Military. Turkey in the 1980s*, and *Elections in the Middle East. Implications of Recent Trends.*

Yılmaz Esmer is Professor of Political Science at Boğaziçi University. He has contributed to such journals as *Sociology of Education* and such collected volumes as *National Development and the World System. Educational, Economic and Political Change, 1950-1970*, and *Local Government in Turkey. Governing Greater Istanbul.*

Deniz Gökçe is Associate Professor of Economics at Boğaziçi University. He has contributed to such journals as *The Middle East Business and Banking* (Istanbul), *Journal of Economics and Administrative Sciences* (Istanbul), and *Türk-Trade. Trade and Business Review* (Ankara).

Metin Heper (Editor) is Professor of Political Science at Bilkent University, Ankara. He has contributed to such journals as *International Social Science Journal, Administration and Society, International Review of Modern Sociology, Res Publica International Journal of Political Education, Governance, International Political Science Review, Comparative Politics, Comparative Political Studies, Journal of Democracy, Comparative Studies in Society and History* and *Government and Opposition*, and is co-editor of *Islam and Politics in the Modern Middle East, State, Democracy and the Military. Turkey in the 1980s*, and *Political Parties and Democracy in Turkey*, editor of *Dilemmas* of *Decentralization. The Municipal Government in Turkey, Democracy and Local Government. Istanbul in the 1980s, Local Government in Turkey. Governing Greater Istanbul* and *The State and Public Bureaucracies. A Comparative Perspective*, and author of *The State Tradition in Turkey.*

Selim İlkin, formerly Director of the Institute of Economic and Social Studies at the Middle Technical University, is now a Research Fellow at the Centre of Economic and Social Studies of Islamic Countries, Ankara. Co-author of seven books in Turkish, he has contributed to such collected volumes as *Die Türkei aufdem Weg in die EG, Turquie, Moyen-Orient et Communaute Européenne*, and *Turkey and the European Community.*

Ersin Kalaycıoğlu is Professor of Political Science at Boğaziçi University. Author of three books in Turkish, he has contributed to such journals as *Legislative Studies Quarterly, Comparative Political Studies* and *International Journal of Political Education* and to such collected volumes as *State, Democracy and the Military. Turkey in the 1980s, Local Government in Turkey. Governing Greater Istanbul,* and *Parliament and Democratic Consolidation in Southern Europe. Greece, Italy, Portugal, Spain and Turkey*

Ziya Öniş is Associate Professor of Economics at Boğaziçi University. He has contributed to such journals as *International Journal of Middle East Studies, Comparative Political Studies, Journal of Development*, and such collected volumes as *The Political Economy of Turkish Liberalization* and *Experiences with the World Bank's Structural Adjustment Lending Programmes, Vol.2*, and is co-author of *Macroeconomic Policies. Crises and Long-Term Growth in Turkey* and *The External Financing of Turkey's Imports.*

Ayşe Öncü is Professor of Sociology at Boğaziçi University. Author of one book in Turkish, she has contributed to such journals as *International Social Science Journal, Current Sociology*, and *International Journal* of *Urban and Regional Research* and such collected volumes as *Dilemmas of Decentralization. Municipal Government in Turkey, Political Economy of Income Distribution in Turkey, Improving the Management of Urban Research, Economy and Society. The State of the Art*, and *Changing Turkish Society*

Ergun Özbudun is Professor of Constitutional Law and Political Science at Ankara University. He has contributed to such journals as *International Journal of Middle East Studies, Journal of South Asian and Middle Eastern Studies*, and *Middle Eastern Studies*, and is co-editor of *Electoral Politics in the Middle East. Issues, Voters and Elites, The Political Economy of Income Distribution in Turkey, Atatürk. Founder of a Modern State*, and *Competitive Elections in Developing Countries*, and author of *The Role of the Military in Recent Turkish Politics, Party Cohesion in Western Democracies. A Causal Analysis*, and *Social Change and Political Participation in Turkey.*

Ümit Cizre Sakallıoğlu is Assistant Professor of Political Science at the Middle East Technical University. Co-editor of a book in Turkish, she has contributed to such journals as *Middle Eastern Studies* and such collected volumes as *Nationalism in Contemporary Europe.*

Index

Bei Fragen zur Produktsicherheit wenden Sie sich bitte an:
If you have any questions regarding product safety,
please contact:

Walter de Gruyter GmbH
Genthiner Straße 13
10785 Berlin
productsafety@degruyterbrill.com